ORGANIZATIONAL ASSESSMENT AND IMPROVEMENT IN THE PUBLIC SECTOR

American Society for Public Administration
Book Series on Public Administration & Public Policy

Editor-in-Chief
Evan M. Berman, Ph.D.
National Chengchi University, Taiwan
evanmberman@gmail.com

Mission: Throughout its history, ASPA has sought to be true to its founding principles of promoting scholarship and professionalism within the public service. The ASPA Book Series on Public Administration and Public Policy publishes books that increase national and international interest for public administration and which discuss practical or cutting edge topics in engaging ways of interest to practitioners, policy-makers, and those concerned with bringing scholarship to the practice of public administration.

Organizational Assessment and Improvement in the Public Sector,
Kathleen M. Immordino

*Major League Winners: Using Sports and Cultural Centers as Tools
for Economic Development,* Mark S. Rosentraub

The Formula for Economic Growth on Main Street America, Gerald L. Gordon

*The New Face of Government: How Public Managers Are Forging a New
Approach to Governance,* David E. McNabb

*The Facilitative Leader in City Hall: Reexamining the Scope
and Contributions,* James H. Svara

American Society for Public Administration
Series in Public Administration and Public Policy

ORGANIZATIONAL ASSESSMENT AND IMPROVEMENT IN THE PUBLIC SECTOR

KATHLEEN M. IMMORDINO

CRC Press
Taylor & Francis Group
Boca Raton London New York

CRC Press is an imprint of the
Taylor & Francis Group, an **informa** business

CRC Press
Taylor & Francis Group
6000 Broken Sound Parkway NW, Suite 300
Boca Raton, FL 33487-2742

© 2010 by Taylor and Francis Group, LLC
CRC Press is an imprint of Taylor & Francis Group, an Informa business

No claim to original U.S. Government works

Printed in the United States of America on acid-free paper
10 9 8 7 6 5 4 3 2 1

International Standard Book Number: 978-1-4200-8420-7 (Hardback)

Library of Congress Cataloging-in-Publication Data

Immordino, Kathleen M.
    Organizational assessment and improvement in the public sector / Kathleen M. Immordino.
        p. cm. -- (American Society for Public Administration book series on public administration & public policy)
    Includes bibliographical references and index.
    ISBN 978-1-4200-8420-7 (hardcover : alk. paper)
    1. Organizational effectiveness--United States--Evaluation. 2. Administrative agencies--United States--Management--Evaluation. I. Title.

JK421.I52 2010
352.3'5--dc22   2009028181

Visit the Taylor & Francis Web site at
http://www.taylorandfrancis.com

and the CRC Press Web site at
http://www.crcpress.com

Contents

Prologue

What do we mean when we talk about assessment and improvement in public sector organizations? Simply put, assessment and improvement are processes through which a government agency—at the federal, state, or local level—can systematically examine its operation and review its performance to determine current strengths and opportunities for improvement and then can apply the information gained to make positive changes. An assessment process, as described in this book, is a structured method of collecting and evaluating information about those areas of an agency's operation that are most closely associated with organizational excellence. The knowledge gained during the assessment is used to determine the relative priorities of the suggested opportunities for improvement from which the agency can initiate improvement efforts. Assessment is often referred to as self-assessment, because it advocates the involvement of employees as the "consultants" who collect the information and assess the current state of the organization.

The process of assessment recognizes that the effectiveness of a government agency's operations depends on many different factors and the relationships between those factors. The ability to effectively accomplish the mission of any agency relies on the organization's leaders, the staff members, and the workforce climate, on the ability to plan, on the use of measurement and information, on the programs and processes that carry out the core functions and the support functions, and on the constituents and beneficiaries for whom they provide these services. Each of these categories makes a vital contribution.

Why is interest in assessment increasing in the public sector? The answer may lie in two words: responsibility and capability. Public sector organizations have an extremely broad scope of responsibility. They provide services for individuals, groups, large and small jurisdictions, and society at large. They are responsible, in many ways, for the services that enable our society to function. The services provided by government agencies impact people's lives every day and cover a breadth of responsibility unmatched in any another sector. These responsibilities range from public safety and national security to protecting children and the elderly, managing the criminal justice system and protecting the environment. At the same time, government agencies operate in a maze of paperwork and processes that are designed to ensure equitable treatment but can also be frustrating to staff and constituents alike and give "government work" a sometimes negative connotation. Government cannot choose its customers; in many ways, it is accurate to say just that they are responsible for everyone. They provide direct services that people need and protect the most vulnerable populations. They also provide services that people may not want but that are necessary for the overall benefit of society.

Government must also have the capability to carry out these responsibilities. There is a continual demand for new and different services and service delivery methods, and the demands of public service are stretching the capability of the public sector to respond. The pressures on public sector employees are complicated by the retirement of the baby boomers who make up a large part of the public sector workforce and the resulting organizational knowledge that leaves with them. Facing decreasing budgets and growing populations for whom to provide services, government must find ways to increase the capability of its agencies, to maximize its available fiscal and human resources, and to increase both effectiveness and efficiency.

The introduction of assessment processes in government is in many ways a response to internal and external demands that agencies become proactive in examining and improving their ability to function at the highest possible levels. At all levels of government, the pressure is on for agencies to develop and implement assessment programs and to address the opportunities for improvement that result. Public sector organizations that do not have a process in place to evaluate their operation and improve their efficiency and effectiveness are likely to find that the measures of their success are being defined and imposed by individuals and constituent groups outside the organization. In many cases, the opinions of these groups about what constitutes effective performance and what should be measured and how could differ greatly from that of those working within the organization. This should provide an incentive to be proactive in examining our organizations and initiating improvements.

Many government organizations are actively engaged in quality improvement and assessment processes. The states of Utah and New Mexico actively utilize the balanced scorecard process developed at Harvard University. Thousands of government agencies at all levels collect and analyze performance data and receive strong support for their efforts from associations such as the American Society for Public Administration, the Association of Government Accountants, the National Center for Public Productivity at Rutgers University, and the International City/County Management Association.

The year 2007 marked a very exciting time for assessment in government, as the first two public sector winners of the prestigious Baldrige National Quality Award were named. The winners, the Army Armament Research, Development and Engineering Center (ARDEC) and the City of Coral Springs, Florida, are not newcomers to the idea of assessment and quality improvement. Both have a long and distinguished history of self-assessment and organizational improvement. They share many common values, including a focus on those for whom they provide services. The people at ARDEC say that feedback from their external environment telling them that they needed to get better was a key factor in their adoption of assessment processes, and their Baldrige application makes very clear their appreciation of the responsibility to serve and protect the nation's armed forces.

There are a number of successful tools available for organizational assessment. Why, then, is it necessary to design assessment processes for the public sector? How is the business of government different from that of the private sector? Government agencies are frequently told that they need to function more like business. In some ways, this can be true. Government needs to become more efficient in the way it conducts its business, and there are some lessons to be learned from the private sector. But what is also clear is that there are significant and important differences. Government agencies have a legislated set of functions and serve broad and far-reaching populations. They often do not have the ability to eliminate programs, even when those programs are ineffective. The mission of government is not grounded in profits and losses; success in government is not defined by financial measures, as it is in the private sector. There is a different relationship between government agencies and the people for whom they provide services than exists between businesses and their customers. As a result, those who work in government agencies may not be totally comfortable in using assessment tools that focus on the private sector. The best answer may be to adopt the use of aspects of private sector assessment programs that are common to all organizations and to customize them to fit the language, the purposes, and the culture of the public sector. The most well-known and successful assessment program is the Baldrige National Quality Program, and that became a starting point in the process of developing a set of criteria specifically for the public sector.

The process of developing a public sector assessment methodology began as the result of an orientation program being used to introduce the Baldrige process to employees of a government agency in preparation for an assessment. The facilitator, who was a trained Baldrige examiner from outside the organization, noted during the program that some concepts should be changed or eliminated to make the process more usable for the public sector. The participants questioned whether, instead, there could be a model that used familiar concepts and terminology and used examples relevant to the work of government. We then realized that having a customized version—what eventually became the Public Sector Assessment and Improvement (PSAI) model—would provide an alternative to having to "translate" the Baldrige criteria for public sector applications and would allow participants to focus more explicitly on the issues that are most relevant to their own organizational contexts.

Other efforts to customize the Baldrige criteria provided guidance and encouragement that this could be done. In particular, *Excellence in Higher Education* (Ruben, 2007a) showed that it was possible to customize the language and culture of the Baldrige criteria to meet a specific, narrower portion of a sector. A study conducted at Rutgers University (Immordino, 2006) demonstrated that the use of a customized assessment process for government (1) facilitated communication about assessment and improvement and about the organization itself; (2) increased the level of organizational knowledge that staff members possess by enabling personal and organizational learning, which, in turn, built support for change; (3) enabled participants to agree on the essential functions of the agency and to focus on a smaller number of critical responsibilities; and (4) essentially "raised the bar" in terms of what staff members believe the agency is capable of achieving.

Assessment serves a number of purposes:

- It provides a method and a common language for talking about the organization and how it can be improved.
- It provides a way to involve employees from all areas and at all levels in improving the organization.
- It focuses the attention of government leaders and staff members on the opportunities for improvement.
- It helps prioritize the challenges facing the agency, thereby providing a "compass" for employees to use in decision making.
- It provides a systems approach to thinking about the organization so that people view and understand the impact of their work operations on the operations of the agency as a whole.

Government is always changing. New constituents and beneficiaries, new programs or funding sources, new expectations and technologies all mean new approaches and reorganized priorities. In this atmosphere of continual change, assessment provides a way to examine critical functions and to determine the best ways to engage employees in identifying and implementing opportunities for improvement. The ultimate goal of organizational assessment and improvement is not only to improve efficiency and effectiveness but also to create a culture of assessment, where continuous improvement is a part of the everyday business of carrying out the work of government throughout the organization.

Foreword

Every week's news brings fresh reminders of the complex array of challenges facing contemporary organizations in every sector. While the realities of organizational life may have actually changed very little over the years, the public perception is otherwise as we are bombarded with reports of inefficiencies, ethical violations, greed, cost overruns, corruption, unwieldy bureaucratic procedures, waste, an absence of planning, and leadership ineptness. The result, and understandably so, is an escalating mistrust of organizations of all kinds, and of their leaders, at a time when precisely the opposite is needed.

For those in government service, issues of public confidence are certainly not new ones. It will seem ironic to some that in the current circumstance, public sector organizations are being asked to play an increasingly central role in addressing the inefficiencies, missteps, and misdeeds of the private sector entities and its leaders. The responsibilities that now fall to government are profound and pervasive. We find ourselves looking to national, state and community leaders to improve the way government works because of the many challenges facing the public sector, and also because we need to provide better models for the private sector.

As a nation we want and need to be reassured that organizations of all kinds can be run effectively and efficiently, can be guided not so much by self-serving interests as a genuine regard for the public well-being, and can operate with a transparency and accountability that will reinvigorate confidence in the potential for organizational excellence and leadership. Because of our unique point in history, it falls to government to lead the way.

Expectations—perhaps better termed hopes at this point—are high. That said, where do leaders who aspire to address these challenges look for guidance, for a standard of excellence in organizational performance? Of the available models, few if any are as helpful as the Malcolm Baldrige framework. First introduced by the Department of Commerce in 1987, the Malcolm Baldrige model has inspired countless scholars and practitioners, and has long since been integrated into the cultural fabric of many of our most distinguished private sector organizations. The model is finding growing acceptance and application within education and healthcare, and has begun, also, to find application in non-profit organizations.*

With the publication of *Organizational Assessment and Improvement in the Public Sector* by Kathleen Immordino, the benefits of the Baldrige framework are extended to the culture, language and needs of government. The Public Sector Assessment and Improvement (PSAI) model, like the Baldrige framework on which it is based, provides both a standard and a strategy.

As a standard for excellence, the Baldrige framework consists of seven categories. Although the language and definitions used to describe the framework have changed over the years, and vary somewhat from sector to sector, the seven basic themes remain constant. In general terms, the framework suggests that organizational excellence requires: [†]

1. Effective leadership that provides guidance and ensures a clear and shared sense of organizational mission and future vision, a commitment to continuous review and improvement of leadership practice, and social and environmental consciousness

2. An inclusive planning process and coherent plans that translate the organization's mission, vision, and values into clear, aggressive, and measurable goals that are understood and effectively implemented throughout the organization

3. Knowledge of the needs, expectations, and satisfaction and dissatisfaction levels of the groups served by the organization; programs, services, and practices that are responsive to these needs and expectations, and assessment processes in place to stay current with and anticipate the thinking of these groups

4. Development and use of indicators of organizational quality and effectiveness that capture the organization's mission, vision, values, and goals and provide data-based comparisons with peer and leading organizations; widely sharing this and other information within the organization to focus and motivate improvement

5. A workplace culture that encourages, recognizes, and rewards excellence, employee satisfaction, engagement, professional development, commitment, and pride and synchronizes individual and organizational goals

6. Focus on mission-critical and support programs and services and associated work processes to ensure effectiveness, efficiency, appropriate standardization and documentation, and regular evaluation and improvement—with the needs and expectations of stakeholders in mind

---

* See Malcolm Baldrige National Quality Program. http://www.quality.nist.gov/
[†] Brent D. Ruben, *Excellence in Higher Education 2009 Guidebook. An Integrated Approach to Assessment, Planning and Improvement in Colleges and Universities*. Washington, DC: National Association of College and University Business Officers, 2009.

7. Documented, sustained positive outcomes relative to organizational mission, vision, goals, the perspectives of groups served, and employees, considered in the light of comparisons with the accomplishments of peers, competitors, and leaders

Because the PSAI model incorporates fundamental, broadly based, and enduring dimensions of organizational quality and effectiveness, the framework has a transferability and portability that usefully transcends particular administrations, organizations, and time frames. To the extent that the model is disseminated and widely understood and used within the department or government entity, future leaders can carry the model forward conceptually and operationally rather than feeling the need to invent their own approach.

In addition to articulating a series of standards for organizational excellence, the model offers a strategy for assessment, planning and improvement based on the standard, and it does so through actively engaging colleagues throughout the organization in the process.

From our experience using a similar model in higher education,* and from available evidence, it would seem that Baldrige-based programs can be very helpful in attaining a variety of important organizational goals, including:

■ Fostering organizational self-reflection
■ Clarifying aspirations and goals
■ Enhancing participant understanding of dimensions of organizational excellence
■ Team building
■ Increasing and enhancing communication
■ Professional and leadership development
■ Promoting comparisons and benchmarking
■ Identifying and creating a shared sense of priority improvement needs
■ Promoting the measurement of performance
■ Energizing members of the organization to possibilities for continuous improvement, even with limited resources

No doubt audiences for *Organizational Assessment and Improvement in the Public Sector* will see great value in having a framework to advance the goals of integrated assessment, planning, and improvement in government. For this reason, in particular, this is an extremely important and timely book. It provides concepts and tools to facilitate the creation of government entities that can come exemplify

---

* Brent D Ruben, Travis Russ, Stacy M. Smulowitz, and Stacey L. Connaughton. Evaluating the Impact of Organizational Self-Assessment in Higher Education: The Malcolm Baldrige/ Excellence in Higher Education Framework. *Leadership and Organizational Development Journal*, 28(3), 2007.

the very best organizational principles and practices, and in so doing can help to inspire renewed confidence in our organizations, our leaders, and our future that is sorely needed.

Brent D. Ruben, Ph.D.

Acknowledgments

This book owes a great deal to Dr. Brent Ruben and the University Center for Organizational Development and Leadership at Rutgers, The State University of New Jersey. Dr. Ruben developed *Excellence in Higher Education* (Ruben, 2007a), an adaptation of the Baldrige National Quality Award Criteria for higher education, which is in many ways the inspiration for what became the Public Sector Assessment and Improvement model. As a doctoral student working with Dr. Ruben, I had the opportunity to see, firsthand, the difference that can be made when the participants in an assessment program are comfortable with the language and the examples being used. My many discussions with him about assessment and about this book contributed a great deal to the end product. In that same way, I owe much thanks to the Baldrige National Quality Program for its long history of promoting and facilitating assessment in organizations. I consider this book to be a supplement to the excellent work that they do and applaud the steps taken to bring formal assessment processes to the public sector.

I would also like to acknowledge the leadership and staff of the New Jersey Department of Transportation, who participated in both a department-wide Baldrige assessment in 2000 and in the first tests of the Public Sector Assessment and Improvement model in 2004. Their comments and feedback helped a great deal in refining the model. Thanks go especially to my former colleagues in the office of the Assistant Commissioner for Administration and its divisions.

I am also grateful to the American Society for Public Administration for its continuous support of all public sector professionals and for developing this book series. Dr. Evan Berman has been an encouraging mentor, as well as editor, throughout this process. I must also thank Patricia Worthington for her thoughtful review and comments on the manuscript and my husband, Howard, and children, Matthew and Jaclyn, for their support. Last, but certainly not least, thanks to my friend, colleague, and longtime ASPA member Warren Barclay for his encouragement and assistance in getting this project off the ground.

About the Author

Kathleen M. Immordino, Ph.D., is the director of organizational research and assessment for the University Center for Organizational Development and Leadership at Rutgers, The State University of New Jersey. Prior to joining the center in 2007, she was a career public sector professional with over 28 years of experience in state government. Dr. Immordino served as the assistant commissioner for administration in the New Jersey Department of Transportation, assistant commissioner for planning and research in the New Jersey Department of Personnel, and executive director for planning and development in the New Jersey Department of Labor following a number of positions in human resources and strategic planning.

A graduate of Dickinson College, Dr. Immordino received a master of arts degree from Rider University and a Ph.D. in organizational communication from Rutgers University. She is a past president of the New Jersey Chapter of the American Society for Public Administration (ASPA) and a recipient of the Joseph E. McLean Chapter Service Award. She is a former vice chairperson of the Personnel Subcommittee of the American Association of State Highway and Transportation Officials and was a member of the publication board for the International Public Management Association for Human Resources. She is a certified public manager and an adjunct professor at Rider University.

Chapter 1

Organizational Assessment and the Public Sector

This chapter introduces the concept of organizational assessment and its value to public sector organizations in addressing the need to provide effective and efficient programs and services. Organizational assessment is presented as a form of organizational development and as an integrated approach to examining all aspects of operation and performance. It discusses the criticality of integrating assessment and improvement and the challenges and opportunities that face government organizations.

Organizations of all kinds, to remain effective, must continuously improve themselves in response to the challenges confronting them. Those in the public sector are no exception. These agencies are subject to both internal and external pressures that result in frequent—some would say constant—pressure for change.

Public sector organizations have a unique opportunity to impact the lives of those for whom they provide programs and services. At all levels—including federal, state, and local government as well as commissions, boards, authorities, and other agencies whose mission is to serve the public[1]—the key question is how best to meet the needs of those constituents. They must respond and adapt to demographic shifts as well as to changes in the economy, their internal workforce, and the priorities of those for whom they provide services. Government agencies constantly interact with their constituents and beneficiaries, and the expectations of those groups for both the type and the scope of services an agency provides change on a regular basis. This creates an ongoing demand not only for new and different services, some of which are needed for new or expanding constituent groups, but also for innovation in the way existing services are provided. Government agencies are under constant pressure to improve their efficiency, effectiveness, and responsiveness. At the same time, there is pressure for increased transparency and accountability in the way that government agencies conduct their operations. For most of these agencies, the increasing demands for accountability and performance measurement are coming from multiple internal and external sources. Coe (2003) notes that accountability is one of the major concepts underlying government service and that those who study public administration have spent much time trying to determine the best ways to hold public agencies and their leaders accountable. The external sources include the public at large, the direct recipients of services, the media, legislators, political leaders at various levels, and advocacy groups. In addition, they face the increasingly stringent requirements of oversight commissions and regulatory agencies. Internally, the push to evaluate performance and improve services comes from both elected and appointed leaders and from the career managers and staff who are trying to stretch limited resources. To make resources available for both existing services and new challenges, they must continually review their ability to achieve their mission and their capability to be efficient and effective in meeting the needs of those they serve.

At the same time that the scope of services provided by government is growing, the critics of government agencies are becoming more vocal about what they perceive to be its problems. These concerns have generated calls from taxpayers, legislators, academicians, and government itself for expanding performance management and introducing a culture of continuous improvement.

To some extent, government agencies have suffered from a public perception of inefficiency and mismanagement. In some cases, this is compounded by reports of corruption and waste. *Excellence in Government*, a 1990 study described part of the problem (Carr and Littman, 1990):

> Government agencies … must cope with seemingly intractable deficits, steady growth in demand for traditional services, new and unusual requirements brought on by a drug epidemic and a highly competitive world economy, and increasing disillusionment with government's ability to serve the needs of its citizens.[2]

Similarly, the statement of "findings and purposes" that precedes the Government Performance and Results Act of 1993 says:

> Waste and inefficiency in federal programs undermine the confidence of the American people in the Government and reduces the Federal

Government's ability to address adequately vital public needs …. The purposes of this act are to … improve the confidence of the American people in the capability of the Federal Government … improve Federal program effectiveness and public accountability by promoting a new focus on results, service quality and customer satisfaction … and improve internal management.[3]

In 2008, the Association of Government Accountants (AGA) sponsored a survey designed to measure public attitudes toward transparency and accountability in government. The survey, titled *Public Attitudes toward Government Accountability and Transparency,*[4] was intended to provide a baseline of public sentiment toward these issues. AGA believes that failure to provide timely and accurate information to citizens on government finances promotes cynicism and mistrust. Although the AGA-sponsored survey focused on financial information, the responses speak to the broader question of public trust. The results showed that there is an "expectation gap" between what citizens believe they should know about federal, state, and local government and the information that is available to them. Citizens reported a distrust of government at all levels based not only on what information is or is not provided but also on the perceived lack of openness and the attitude of government toward making this information available in user-friendly ways.

The very public nature of these concerns has created what is often referred to as a crisis in public confidence. Thinking about the well-known adage that "perception is reality," the public may well believe that there is no good news to be had when it comes to talking about government performance. However, in many ways, they are missing a big part of the story. This "crisis" perspective often fails to recognize what those who work in the public sector know to be true: An overwhelming number of positive performance outcomes are generated by government, and government itself is leading the charge toward improved organizational effectiveness. Government agencies are often the strongest advocates for undertaking assessment and improvement initiatives. Many of the most successful assessment processes are initiated from within these organizations by staff members, managers, and leaders who are committed to continuous improvement. In addition, organizations with close ties to government and its employees such as the American Society for Public Administration are some of the most vocal supporters of efforts to educate the public about government and to increase public confidence. When viewed this way, the issues that impact the public perception of government provide both a challenge and an opportunity for public administrators.

The Demand for Effectiveness and Efficiency

Being effective is difficult. This is true for people in any complex organization; it is especially true for those in government and public sector jobs, which tend to have overlapping jurisdictions, little autonomy, and multiple constraints. (Haass, 1994, p. xii)

The successful operation of any government agency, regardless of the type or size of the jurisdiction, presents a four-part challenge for public administrators. The challenge at all levels of government is to function in a way that:

- Makes the best use of available resources.
- Serves the broadest possible population.
- Accomplishes the goals of society and of government leaders.
- Sustains a workforce that is energized and able to meet these challenges.

The ability to fulfill the organization's mission and to meet its goals and objectives is measured in terms of both *effectiveness* and *efficiency*. Although these words are frequently used to discuss organizations, it is important to clearly define both of these terms as they relate to the performance of government.

Effectiveness can be defined as the degree to which a government agency meets the perceived need for services at an acceptable level of service quality. It is not always easy to measure, as both parts of the equation can be subjective and dependent on the perspective of the group who is doing the measuring. As Haass (1994) points out, "Being effective is difficult. This is true for people in any complex organization; it is especially true for those in government and public sector jobs, which tend to have overlapping jurisdictions, little autonomy, and multiple constraints."[5] Being effective becomes especially difficult in the face of calls to "do more with less." Part of the problem is that those who are served by government go beyond the traditional definition of "customer." The beneficiaries of government activities include not only the individuals and groups that directly use the services they provide but also society as a whole. When a municipality provides efficient trash pickup, it is not serving just individual homeowners; the entire town benefits because the sidewalks and roadways are free from trash, enabling them to sustain a community that will attract homeowners, workers, and businesses. Most people will never come in contact with anyone who works for the Centers for Disease Control and Prevention, but they benefit every day from the research being done there. In many cases, these constituents come to government because they have no choice of provider. Government is the only source of the services these groups require, for example, those who wish to obtain a driver's license or a social security number. In other cases, constituents and beneficiaries[6] are a "captive audience" who have no choice but to participate in certain government processes, such as paying taxes.

Although we most often think of the public when we talk about the constituents for whom government is responsible, it is important to remember that public sector organizations have internal as well as external constituents. Many of the administrative functions, including human resources, information technology, facilities, mail processing, and motor pools, generally do not deal with the public in any substantive way, but that doesn't mean that they don't have constituents. Instead, they are responsible for a set of internal customers who also have expectations for the level of service they receive.

Efficiency can be defined as making the best possible use of the resources available in meeting the needs of constituents. Schachter (2007) says that efficiency has been one of the most prominent administrative goals in government for more than 25 years and is a key part of every report on government reform in this century. Efficiency takes into account many different types of resources. The typical things that come to mind are time and money, but the resources of government are not limited to funding streams, equipment, and taxpayer dollars. They also include the energy and talent of the staff and the goodwill and trust of the constituents.

The concepts of effectiveness and efficiency can be considered in the context of the four challenges of government. If we look at the challenges of government as a model (as shown in Figure 1.1), then effectiveness and efficiency each pertain to one half of the diagram. Effectiveness is related most closely to the two challenges on the left side of the diagram: serving the broadest possible population and accomplishing the goals of society. The two challenges on the right side of the diagram, making the best use of available resources and sustaining the workforce needed to carry out these goals, represent efficiency.

Effectiveness and efficiency are without question impacted by the demand for increased government services. One of the considerations for government agencies

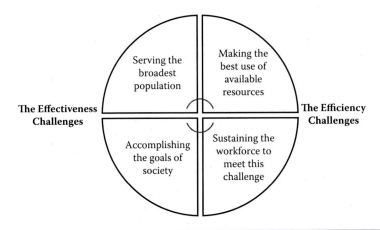

Figure 1.1 The challenges of government operations. The four challenges of government are represented as parts of a circle, which demonstrates the way that they are all interrelated. While all of these challenges contribute to the overall performance of government, those on the left side of the diagram (serving the broadest population and accomplishing the goals of society) are related to the effectiveness of government performance whereas those on the right side (making the best use of available resources and sustaining the workforce to meet this challenge) are related to the efficiency of government.

that are asked to take on responsibilities for new and increasingly diverse services is that most of the time the existing range of programs and services must also be maintained. Often, decisions to add services or increase the population served are made without evaluating whether the existing services meet the test of effectiveness and efficiency. Decision makers may not adequately anticipate whether the new responsibilities will change their ability to sustain the effectiveness and efficiency of previously existing services and whether the agency can meet the new expectations. Although efficiency and effectiveness seem to go hand in hand, they are not necessarily dependent on each other. It is certainly possible to be effective without being efficient; in fact, this is one of the charges most frequently leveled at various government agencies. It's also possible to be efficient and not effective. While the goal is to achieve both effectiveness and efficiency, they may at times seem to be incompatible concepts or mutually exclusive. Often, government programs and the laws or regulations that implement them contain complex regulatory provisions that all but ensure that these services will never be completely efficient. Initially, it may seem logical to think that it is more important to be effective. The mission of any agency presumes effectiveness. However, efficiency can't be overlooked. Being efficient maximizes the available resources and can also free up resources, which in turn can lead to expanded services and an increased ability to meet goals. It's no wonder that the challenge of evaluating government performance is so difficult. The important question facing public administrators in such situations is how to achieve both efficiency and effectiveness.

Organizational Assessment

While government itself, as well as legislators, the public, and various other constituents, traditionally measure the effectiveness and efficiency of government programs and services in terms of distinct programs and projects, the level of organizational performance required to meet the expectations of these groups requires an integrated approach to the organizations and their systems, programs, and operations. In response, government organizations are increasingly adopting the methodology of assessment and continuous improvement. The staff of a government agency can measure its current level of performance, but it cannot fully evaluate what it will take to achieve the highest level of effectiveness and efficiency without a systematic examination of the organization. The question becomes how to determine whether a government organization is functioning in a way that is efficient, effective, and capable of addressing the needs of constituents and beneficiaries or, from a broader perspective, the needs and requirements of society as a whole. The process of making this determination must begin with a clear understanding of the entire organization, its people, and its programs. We often assume that this information is generally available and well known, but in reality, this type of comprehensive knowledge can be elusive. This understanding must be grounded not just in the perceptions of a few decision makers but in real, observable, and documented information that clearly outlines, in a structured manner, the current state of the organization. The process through which this evaluation takes place, and through which the needed information is obtained and considered, is called *organizational assessment*.[7] Those who lead, manage, or work in government, as well as the beneficiaries and constituents who have an interest in the performance of government, need to understand organizational assessment: what it is, how it works, and how it can be applied in a way that addresses the needs of the public sector.

What Is Organizational Assessment?

The word *assessment* is one frequently used in government. It has a number of different meanings depending on the context in which it appears. One of the more commonly seen uses is to describe the process of apportioning costs or of determining the appropriate level of taxes based on the value and use of property. Assessment can also be used to mean a test, interview, or other similar tool used to evaluate candidates for employment or promotion in a civil service or merit employment system. It can describe the process of evaluating progress toward learning outcomes, competency development, or skill acquisition in an employee development initiative. On a broader scale, it can apply to the process of determining the need for training throughout an organization. It can be used to mean evaluating the accuracy and importance of data, such as intelligence information, or determining the level of risk associated with climate, infrastructure conditions, or pandemic disease. Assessment can also be used to describe the accreditation processes used by organizations such as the Joint Commission on Accreditation of Healthcare Organizations, which (within its broader commitment to the health-care sector) reviews government medical facilities and medical program providers.

Despite the different meanings, all of these examples of assessment have something in common: a shared foundation. Each example describes a way of comparing people, practices, or information against agreed upon standards, past performance, perceived need, or known information. When the word *assessment* is used in the context of an organization and its goals, purposes, and performance, making comparisons becomes very important. Comparisons are made as a way to determine and evaluate the current operations and level of effectiveness and efficiency of the organization. Those comparisons might be internal, comparing the organization's performance with that of previous years or comparing the outcomes of one program or service delivery method against another within the same agency. The comparisons can also be external, such as comparing the organization with others—in the public sector or in other sectors—that perform similar functions. Organizational assessment, in this context, is *a systematic process for examining an organization to create a shared understanding of the current state of the elements that are critical to the successful achievement of its purposes.* Breaking this definition down into its component parts helps identify the key principles of organizational assessment.

Assessment is, first and foremost, a *systematic process*. It provides a structured framework for collecting, combining, and evaluating information that exists throughout the organization. All too often, decisions about the performance and capability of an organization are based primarily on anecdotal information. Decisions based on this type of information can be very subjective.

> Organizational assessment is a systematic process for examining an organization to create a shared understanding of the current state of the elements that are critical to the successful achievement of its purpose.

Like any other type of performance evaluation, decisions about organizational effectiveness can be heavily influenced by the organization's most recent performance, whether that performance was good or bad. Being systematic means having a structured way of collecting information in which decisions are carefully and conscientiously made about the scope and depth of information that is available, how it is to be obtained, and how it will be used. The word *process*, meaning a sequence of steps and a planned methodology for carrying them out, is also a significant element in this definition. The process of conducting an assessment is in many ways equally as important as the results obtained. It provides a way to involve members of the organization in seeking out needed information and encourages them to use that information to create new knowledge. The process of assessment is action oriented and extends beyond reporting performance and monitoring the status of the organization. It is the first step in a cycle that begins with assessment and continues to include improvement. It provides a way to stimulate discussion and to generate opportunities for improvement and a methodology for acting on the information obtained. Because it is a systematic process, assessment is:

■ Consistent.
■ Reliable.
■ Repeatable.

This means that the results, or outcomes, can be compared over time.

The assessment process focuses on the *organization* as a whole. Introducing and sustaining a program of real continuous improvement in any organization goes beyond examining and improving individual processes or specific work units. Historically, government has been very good at segmenting itself based on the functions and services it provides. It's very common to find that individual programs are monitored and that their performance is evaluated based on the discrete functions that they use to conduct their operations rather than on the part they plan in larger,

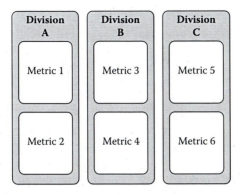

Figure 1.2 Evaluating programs and services in silos. In this example, each division is focused on collecting data or metrics that deal with specific activities that take place within its unit.

organization-wide processes. The example in Figure 1.2 provides a demonstration of how this works. Imagine looking at three divisions that perform different functions in a government agency. Typically, each of the three divisions shown will have developed its own sets of metrics to reflect the performance of its programs or functions. While these metrics may be useful to the individual offices or programs, none of the metrics crosses division lines or measures the impact of processes that involve more than one division.

This is often referred to as examining programs in *silos*. The result of this kind of monitoring can be a collection of metrics that do not reflect the efforts of the whole organization. It's much less common to find organizations that assess themselves across programs and work units and focus on the overall performance of the organization as a working entity. When this broader approach is taken, the result incorporates measures, metrics, and performance into a comprehensive study of the overall management and operation. That's not to say that assessment must always take place at the organization level. While the most useful application of assessment is the analysis of an entire organization, the process can also be applied to subsets, such as divisions, geographically separate offices, or other units. In this case, the assessment process is still conducted within the context of the larger organization.[8] It considers whether the mission and goals of the subunit are consistent with those of the organization as a whole.

Assessment *creates a shared understanding* by enabling the members of the organization to collect, review, and compare information so that together they have greater knowledge of the organization than they would have individually. Creating a shared "pool" of information assists them in reaching consensus about the organization. The assessment process brings together the perspectives of people who work in various jobs in different areas and at many different levels. It is often referred to as organizational self-assessment, since the participants in the assessment process are the members of the organization: the employees, managers, and leaders. It involves them in evaluating or diagnosing the organization and recognizes that they have unique information about what they do, their role in the organization, and how they interact with others. An analogy commonly used to describe assessment is that the process produces a snapshot of the organization at a specific point in time. A more accurate way to consider it might be to think of a jigsaw puzzle. Bringing people together to participate in an assessment is like inviting a group of people to join in putting together a puzzle, but in this case, each person owns some of the puzzle pieces. There is no picture on the box for guidance, but everyone believes he or she knows what the finished puzzle should look like. It's very likely that everyone's idea of the finished picture has some elements in common but differs in many respects based on each person's knowledge and his or her interpretation of that information. As group members negotiate how the puzzle pieces fit together, a picture gradually emerges that all the contributors can see and understand.

Assessment focuses on the *current state* of the organization. It is a forward-looking process that focuses on where the organization is now and the way that it currently operates rather than on how it got there. Many traditional forms of performance measurement rely on historical data. Assessment may at first seem historical in nature, since one of the inputs to the process can be a comparison of current data with information from previous years. Such data can be used to consider trends, but the emphasis is on how the operations are currently being performed and how they can be improved.

Assessment identifies the *critical elements* that enable the organization to function. In this way, it can also be thought of as a measure of organizational health. It is grounded in the mission and vision of the organization and incorporates the structure, leadership, processes, plans, and constituents in the evaluation of overall performance. The assessment process facilitates a review of the organization's priorities and provides a way to examine whether actions and critical support, including the allocation of financial resources and workforce planning, are aligned with the organization's mission, goals, vision, and plans. Assessment considers major cross-functional issues including strategic planning, human resources, knowledge management, and performance measures that are keys to the success of the organization.

Assessment and Organizational Development

To understand how and why assessment works, it's important to consider assessment as a form of organizational development. The classic definition of organizational development comes from Richard Beckhard (1969),[9] who in his 1969 book *Organizational Development: Strategies and Models* said, "Organization development is an effort planned organization-wide, and managed from the top, to increase organizational effectiveness and health through planned interventions in the organization's 'processes' using behavioral science knowledge." Organizational development efforts are often described as interventions, because they are used to intervene in the life of the organization as a way to introduce change.

As the field of organizational development has evolved, several common elements have emerged. Organizational development:

- Views organizations as systems and considers how the parts of the system work together.
- Includes the members of the organization in the diagnosis and recommends change that can be implemented by its members.
- Helps individuals understand and initiate change.
- Educates employees about how the organization functions.
- Encourages a long-term view of organizational improvement.
- Requires and supports personal and organizational learning.

These elements can be incorporated in an updated description of organizational development as a process that enables participants to create organizational and personal learning and to build a case for change in organizations. Organizational assessment is one of a number of organizational development processes including surveys, communication audits, and consultant studies through which an organization can learn about itself.

The major steps in organizational development are diagnosis, feedback, discussion, and intervention. These activities are often performed by external consultants. In contrast, the assessment process uses the members of the organization, rather than an organizational development consultant, to perform this work.[10]

How Does Assessment Work?

When a public sector organization decides to engage in a self-assessment process, the goal is to produce a realistic understanding of the agency's current strengths and opportunities for improvement, along with agreement on the actions that can be taken to move the organization forward and to improve its ability to achieve its mission. The assessment process itself is not prescriptive. It does not dictate how an agency should be organized or how many levels of management it should have. It does not recommend what measures should be used or how leaders should act. It is a tool that provides the information that organizations need to make decisions. Assessment is often undertaken as a prelude to preparing a strategic or business plan by providing the organization and the participants with knowledge about its current state. An assessment initiative can also be part of an actual strategic planning process by providing a model to be followed by the participants in defining the strengths, weaknesses, opportunities, and threats facing the organization.

Several common elements, as shown in Figure 1.3, go into the design of a comprehensive organizational assessment:

1. Grounding the assessment process in the mission of the organization: The starting point for any assessment is in the mission of the organization. While the performance of any group, individual, or program can be assessed, the most fundamental issue is whether it makes a contribution to the core mission and purpose for which the organization exists. It's possible to be highly effective in a program that has long outlived its original purpose and no longer has a positive impact on the overall goals of the agency in which it exists.

2. Using structured categories to guide the process: In any complex organization, there are innumerable "things" that can be measured and studied. An effective assessment process focuses on those things that have the greatest impact on the way the organization functions. It often does so by identifying a set of categories for review and analysis. The identification of specific categories serves as a way to focus the attention of the participants, as well as those who review the outcomes, on the areas that will make the most difference in improving operations. These categories are often broken down into a format that uses a series of questions to identify the information the organization will need for the assessment. This type of format provides a road map of important considerations.

3. Involving and engaging members of the organization: The scope of participation in an assessment process can vary greatly, depending on the agency, the particular reasons for the assessment, the resources available to conduct the assessment, and the time that can be devoted to it. Whatever the scope, at some level it must include the participation of people in the organization. Participation can range from very active involvement in the process to more passive involvement, such as the use of surveys. The most successful assessment processes involve a broad range of individuals from across the organization to facilitate the broadest possible information inputs. As Weisbord (1987) points out, "It is a mistake to assume we know any system's productive capacity before we involve people in shaking out the bugs."[11]

An organizational assessment process should:

- Be grounded in the mission of the organization
- Use structured categories as a guide for examining the most important concepts
- Involve the participation of members of the organization
- Balance qualitative and quantitative measures

Figure 1.3   Common elements in organizational assessment processes.

- Stage 1: Understanding the current state of the organization
  - Information collection and exchange
- Stage 2: Visioning and Gap Analysis
  - Identifying strengths and opportunities for improvement
- Stage 3: Improvement Planning and Prioritization
  - Prioritizing the opportunities for improvement
  - Developing improvement plans
- Stage 4: Outcomes and feedback
  - Communicating assessment outcomes
  - Implementing improvement priorities

Figure 1.4   The stages of organizational assessment.

"It is a mistake to assume we know any system's productive capacity before we involve people in shaking out the bugs."
Marvin Weisbord

4. Balancing qualitative and quantitative assessment: A thorough assessment must be based on the incorporation of both qualitative and quantitative information. Much of the information developed in the information-gathering parts of an assessment process is qualitative; that is, it includes not only information about the organization but also people's reaction, feelings, impressions, and descriptions. It considers the organizational culture and the workforce climate. This qualitative information is very much a part of understanding how the organization functions and is very useful in determining the impact of all the information collected. However, it must be balanced by the use of quantitative, verifiable information to facilitate the comparison and prioritization of opportunities for improvement.

There are four major stages in the assessment process, as shown in Figure 1.4.

Stage 1: Understanding the Current State of the Organization

In the language of organizational development, this stage would be called diagnosis and feedback. The concept underlying this stage is to find a way to provide a common background to those who are studying the organization so that everyone participating in the assessment has the same "picture" as a starting point. Because people may differ on how they see the organization, based on the information that may have been available to them in the past, this stage involves both collecting and exchanging information and negotiating an agreement on what represents an accurate picture of the organization and where it is now.

Information Collection and Exchange

Two types of information are collected and used in conducting an organizational assessment. The first type is information about the organization itself. Also referred to as an organizational description or profile, it includes its purpose or mission and basic structural and demographic information. The second type is information about how the organization functions and the outcomes that are achieved relative to its goals. A structured assessment process provides a method to locate and bring together data and information from across the organization as well as information that resides outside with other organizations or with the constituents and beneficiaries of its programs. This information is used to create an accurate picture of where the organization is now, where it would like to be, and the gaps that exist between those two points. After the collection of information, the next step in the organizational assessment process is to share it among the participants so that there can be an assessment or evaluation of what it represents (Figure 1.5).

Stage 2: Visioning and Gap Analysis

The goal of this stage is to assess the difference between where the organization is now and where it feels it should be. As participants begin to exchange the information collected and a shared understanding starts to develop, they begin to identify what things constitute the organization's strengths—things that are done well and that provide a basis for further improvement—and what things constitutes opportunities for improvement. One of the benefits of the assessment process is that all the participants are being presented with the same information. Hutton (2000) in his research on consensus-building suggests that when people are being presented with the same set of information, they become more likely to reach similar conclusions about the current state of the organization and what it needs to move forward. Realistically, people may still disagree about the validity and relative importance of some of the information being exchanged. As a result, participants use two related communication processes—negotiation and consensus—to resolve the differences in their perceptions and to reach agreement on the strengths and opportunities.[12]

Stage 3: Improvement Planning and Prioritization

The third part of this process calls for prioritizing the opportunities for improvement and for developing plans to implement those improvements. This could be

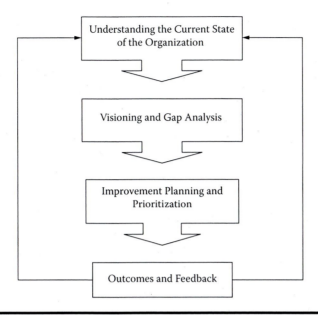

Figure 1.5   Assessment and Improvement process model. This model illustrates how the four stages of assessment are related to each other. The stages are sequential, and the information generated at the conclusion of the process becomes part of the feedback used to restart the next cycle of assessment.

called the intervention stage of organizational development. It looks at how the information learned during the assessment can be put to work to initiate changes. Once participants have reached consensus on the opportunities for improvement, the question is how to determine which of the opportunities are the most important and what actions should be taken. As these priorities are negotiated, the result is a common agreement on an agenda for improvement.

Stage 4: Outcomes and Feedback

This stage involves two critical areas: making people aware of the outcomes of the assessment process, and actually implementing the improvement priorities. This makes the assessment process "real" for many of those who have either participated or who were aware that the process was taking place but did not have the opportunity to be part of it. Depending on the scope of the assessment effort, some or all of the organization's members may have participated. In large organizations, it may not be possible or practical to involve everyone in all aspects of the process. These two action items make the assessment more than just a document or report and provide evidence of tangible results.

Challenges in Public Sector Assessment and Improvement

Government agencies face some challenges that differ in scope and perspective from those faced in the other sectors: business, education, and health care. In early 1999, the New Jersey Department of Environmental Protection (NJDEP) began a self-assessment process using the Baldrige criteria.[13] The department's objective at the time was to apply for the Governor's Quality Award, which was administered by an organization known as Quality New Jersey. At the end of 2000 NJDEP was notified that it had been selected for the Governor's Bronze award, and two years later, it achieved the highest level of the Governor's Award. Motivated by this success, in 2002 it applied for and received the National Public Service Excellence Award, becoming the first public agency in the state to achieve this award. In the years since then, in the words of one NJDEP executive, the assessment process has "dropped off the radar screen." Without a doubt, somewhere along the way it encountered some of the many challenges faced by public sector organizations in implementing and sustaining assessment processes.

Dealing with Public Perceptions of Bureaucracy

Complicating the way that the public sector is assessed is the difficulty of dealing with the public perception of bureaucracy. There is a traditional and widespread view of government as a bureaucracy and government workers as bureaucrats—terms that both carry negative connotations and imply a resistance to innovation. The term *bureaucracy* brings with it a picture of endless, inefficient processes and a strict adherence to procedures rather than a focus on results. By contrast, professional public administrators reject the concept of bureaucracy as an inefficient process or of bureaucrats as people whose job it is to prevent others from accomplishing their goals. Going back to the origins of public service, bureaucratic processes were developed as a way of ensuring equal treatment in the provision of government services. Government workers are dedicated and highly skilled people who often devote their professional careers to helping the neediest and most vulnerable in our populations. Assessment provides an opportunity to educate the public about the complexities and professionalism of government's operations.

Understanding the Complex Nature of Government Service

The public sector, compared with other types of organizations, is less able to control the type and amount of services it must provide. It must deal with an inability to shed unproductive or financially unsuccessful programs or even to choose or reject its beneficiaries and constituents. Not only are government agencies being asked to perform at a higher level, but they are frequently also being asked to take on responsibilities for an increasingly diverse set of services. Anyone who has worked in government knows that it is much easier to add new programs than it is to ever let one go. Rarely, if ever, does government stop providing a service. Since government performs functions on behalf of the larger society, it often finds itself in the position of not being able to support all the services wanted or needed by its constituents. Compounding the issue is that, unlike private sector companies, government offers services that people don't necessarily want but that need to exist either for the benefit of individuals or to meet the broader needs of society. There are few people who, if given the choice, want to pay taxes, yet tax dollars are needed to fund the services that impact people's lives. No one, we suspect, would choose to go to prison, yet few people would argue that correctional institutions are unnecessary. Still other government services are those that people find attractive and useful but that may not be seen as being paid for directly, such as libraries, open-space preservation, or national parks. At every level of government, there is a finite amount of funding available. Questions about how to best provide services are also questions of public policy, as government administrators attempt to balance the needs of their constituent groups. How do you compare the need for roads and bridges with the need to serve families in crisis? How do you balance the need to preserve farmland or open space with the need to provide affordable housing? In many ways, these needs can be in direct competition. In too many cases the cost of delivering services is far outpacing the available revenues. To function in this environment, government agencies must clarify priorities.

Government services are not typically restricted to the residents of the jurisdiction or even to citizens. Services such as environmental protection, libraries, or national parks benefit a much broader section of society. As a result, agencies often have difficulty gaining consensus on what problems exist and which ones are most critical. Although some studies have suggested that taxpayers are willing to pay more in taxes if they are satisfied with the services received, more often than not government is caught in between the competing priorities of the people they serve. Some constituents are unwilling to accept a decrease in services but at the same time are unwilling to support the additional funding needed to maintain existing service levels.

Lack of Control over the Inputs

There are two ways government lacks control over inputs. The first applies to the costs of the goods and services that enable government to do its job. Whenever the cost of manufacturing a consumer product goes up, the manufacturer can generally increase the final cost of the item and pass that cost on to the purchaser. When that happens, the laws of economics govern whether the consumer will continue to purchase the product at the increased cost. If consumers do continue this behavior, the level of production and presumably the bottom-line finances can stay the same. Government is subject to the same type of increases in the cost of providing services. Like businesses, it must pay increasing costs ranging from the cost of steel for public works projects to the cost of fuel for the cars used to transport workers to various assignments. Unlike business, the idea of government agencies increasing the cost of services and passing that cost onto its beneficiaries is not as easy to explain or to implement. It's not easy to make the case that taxes must be increased to sustain an existing level of service. Unlike the example of the manufacturer, the decision to raise taxes and to increase revenue rarely rests with the government agencies that are incurring the costs and demands. These decisions are made by legislators who listen carefully to the concerns of the taxpayers and often call instead for "leaner government."

The second problem related to inputs is the inability to control who or what will drive the need for services. In the same way that government lacks control over its fiscal inputs, it cannot control many of the external inputs that drive the demand for its services. For example, it cannot control the amount of snow that falls, nor can it predict the amount. It can't control the damage caused by other weather emergencies such as hurricanes or floods,[14] nor can it control or necessarily anticipate the number of people who will require their services, such as the number of children who will need foster care, the number of inmates in federal, state, or local prisons, or the number of students to be educated.

Balancing Competing Perspectives

People think about government in terms of individual transactions that they personally experience. They judge whether the process for obtaining a building permit took less time than they expected or whether the motor vehicle agency was open on Saturday when they needed to renew their driver's license. People may not see or consider the broader mission of the organization or make the connection between themselves and most of the work of government. The responsibilities of government are as diverse as the constituents that they serve, and there is much at stake in the allocation of funds and services. Many of these constituent groups are competing with each other for the limited services and resources government provides—for example, grants to communities, funding for the arts, or provision of infrastructure improvements. Every service or program has a constituency with a vested interest in lobbying for its retention, and services are often maintained even after their funding streams have been eliminated. For every program that serves millions of people, there are others than serve a much smaller group. If there is a fixed pool of resources available for government programs, then the inability to eliminate programs necessarily means that new programs shrink the available pieces of the pie for existing programs. Traditionally, government agencies are not used to thinking in these terms and rarely consider that they are forcing their constituents to compete against each other for access to resources. In times of reduced resources, agencies often "share the pain" equally by making across-the-board cuts rather than making decisions to eliminate programs. As a result, it is difficult to reach consensus on the problems that exist and their relative priorities (Haass, 1984).

Consequences for Poor Performance

The consequences to government for poor performance are also different. With few exceptions, government agencies are not going to go out of business, even if they are not meeting accepted standards of performance. In the private sector, customers who are not happy with the level of service they are receiving can choose to seek services elsewhere. In government, dissatisfied constituents may not have that option. They still need the services, and in many cases, government is the only provider. Instead of seeking a new service provider, these constituents take their complaints to legislators, who may react by decreasing the budget allocation to that agency, leading to a situation where public administrators are left trying to do even more with even less.

A Culture of Risk Aversion

Government tends to be extremely stable. As a result, it often suffers from a culture of risk aversion, which can discourage innovation, experimentation, risk taking, and entrepreneurial efforts. It's often the case that any public mistake is buried in the rush to generate new regulations. A typical yet frustrating response to mistakes or to failures is to write a new procedure to make sure no one ever tries them again. Faced with this culture, it should not be surprising that government's reaction to such efforts is often to develop a more entrenched bureaucracy.

The Public Nature of Work, Successes, and Failures

Sunshine laws and Freedom of Information/Open Public Record laws have brought many government processes into the public view. Though people might not agree about the extent of this visibility, much of the public sector's business is relatively transparent. Budgets are available for everyone to see. Public records acts, from the federal Freedom of Information Act to state and local public access laws, have made hundreds of thousands of documents available to the media and the general public. Government salary information is a matter of public record, and there certainly are no hidden stock options or golden parachutes. Sunshine laws require that many of the meetings of government be conducted in full view of the public. This is not to say that the public has access to everything that goes on in government. Many deliberations must, as they would in any business, be conducted out of the view of the public. But, to a greater degree than would occur for all but the most visible of businesses, government's actions are debated in the public forum and its failures dissected while its successes often go unnoticed.

Reconciling the Priorities of Elected Officials and Career Staff

Elected and appointed government officials and the career professional, administrative, and support personnel in government agencies typically have different priorities and responsibilities. A turnover in leadership is always possible in any organization, but government organizations are almost assured of a change in leadership at regular intervals following every election, yet the performance of the organization's leaders is rarely assessed. Public leaders, especially those who are appointed and serve at the pleasure of a chief official, are generally considered transitory and unlikely to stay for more than a few years at best. This short tenure often causes them to be focused on a few specific policy issues, and they are not perceived as being involved with the operation of the organization. Despite this perception, many of these top leaders recognize the need for strong organizational involvement. An example of this is provided in the NJDEP application for the Governor's Quality Award in which they say:

> … the Commissioner is responsible to the Governor for the implementation of the administration's environmental policy. Because the Commissioner is appointed by the Governor; the Department is subject to periodic change in leadership as administrations change. Naturally, such changes can impact the Department's organizational structure, business and regulatory approaches, and strategic and public policy priorities. However, Commissioner (Robert) Shinn has had the longest tenure of any Commissioner in the Department's 30 year history. This has provided not only consistency in strategic focus, but also fostered a stronger sense of stability throughout the Department.[15]

Similarly, in a study based on the Government Performance and Results Act, Harsell (2003) says that "although GPRA mandates the use of a number of managerial tools to improve internal agency management, it does little to redress the barriers between political appointees and career managers."[16] Additionally, most government agencies have a layer of career, nonappointed managers who provide the stability between transitions and should also be counted as part of the leadership. Dubnick (2005) describes a change in recent reform efforts to focus less on the elected officials as the point of accountability and more on the nonelected administrators. The timeline on which elected and appointed officials operate is different from that of the career worker. The elected official is trying to accomplish high-profile change in a relatively short period of time because of commitments made in his or her campaign and the need to create a resume for reelection. The career worker is typically trying to maintain and improve systems and processes that have and will exist for a very long time. An analogy might be that the elected official is running a sprint, while the career employee signed up for the marathon. Oftentimes, neither understands the viewpoints or goals of the other. The challenge is to find ways to integrate the needs of the elected and appointed government officials with those of long-term career professionals and to provide ways through which their goals and objectives can be linked.

Opportunities in Public Sector Assessment

Despite these challenges, implementing assessment processes offers some very interesting opportunities for public sector organizations, in addition to the obvious benefit of improving the way an organization functions. Among them are the following.

Focusing Attention on the Organization, Not the Discipline

The missions assigned to public agencies involve diverse fields such as environmental protection, transportation, commerce, or social services, which can be considered their "technical" disciplines. People who work in these disciplines and their constituents have a tendency to define them in terms of these individual specialties, which become a kind of shorthand for the agency's mission. A transportation agency is thought of primarily in terms of engineering, construction, and maintenance. We forget that each organization includes many other, different functions, including administrative, legislative liaison, and communication responsibilities. Rather than looking at the way the organization functions, each group focuses on its "piece" of the process, which can result in ineffective use of available resources. It is important to realize that the combination of all of these services is what creates the organization. From the perspective of external constituencies, program, job, and role distinctions are generally irrelevant. They are not interested in whether a certain process is done in Division X or Division Y. They are looking at outcomes: the results of the processes. A broader perspective ultimately contributes to improving the satisfaction of the groups for which programs and services are being provided. Frustrated taxpayers whose calls have been transferred four times do not care who they are talking to: They want their problem solved. Providing excellent service means that individual roles and functions must be transparent to the constituent. What matters are results.

The challenge for leaders and managers is to look past the specific discipline for which their agency is known and to think about the organization: a series of systems that interact to accomplish their goals. Organizational assessment processes facilitate this perspective by looking at the whole organization and how it functions. Cross-organizational communication, which is a key component in organizational assessment, can help create an organization-wide perspective. An assessment process would gather information not just about the organizational structure of an agency but also about the interaction of its various units and its major operating processes. Take, for example, a Parks and Recreation Department in a city government. In addition to identifying the various sections of the department such as park maintenance, recreation planning, community outreach, and grants and accounting, it would generate information about how those units interact. Similarly, it would provide information about the way each of those units, and the department as a whole, relate to other constituents including the Office of the Mayor, the police,

Figure 1.6 These four items form the basis for informed decision making in organizations.

the local school district, volunteer organizations, and those who use the services of the department.

Creating a Basis for Improvement

The information developed through an assessment can help determine how successful an agency is in carrying out its mission and what changes would improve the ability to do so. To make informed decisions about how and in what way to improve an organization, it is important to determine several key pieces of information:

- What are the current strengths of the organization?
- What opportunities exist for improvement?
- To what degree are the mission, goals, and resources currently aligned?
- What support is available to those who carry out the work of the organization on a daily basis?

Only after considering this information can meaningful decisions about the organization be made (Figure 1.6).

Providing Ways to Measure Success: Defining Success Factors and Measuring Results

Before you can measure success you must be able to define what it is. This is a major challenge for any government organization. The ability to determine whether a public sector organization is successful can depend on the ability to create agreement on the meaning of success—meanings that can differ from organization to organization, and sometimes office to office. While success can, overall, be defined as accomplishing the mission and goals of the organization, there is frequent and very public debate over what the mission and goals should be. The mission of a government agency is initially determined by its enabling legislation. General statements of purpose can often be subject to interpretation by the legislators who created them, the staff members who carry them out, and the members of the public who become the constituents and beneficiaries. The result can be a lack of consensus as to what constitutes the mission of the organization. In the private sector, financial measures are a recognized method of assessing organizational performance. In the public sector, financial measures are not necessarily good measures of success. Schachter (2007) describes the difficulty of measuring the financial aspects of government, noting that the "long term inability of scholars to agree on how to maximize governmental efficiency suggests the difficulty of measuring public sector cost-benefit ratios."[17]

Many times, success in the public sector means dealing with avoidance or prevention. Government agencies should be considered successful when they avoid a bridge collapse because of a sound program of inspection and repair or when they prevent an epidemic because flu vaccine was made available and distributed timely and efficiently. Similarly, government programs could be considered successful if they maintain desirable levels of services. Other programs might define success, ultimately, as putting themselves out of business by eliminating child abuse or finding ways to decrease the prison population. Organizational assessment can provide a starting point for establishing new measures of success.

Creating Awareness about Effective Practices in Other Sectors

Government officials are weary of frequent admonishing to "be more like business" when that advice is well intended but applied inappropriately to incomparable situations. Still, there are situations where government, health care, business, and education have common practices and could learn from each other. Many of the administrative and support functions in government are similar to those that exist in the private sector. Using them as "benchmarks" can provide new ways of looking at the organization as well as a source of new practices that can be adapted for government use. For example, when the Robert Wood Johnson University Hospital at Hamilton wanted to improve the way that it addressed patient care, service, and accommodations, it sent a team to study not only other hospitals but also the Ritz-Carlton Hotel (a previous winner of the Baldrige National Quality Award) to determine what practices might be applicable to its environment.[18] This type of creative thinking enabled it to win a Baldrige Award of its own.

The Role of Constituents and Beneficiaries in the Assessment Process

The idea of incorporating constituent feedback into assessment programs is being used increasingly at different levels of government. The demand by citizens for increased levels of government services and similar demand for better-quality services is linked to increased demands for administrative reform. The National Center for Public Performance at Rutgers University–Newark, which is devoted to improving productivity in the public sector, advocates "citizen-driven government performance."[19] Programs such as the Government Results and Performance Act recognize the need to include customer involvement in the assessment process, as does the Baldrige process.

One of the critical success factors in achieving a high level of organizational performance is to have a clear understanding of the needs and wants of those served. This includes those who benefit directly from products and services and those who benefit indirectly. It applies to others who also have an interest in these services. Many of the existing tools for assessing organizations, including the Baldrige program, specifically include customer feedback as part of the assessment process. Government is becoming increasingly more sophisticated in identifying constituents and beneficiaries and figuring out how to incorporate them into the process.

Considering these opportunities and challenges as a whole provides an illustration of the potential impact that an organizational assessment process can have. With an understanding of its potential to help move an organization forward, it can be an important strategy in many ways. It has benefits both for the organization as a whole and for the individuals who have the opportunity to participate. An organizational assessment can:

- Provide a structured communication process that takes existing information from across the organization and creates new knowledge through the exchange of information.
- Define organizational excellence and continuous improvement.
- Identify the strengths of the organization.
- Provide a realistic picture of the challenges and opportunities facing the organization.
- Provide a common understanding of the measures of success.
- Help clearly identify for employees both the critical issues and what the relative priorities are for those issues.

Assessment enables participants at all levels to look at the organization and to ask if the pieces are in place to create the type of organization it aspires to be. At the same time, it provides leaders with an opportunity to create a case for change to meet the increasing and evolving demands of their constituencies. A commitment to assessment and to the use of assessment processes will provide government with ways to increase organizational performance, to maximize resources, and to be able to "tell its story"—to communicate with its many and varied constituencies and beneficiaries in a positive way about the good work that is being done.

One of the long-term goals associated with the implementation of an assessment program is to make assessment a regular part of the way that the organization does business. The idea is to create a collective understanding of the benefits of assessment and improvement. Public sector organizations need to find a way to create a culture in which, even in the absence of a formal assessment process, people think about whether there are better, more efficient, and more effective ways to serve the public.

The challenge for government leaders, managers, and staff, then, is to change the culture of these organizations to integrate the concept of assessment and to instill a commitment to continuous improvement.

Summary

The leaders of public sector organizations at all levels of government are continually faced with the need to improve their agency's performance to increase the level of both efficiency and effectiveness and to address the public's expectation for the way that programs and services are provided. The ability to make such decisions and to initiate significant and substantive changes must be grounded in a comprehensive understanding of the agency and the way it functions. While government agencies face challenges that may differ from the issues in other sectors, they also have a different set of opportunities.

Organizational assessment provides a structured program for examining both operations and outcomes. Assessment is a systematic process that results in the development of cross-cutting information on issues that are most critical to the success of any organization. It relies on the participation of those who work in an agency, and, as a result, it builds an internal case for change. It is a comprehensive program that begins with understanding the current organization. This information is compared with the vision that leaders have for the organization so that a determination can be made of the gap that exists between the current and the desired way of operating. Opportunities for improvement are identified and prioritized, and, finally, project plans are developed and implemented. The feedback from this process forms the starting point for a new cycle of continuous improvement.

Notes

1. The terms *public sector organization* and *government agency* are used interchangeably through this book to refer to federal, state, and local governments and to other entities such as boards, authorities, and commissions. When an example pertains to a particular type of government agency, the language will include a reference to a specific level.
2. p. ix.

3. This quote is taken from the "Statement of findings and purposes" that precedes the Government Performance and Results Act. The text of the act can be found at the White House Website: http://whitehouse.gov/omb/mgmt-gpra/gplaw2m.html#h2
4. http://www.agacgfm.org/harrispoll2008.aspx
5. p. xii.
6. The words *constituents* and *beneficiaries* are used throughout this book. Beneficiaries are those who directly benefit from a service, for example, someone who obtains a driver's license or receives a grant. Generally speaking, beneficiaries are a subset of constituents, a broader group that includes beneficiaries and other stakeholders who are impacted by or who have an interest in the operations of government.
7. The term *organizational assessment* is used here as a generic term. It includes many types of assessment programs and is not limited to a specific model.
8. Assessment processes can be used by entire organizations or by subunits such as divisions, offices, and programs within a larger unit.
9. p. 9.
10. This book focuses on self-assessment processes, in which the members of the organization are used to conduct the assessment. While assessments can be done by consultants or others external to the organization, the organization loses a valuable opportunity: the benefits that accrue from the organizational and personal learning experienced by the staff and leaders who take part in an assessment process.
11. p. 93.
12. Negotiation and consensus are discussed in more detail in Chapter 2, "Assessment as a Communication Process."
13. The New Jersey Governor's Award for Quality, administered by Quality New Jersey, used the Baldrige criteria as the format for its assessment and award process. More information about the New Jersey Department of Environmental Protection is available in Chapter 7.
14. Government agencies can and should track trends over time and incorporate that information into planning. However, some of these inputs are difficult to use in predicting resource allocation for a particular year. For example, you can track snowfall amounts for the last 10 years and predict the amount of salt that will be needed for snow and ice control. You cannot eliminate the possibility that the salt that you purchase will not be needed and that the funds could have been used for another purchase.
15. New Jersey Department of Environmental Protection application for the 2002 Governor's Award.
16. p. 2.
17. p. 801.
18. Robert Wood Johnson University Hospital at Hamilton (2004).
19. Rutgers University–Newark, School of Public Affairs and Administration website, http://spaa.newark.rutgers.edu/

Chapter 2

Assessment as a Communication Process

This chapter examines assessment as a communication process and considers the types of communication that occur during an assessment and their benefit to the organization. Assessment facilitates the creation of new organizational knowledge by bringing together the knowledge held by diverse participants. Breaking down assessment into its component communication processes (information gathering and exchange, negotiation and consensus, information dissemination) demonstrates how assessment can change perceptions about the organization itself and how the organization can achieve its mission. Assessment can also create a focus on organizational priorities and can change what people inside the organization and constituents see as the priorities. It includes research that supports the ability of the process to create convergence, or a shared sense of the critical issues and priorities facing the organization.

Communication, which can be described as the exchange of information to create shared meaning, is one of the most significant factors in the ability of an organization to accomplish its mission, goals, and objectives and to achieve its vision. It is a continuous process of interacting with others, both inside and outside the organization. Communication—the amount, the type, and the quality—is one of the most important determinants of organizational performance. Communication can be a positive force or an obstacle to progress. It enables our daily work when it is effective and invariably impedes our work when it isn't. It is multidirectional: horizontal, vertical, top-down, bottom-up, internal, and external. In its many forms—verbal, written, nonverbal, and, increasingly, electronic[1]—it plays a major role in determining the effectiveness and the efficiency with which an organization can function. Organizational communication is the vehicle through which knowledge and information are disseminated, and, in large part, it determines how work gets done, how decisions are made, who has access to information, and, sometimes more importantly, who does not.

Communication is the exchange of information to create shared meaning.

Public agencies exchange information in myriad ways, and a structured organizational self-assessment can be considered one type of organizational communication process. The act of initiating an assessment can also be viewed as introducing a structured communication process into the daily life of an organization. Communication can be thought of as the engine that drives assessment, and the success of the assessment relies on the quality of the information that is exchanged. If the communication that takes place in an assessment is effective, it increases the likelihood that the process will result in meaningful outcomes. That, in turn, can facilitate change.

Assessment and communication intersect in several different but important ways:

- An assessment process is conducted by collecting, exchanging, and interpreting information.
- The participants in the process communicate with each other and with others inside and outside the organization in both the collection and the exchange of information.
- Participants use the communication processes of negotiation and consensus-building to consider the information presented and to reach agreement on the strengths, opportunities for improvement, and future actions.
- The quality of the communication that takes place in the organization is one of the factors that can be measured during an assessment.
- Communication before, during, and after the assessment process is the most important factor in keeping nonparticipants—the rest of the organization—informed about what is taking place.
- Communication to constituents during the process (as part of information collection or as participants) about the outcomes of the process can build and enhance relationships, and communicating the outcomes can be an important first step in engaging constituents in improvement efforts.

In addition to these more visible communication activities, the assessment process also has the potential to have a positive impact on future communication. During the assessment process, participants develop new communication channels as they seek out information. The process also creates interpersonal and cross-organizational working relationships. Both of these can have lasting impacts and can facilitate and enhance the amount, type, and level of communication that takes place in the organization long after the assessment process is completed. When these factors are taken into account, it becomes apparent that communication facilitates the assessment process and is itself an outcome of the assessment process.

Communication Processes in Self-Assessment

Communication is an integral part of an assessment, and several different communication processes are incorporated in the structure or framework of an assessment process (see Figure 2.1). This framework is designed to maximize the ability of the organization to acquire information, to make it available to participants, and to use it for analysis. This is accomplished through the use of four communication processes:

■ Creation of a common language.
■ Information gathering and exchange.
■ Negotiation and consensus-building.
■ Disseminating information and outcomes.

Communication Process 1: Creation of a Common Language

One of the challenges in undertaking an assessment is to provide a common frame of reference for four key groups: (1) the participants; (2) people who, while not participants, provide input and contribute information; (3) those involved in implementing the resulting improvement opportunities; and (4) those simply interested in the process and its results. Using a structured process gives all of these groups a way to talk about the process, regardless of their level of personal involvement, by helping to establish the following:

■ A common language to describe, discuss, and share information about the organization.
■ A common vocabulary of assessment and continuous improvement terminology.

Haavind (1992) writes about the use of assessment processes at the Xerox corporation and quotes a product manager who stated that before engaging in quality processes "… everyone had their own ways of solving problems…. We were all speaking different languages."[2]

Communication in the Assessment Process

Creation of a common language

How do we define the key concepts about our organization?

What is the terminology of quality and continuous improvement?

Information collection and exchange

What would a profile of our organization include?

What information do we have?

What do we need to learn?

What are the key values that define our organization?

Who has the information that we need?

How do we collect it?

What information do we need from constituents?

What are our trends?

With whom should we compare ourselves?

Negotiation and consensus

What is the most accurate picture of our current state?

What are our strengths?

What are our opportunities for improvement?

What are our priorities for change?

What can we reasonably do?

What resources will it require?

What will we do?

Who will be responsible?

How will we measure our accomplishments?

Communication and dissemination of assessment outcomes

How will the outcomes be disseminated?

To whom will the information be provided?

What communication methods are most appropriate for different audiences?

How will feedback be incorporated in the assessment process?

Figure 2.1 Communication in the assessment process.

Providing a Common Language to Talk about the Organization

It may seem somewhat strange to talk about creating a common language to discuss the organization. After all, people work for the same agency, perform activities related to the mission of their workplace, and work toward the same goals, so it seems logical that they would have common ways of describing the organization and its structure, its people, and its way of doing business. However, this is not always the case, especially in an agency where people may not have opportunities to interact or share information with others outside their own part of the organizational structure. *Getting Started* (Baldrige National Quality Program, 2003a), a guidebook for conducting a self-assessment using the Baldrige program, lists "building a common language" as one of the principal reasons organizations initially undertake a self-assessment, saying "… You create opportunities for people across the organization to communicate with one another, perhaps for the first time. In effect, you are providing a common language so they can develop a common understanding of their organization's purpose, activities, and environment.[3]"

> "…You create opportunities for people across the organization to communicate with one another, perhaps for the first time. In effect, you are providing a common language so they can develop a common understanding of their organization's purpose, activities, and environment."
>
> *Getting Started*

Public sector organizations are very diverse, not just in terms of the people who work there but also in terms of the occupations, professions, and disciplines that they represent. As a result, people often have very different ways of talking about what goes on in their workplace and how they get it done. Within organizations there are multiple languages where the terminology, or jargon, reflects the many differences in people and professions. Although we may not often stop to think about it, several types of language factor into daily work operations.

First, every organization has a language or vocabulary that its members use to describe the organization itself, its people, and its work processes both internally to staff members and externally to constituents and beneficiaries. This includes the commonly used terminology appropriate to the major profession or industry that it represents. Those in a transportation or public works department will use the language of engineering and planning. The staff of a commerce department will use the language of economics. This type of language also, without a doubt, includes its share of abbreviations, nicknames, and acronyms. Government agencies are particularly well known for their innumerable and sometime indecipherable acronyms, so much so that some agencies provide new employees with lists of acronyms and their meanings as part of their orientation. It can be difficult to remember that these terms have little or no meaning to internal and external groups that are not familiar with its abbreviations and acronyms and those who are not exposed to the "industry" terminology on a regular basis.

Types of Language in Organizations

- The terminology of the agency's primary profession or discipline, including acronyms, abbreviations, and nicknames
- The terminology of different occupational groups within the same agency

Those in different occupational groups have language they use both to describe and to conduct their work. Managers, professionals, technical, and administrative staff all have different perspectives and different ways of looking at and describing their workplace. There are specialists not only in the core functions of the agency (e.g., social work, health, or environmental science) but also in the many other disciplines necessary for them to operate effectively. Within each organization, people work in many other types of jobs and functions that support the core technical mission, and they use language appropriate to their own profession. This includes occupations such as accounting, records management, or grant administration. Some government agencies may have librarians or mechanics and fleet managers. Each of these groups has a different way of talking about work. Accountants speak a different language from social workers, and human resource professionals use different terminology from engineers. Individuals and groups assign different words and meanings to workplace terminology. All too often, these differences become a barrier to sharing information between groups. Even though it can create shared understanding, language can also be used to include or exclude groups of people, both employees and constituents, based on whether they can decode the meanings.

The engineer in Figure 2.2 works in a field office. When asked to identify the "leadership" of the agency, she thinks of the overall leader and her field manager but not the other managers who work in the central office. The accountant in the second example works in a central office. He thinks of "leadership" as the overall leader and all the managers. A third person who is asked the same question might think of only the top leader. Before beginning an assessment process, the participants discuss who specifically they are talking about when they consider the

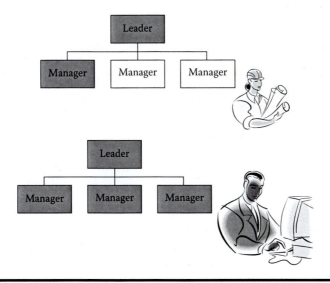

Figure 2.2   Defining leaders.

leadership of the agency so that they have a common frame of reference for purposes of their discussion.

In an assessment process, participants are charged with examining and talking about the functions of a public sector organization in a much broader way. A structured assessment process requires specific categories of information as the topics to be considered and discussed. This provides a framework in which participants can discuss the organization as a larger system of interrelated functions. Rather than talking about individual offices, programs, or occupations, those who participate in an assessment are talking about leadership, planning, constituents, and other concepts that cut across all areas.

For example, the process:

- Encourages participants to describe work processes rather than work units.
- Calls for an answer to the question of what we mean when we talk about information usage or about having a workforce focus.
- Requires a common definition of who people consider to be the leaders or managers—something that can vary in the minds of the participants (see Figure 2.2).
- Helps define not only what leadership is but also what it means to have effective leadership—and what components go into evaluating it.

This common language allows people from across the organization to effectively communicate during the process about such things as the mission, goals, and key functions.

The Vocabulary of Assessment and Continuous Improvement

The assessment process also provides a framework for developing an understanding of the concepts of quality and continuous improvement, which also have their own terminology. It can be difficult to convey to the assessment participants and non-participants (who may be curiously observing the assessment process) what these terms mean, starting with the word *quality* itself. What do we mean when we talk about having or identifying a quality organization? Different people, based on their experience in the workplace or with other quality initiatives, may have very different definitions. Quality, to one person, might be perceived as a formal process for measuring performance. To another, it might mean achieving a certain targeted level of results, without considering how those results were obtained. People may perceive quality as "simply a buzzword" that causes them to react to the words rather than the concepts. They may respond by saying, "We've already done quality circles," or "We tried total quality management," and not understand that quality and continuous improvement are actually a way of doing business. Haavind (1992) cites the difficulty of communicating the concepts of "total quality management" and "continuous improvement" as one of the obstacles to be overcome in "achieving … major change in corporate culture."[4]

The assessment process provides a way to operationalize, or define, the concept of quality for the members of the organization. In effect, the categories that form the assessment structure and the questions or criteria that are used to examine the organization during the process provide a definition of quality. It says to leaders, employees, and constituents that being effective in these areas "is the way that quality is defined in this organization." Because the assessment process examines several different categories, it also reinforces the idea that quality is an overall measure of organizational performance and that effectiveness in one category is not sufficient to create a quality organization. It is the combined effectiveness across all categories that really represents the level of quality for which a participating agency is striving.

The assessment process also introduces participants to a common vocabulary of quality and continuous improvement terminology.[5] It is often the case, especially in agencies that are conducting their first assessment, that participants will not be familiar with much of the terminology. For this reason, assessment processes often include an educational component. Participants may vary in the level of prior knowledge about assessment or continuous improvement. Even though definitions may be provided to them, George and Weimerskirch (1994) suggest that a shared understanding of quality concepts can exist effectively only if participants are trained in those concepts. An option for accomplishing this is through the use of a trained facilitator or designated process leader, who can be either internal or external to the agency. One of the roles this person can play is as an educator who teaches the participants about the assessment methodology to be used; this process also provides them with a common language of assessment. The facilitator can educate participants on quality terminology and how these terms relate to the process by providing definitions and examples that will enable them to understand and apply the most important concepts.[6]

When people are provided with definitions of quality terminology, it establishes a common understanding of these terms, which they can use consistently throughout the process to make judgments about the performance of the organization. Not only does this facilitate the internal assessment process, but quality terminology also becomes a way to extend comparisons outside the organization by providing a way to benchmark[7] its performance against other comparable government or nongovernment agencies using consistent quality language and meanings. An additional benefit is that it provides a way for staff members to talk about the work of the agency outside the assessment process, which contributes to integrating quality as a normal part of how they think about the workplace.

Communication Process 2: Information Collection and Exchange

The ability to conduct a thorough assessment of any government agency relies on three factors related to information and communication:

- The existence of information about the organization and its availability and accessibility.
- The willingness of the people who have access to that information to make it available to create a shared picture of the organization.
- The ability to analyze the information so that informed decisions about the state of the organization can be made.

An organizational assessment begins with the collection of information and data from different areas of the organization that is to be the subject of the process, whether it is the entire organization or a smaller unit. The better the quality of the information gathered, the clearer the picture of the organization that will be created. The decision about what information will be collected is not random. Structured self-assessment processes specify a series of categories to be considered and provide a framework of questions within each category. By answering those questions, participants construct a picture of the organization and the state of its activities. The collection and subsequent exchange of information needed to answer the questions in each assessment category constitute a communication process in which information is shared with all participants to construct a more complete picture of the organization.

The process of organizational assessment uses a combination three types of information, as shown in Figure 2.3:

- Information that already exists in the organization, such as records, statistics, written policies and procedures, and measures.

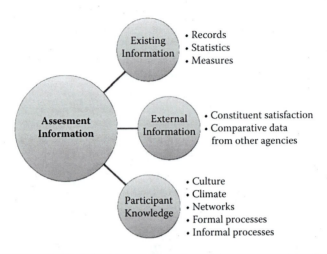

Figure 2.3   Communication inputs.

■ Information that can be collected or obtained from sources external to the organization, such as comparative data or benchmarks from similar organizations, and satisfaction levels of beneficiaries and constituents.

■ Knowledge that exists within the members of the organization, such as an understanding of the culture, climate, networks, and formal and informal processes.

These three types of information become the inputs in the information collection process.

The process of answering the questions that form the basis for the self-assessment incorporates two types of knowledge: personal knowledge and organizational knowledge. Personal knowledge is the sum of the information that participants have collected as a result of their own personal experiences in the organization. This can be made up of communication, experiences, and perceptions, including interactions with coworkers, supervisors, and subordinates. It can also encompass experiences in dealing with constituents either firsthand or by observation of the way others manage their interactions. The nature of the questions also requires that participants reach outside their personal knowledge to other sources inside and outside the organization to gather knowledge and data with which they may not be familiar. The information needed to respond to the questions may not be readily available or known to the participants. Organizational knowledge can be defined as data and information about the organization itself: processes, policies, procedures, and structure.

The Importance of People in the Information Collection Process

This structured approach to assessment depends almost completely on the contributions of employees, either through knowledge that they already possess or through their ability to assemble the needed information. Information collection of this kind requires participants to find, bring together, and exchange information from all parts of the workplace to create a complete description of the current state of the organization. This, in turn, requires that people from across the organization be involved in the information collection process. Why is it so important to include a cross-section of people? Simply put, it's not possible for any one person, regardless of his or her job, rank, longevity, or location to know everything that there is to know about the workings of the organization. Much of the information needed to conduct an assessment already exists within the organization, but not necessarily in a form that is readily known by all or easily available. The information can reside in many locations, based on the function or unit where the work takes place, and can exist in many different forms—for example, written, verbal, electronic, and visual. It can include data and statistics, written reports, flowcharts, and stories about practices. Think of the vast quantities of information that are present in every organization. This information is generated every day in the course of doing business, but it may be known only to those people involved in a specific pro-gram or procedure. Additionally, though much of the information resides within the agency, some of it may also be external, residing with constituents, regulatory groups, legislators, or the community.

The success of the information collection stage relies heavily on involving peo-ple who know about and have access to different pools of information. For that reason, the best results can be achieved by engaging a diverse group of participants with access to different parts of the organization and different types of knowledge. The most successful assessment processes will select participants that reflect the demographic makeup of the organization, since the required knowledge resides with people at all levels. The limits on the knowledge that any individual possesses can be both horizontal and vertical. People may know a great deal about how their own division or unit works but not about the other units that make up the agency. Participants are empowered, enabled, and encouraged to collect information about their own area and other parts of the organization. In the example shown in Figure 2.4, someone who works in Division A of the Department of Public Works may understand what goes on in that division but may not interact with Division B or Division C. This person's organizational knowledge, therefore, is limited to the vertical structure in which he or she works.

People may have very specific knowledge about their role and the specific pieces of processes in which they are involved. Every organization has a person who knows everything about a particular area or process—the "go-to" person. When people need information, they'll say, "Ask Mary—she knows all about that," or, "John is the only one who understands how that works." Yet those people may never have had the opportunity to learn any information about other areas. They may not understand how their particular process (or piece of a larger process) fits into the overall scheme of things, including what happens to their piece of the process once

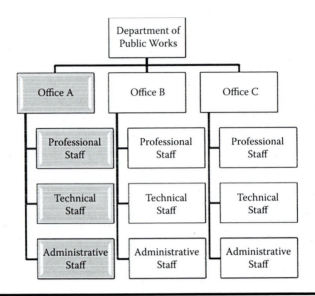

Figure 2.4 Example of vertical knowledge in organizations.

it leaves their hands. At the same time, people at different levels have access to different types of information.

In the example in Figure 2.5, administrative staff members may have common work activities and shared practices. They may interact with each other on a regular basis to accomplish those processes, giving them certain knowledge that might not be available to the professional or technical staff. Similarly, they might share access to constituents that differs from the access that others have. The frontline person who has direct contact with the agencies' clients, such as the person processing registrations or driver's licenses at a Motor Vehicle agency or voter registration documents at a County Clerk's office, has an understanding of the constituents' needs and expectations that may be very different from the information that the chief executive has. Technical staff members may have information about systems and processes that may not be available to others. A good example of this is an understanding of programming, hardware and software, systems, and database management information. Senior executives who are responsible for policy decisions will have access to information on which those decisions are based and will understand the intent of the decisions. They will have information about the external environment that may not be widely known to the staff.

Once this information has been collected and brought to the table (literally and figuratively), the participants in the assessment process pool the information to create a picture of the organization. Combining the information that has been collected in this way allows participants to compare their individual knowledge and understanding with that of coworkers. While doing this, they increase the scope and depth of knowledge they have about the organization.

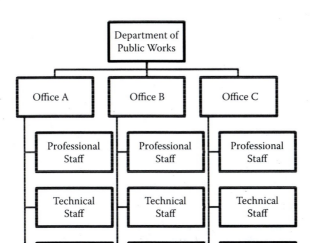

Figure 2.5   Example of horizontal information in organizations.

Since assessment is a fact-based process, the information that is finally incorporated into the assessment must ultimately be objective and verifiable rather than simply anecdotal. The usability of the outcomes from the assessment depends in large part on the quality of the information collected during the process.

Communication Process 3: Negotiation and Consensus-Building

When all the information has been collected, it is important to make sure not only that the information is shared with others but also that there is agreement on what the information means and represents. This is accomplished by negotiating a common interpretation. Negotiation, in the context of organizational assessment, is a communication process in which people discuss the differences in their perceptions of information and its meaning to come to a consensus, or a common, agreed upon definition of what the information represents. Everett Rogers (1995), in his work on the diffusion of innovation in organizations, describes communication as:

> … a process in which participants create and share information with one another in order to reach a mutual understanding. This definition implies that communication is a process of convergence (or divergence) as two or more individuals exchange information in order to move toward each other (or apart) in the meanings that they give to certain events.[8]

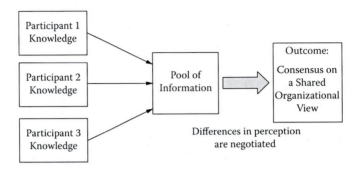

Figure 2.6 Negotiation in the self-assessment process.

The negotiation process provides a way to compare the information that has been collected and pooled to reach agreement on a picture, or collective understanding of the agency. The goal is to reach a consensus on a shared view of the organization and its needs. People can consider the same information but assign different meanings to it. Applying Rogers's (1995) definition to the assessment process, the purpose is to use communication to foster convergence about the information and what it means.

The negotiation process allows participants to find common ground from which to start in identifying the strengths and opportunities for improvement. The diagram in Figure 2.6 shows how this negotiation process takes place. The individual participants contribute the information they have collected (based on their personal knowledge combined with other data to which they have access) to create a pool of information. Within that pool, there may be information and descriptions that do not match. The information contributed by Participant 1 and the information contributed by Participant 2 may represent different perspectives on a process, or the relationship between units. As they discuss the information, they negotiate a shared meaning. For example, in an assessment process in a state agency, the following conversation took place. It concerned constituent information and whether the staff received any feedback from constituents.

Participant A: We don't get any complaints from people.
Participant B: Are you kidding? Am I the only one who sees the complaints come in? I open the letters, and people do have complaints sometimes.
Participant A: Well, I never see those letters.
Participant C: Maybe we need to have a process so that people know when a complaint or question comes in.

If you had asked the participants prior to this exchange whether they ever receive critical feedback from constituents, Participants A and C would have said no, and Participant B would have said yes; each individual's perspective would have been accurate. The difference is that only Participant B had access to the information about participant feedback. This brief conversation was, in fact, a negotiation.

Participant A presented his or her information. Participant B countered with different information. The result of this negotiation/discussion was a shared understanding among the participants that their unit did, in fact, receive complaints from constituents but also that this information was not being made available to staff. In this case, the negotiation also directly contributed to a recommendation for improvement: the creation of a feedback process.

The negotiation process also encourages the development of systems thinking among the participants. The process of presenting and comparing information to identify the degree to which there is agreement and the degree to which differences exist and must be resolved is intended to get people out of their organizational silos and to create a picture of how all the various pieces fit together in a system. They learn how the parts of the organization interact to accomplish the work, where links exists, and where they might be missing. Deming speaks of the potential of cross-functional teams, such as those often used in assessment processes, to "break down barriers between departments" (Cornin, 2004).[9]

Once the negotiation process has been completed and a shared organizational view has been created, the next step is to examine the information to identify the existing strengths and the opportunities for improvement. The communication strategy used at this stage is consensus-seeking. Participants review the shared organizational information that has been negotiated and identify things that they believe represent the strengths of the agency and things that could be improved. Given the volume of information that can be developed in the earlier, information-gathering stages, identifying these factors can be a challenging process. Even more challenging is the next step, which is to discuss and reach consensus on factors that are strengths and, perhaps more importantly, factors that represent opportunities for improvement. There is a commonly used expression that "where you stand depends on where you sit." Depending on a person's location and role in the organization, one might see certain information as a strength while another may believe that it requires improvement. Once these opportunities have been identified and agreed upon, participants must then evaluate the relative importance of the opportunities. This may not be an easy process. People may see the opportunities for improvement that affect them or their ability to get their jobs done as the highest priority. The goal is to keep the attention focused on the whole organization and what would provide the biggest benefit. The communication processes of negotiation and consensus-building can be used again to reach agreement. It is then possible to begin the development of action plans for implementing improvement. The result of this process is the beginning of an agenda for improvement.

Communication Process 4: Communicating Assessment Outcomes

One of the other major functions of communication in an assessment process is to provide a mechanism to inform the organization as a whole about both the progress and outcomes of the assessment. While smaller organizations or units may involve their entire staff, many organizations find it difficult, if not impossible, to include every employee in the assessment process because of the sheer size of the staff or the available time frame. In this case, it is particularly important to share the outcomes. Disseminating the information that comes out of the assessment process is important for a number of reasons:

- The purpose of collecting the information used in the assessment is to provide the most comprehensive view of the current state of the organization so that it can be used for decision making. Sharing this information can have a positive impact on decision making, outside the assessment process, by ensuring that people have access to more information than they might normally receive in the course of doing business.
- It creates ownership of the process by the organization as a whole. Rather than being seen as the work product of a limited group or team of employees, sharing the outcomes makes everyone a part of the process.
- It sets the stage for implementation by presenting the underlying logic for changes resulting from the assessment process.
- It gives people an internal benchmark from which they can compare the impact of changes on future performance and effectiveness.
- It demonstrates seriousness of purpose to constituents and beneficiaries. It indicates a willingness to change and demonstrates that their input was incorporated into the process and that their concerns were addressed to the greatest extent possible.
- It provides a way to get information to those who, because of their role in the organization, might not otherwise have the opportunity to learn this information.
- It provides an educational element by sharing information that will shape both staff and constituent perspectives on the way that the organization operates.
- It opens the process to feedback and can be used as a first step in establishing a feedback loop within the agency.

Disseminating information creates a basis for moving forward into implementation and periodic reassessment. Perhaps the most important aspect of providing this information is to educate staff about the process and its benefits, which in turn begins the process of creating a culture of assessment.

Agency staff members are not necessarily the only audience for communicating the outcomes of an assessment. These results can also be presented to constituents. Constituents are, on a regular basis, making their own assessments of public sector performance, but those assessments may have little to do with actual performance and more to do with how they perceive their access to government decision making. Proactive communication of assessment results can build trust in government's efforts to engage constituents in organizational improvement efforts. This can also apply to regulatory agencies or governing boards. In a 2008 audio conference sponsored by the International City/County Management Association (ICMA), Ellen Liston of Coral Springs, Florida, winner of the Baldrige Award, talked about how they provide assessment information to their commission members in a workshop format where it can be reviewed and discussed.

Many government agencies have begun efforts to communicate performance outcomes and results to constituents. At the same time, external groups have engaged for some time in presenting and comparing government performance information. One of the most well-known groups is *Governing Magazine*'s "Grading the States" initiative. For nearly 10 years, *Governing Magazine* and the Pew Center on the States have collaborated on the Government Performance Project, which is described as an "effort to evaluate all 50 states' managerial capacity."[10] It displays comparative information for all 50 states in a report card format, which provides an easy-to-use diagram showing the performance measures of one or more organizations. Figure 2.7 shows the 2002 report card prepared as part of the Federal Performance Project of *Government Executive Magazine*. The report card shows the relative rankings for six federal agencies on five dimensions of performance. The information is available not only to the agencies involved but also to a wide group of constituents.

2002 REPORT CARD	Agency Grade	Managing for Results	Financial Management	Human Resources Management	Information Management	Physical Assets Management	
Social Security Administration	B	B	A	B	A	N/A	Disability insurance and staffing problems, lack of involvement in policymaking tarnish reputation for excellent management.
Federal Aviation Administration	B	B	C	B	B	B	Significant progress in creating tools for accountability and in technology upgrades offsets regulatory weaknesses.
Environmental Protection Agency	B	B	B	C	C	N/A	Major effort to improve performance measures and tie them to budget paying off; data reliability and staffing challenges persist.
Internal Revenue Service	B	B	C	C	C	N/A	Restructuring, pay-for-performance improve accountability; manual accounting, staffing mismatches and inability to measure voluntary compliance hurt performance.
Centers for Medicare & Medicaid Services	C	D	C	C	C	N/A	Lack of mission clarity, tradition of poor management dog efforts to tighten controls, improve relations with clients.
Immigration and Naturalization Service	D	D	C	D	D	C	Medicare to poor performance in every management area persists except on services side, where fees support improvements.

Figure 2.7 *Governing Magazine*'s **Grading the States Initiative.**

Communication as a Subject of Assessment

An assessment process can also provide a basis for examining and improving internal communication. The type and the quality of communication that exists in the organization is one of the factors that can be measured as part of an assessment. Communication is a process of critical importance in the daily work activities of quality organizations. Blackburn and Rosen (1993) describe the existence of extensive top-down and bottom-up communication processes, including the use of cross-functional work teams, in Baldrige Award-winning companies. Their work provides evidence that the quality of existing communication in an organization is one of the factors affecting organizational excellence.

Communication can also be an outcome or benefit resulting from self-assessment. Enhanced organizational communication processes can be implemented after being identified as an "opportunity for improvement" in the assessment. Hart and Bogan (1992) say that the establishment of a "new level of communications within companies" is a "major consequence" of the Baldrige process.[11] The communication that takes place during the assessment can provide a good basis for increasing and improving the quality of communication that takes place during the ongoing daily operation of the organization. The process brings together people who may not work together on a regular basis and gives them a format to discuss their different roles and responsibilities. It provides an opportunity to build links with others and for them to carry on those conversations long after the formal assessment process has ended. Deming speaks of the potential of cross-functional work teams to "break down barriers between departments" (Cornin, 2004).[12]

Defining Assessment Terminology

When we say that a practice is "widely deployed" throughout the organization, what does that mean to people? They need to have a common understand that deployment refers to a way of measuring the extent to which a particular practice has been successfully implemented in various units across the organization. Examining the extent of deployment is a form of measurement or quantification. In the same way, while it may sound strange to hear people talking about a "robust" process, it refers to a process that is well understood and implemented throughout an organization. By the end of the assessment, that phrase will have a specific meaning that is shared among all the participants.

Summary

Communication is the foundation of organizational assessment, and in many ways a structured organizational process is actually a communication process. The effectiveness of an assessment process relies on the ability to collect, exchange, analyze, and prioritize information. There are four component communication processes: (1) creation of a common language; (2) information collection and exchange; (3) negotiation and consensus-building; and (4) dissemination of assessment information. Organizations are often complex structures, made up of many overlapping systems and processes. Unfortunately, many people are aware only of their own area, which causes them to think, act, and plan within their organizational silos. To fully appreciate and understand the way any government agency functions, it is critical that information be gathered from across the agency. It also requires willingness to negotiate the meaning of the information so that agreement can be reached on a shared picture of the organization. The process increases the internal level of knowledge about the organization across areas and across employee groups.

Assessment creates a common language across multiple work units and facilitates discussion of assessment and continuous improvement, and the framework of the process helps to provide a shared definition of quality.

Notes

1. Electronic communication most often refers to the use of computers to communicate. Forms of electronic communication can include e-mail, instant messaging, and texting. It is also referred to as mediated communication.
2. p. 43.
3. National Institute of Standards and Technology, p. 10.
4. p. XI.
5. Many of the concepts used to describe various parts of the assessment process are contained in the glossary of this book.
6. Many organizations decide to conduct a training or orientation session for participants prior to an assessment process. The training can be provided by an internal or external facilitator, a team leader, or a training professional. The purpose is to familiarize participants with both the assessment terminology and quality terminology so that all participants have the same understanding of what is meant by these concepts prior to engaging in discussion and evaluation. This can also be done as part of the assessment process.
7. Benchmarking refers to the process of comparing an organization or its processes, services, or outcomes with those of another organization.
8. pp. 5–6.
9. p. 46.
10. *Governing Magazine,* March 2008. Can be retrieved at: http://www.governing.com/gpp/2008/index.htm
11. p. 23.
12. p. 46.

Chapter 3

Applying Assessment Practices in the Public Sector

This chapter discusses the importance of adapting assessment processes to fit the language and culture of the organization, including recommendations for language and criteria suited to the public sector. It begins with descriptions of performance measurement and assessment programs in government. Emphasis is placed on the Baldrige National Quality Program and its Criteria for Performance Excellence, describing the evolution of the award and its expansion into other sectors, including the recent addition of nonprofit questions to its criteria and the first awards to government agencies. The chapter reviews the scope of public sector assessment programs that have developed in the Baldrige model and how they are applied at various levels of government. It discusses the importance of learning from other sectors where there are commonalities and of adapting existing models to address differences.

Public sector professionals are very aware that there is no shortage of interest in examining the performance of government. The ability of those who work in government to carry out the core functions of their agencies is the subject of review and evaluation from many different groups, including taxpayers, legislators, researchers, and academia. At some levels of government, performance is analyzed on a daily basis in the media: in newspapers and on television and radio. There are websites and blogs devoted to examining government, and it often seems that every agency or program has a dedicated watchdog group or set of critics. The reality is that the overwhelming majority of government agencies do an excellent job of carrying out their mission and balancing needs with available resources. Public sector leaders are well aware, though, that it is often very difficult to convey that message in a way that engenders credibility and support.

However, for all the interest that exists externally, the most meaningful assessments of government can come from government agencies themselves. Many public sector organizations are, in a very positive and proactive way, actively engaged in assessing and improving their organizational performance. More agencies at the federal, state, and local levels are realizing just how important it is both to evaluate how well they are doing and to convey that information internally to staff, leaders, and decision makers as well as externally to constituents.

While bureaucratic organizations like government thrive on process, the examination of those processes to improve efficiency and effectiveness has not always been part of the organizational culture. As previously discussed, there are certain challenges that go along with assessing the public sector workplace. Ruben (2005) describes the frustrating nature of conducting organizational development work in the public sector, which is generated in part "as a result of the ultrastability of the workforce, limited incentives and disincentives, complex bureaucratic structures, and the absence of a consensual view as to what constitutes the mission of the organization."[1] The question facing government agencies is how to measure their processes, major work functions, and outcomes in an objective way that can:

- Tell the story of government's successes and accomplishments.
- Be replicated so that results can be compared from year to year.
- Enable comparisons with public and private sector organizations.
- Measure the right things, that is, obtain information and examine outcomes that represent the most important functions of the agency and that can lead to improvement.
- Identify the most critical needs for improvement.
- Measure progress in a way that is meaningful to constituents, legislators, and other groups.

The process of examining government performance involves three progressively more thorough levels of analysis: collecting information, comparing information, and analyzing information (Figure 3.1). These levels can be thought of as markers along a continuum, from the most basic processes to the most complex. Most government agencies will fall somewhere within one of these categories. At the primary or first level, information about the performance of the agency, both in terms of processes and outcomes, is collected. This information collection can be the result of internal or external reporting requirements. It is often part of a budget process and may be

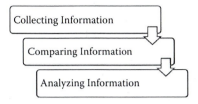

Figure 3.1 Levels of information usage in government agencies. As government agencies become more sophisticated in using data to evaluate their performance, they "dig deeper" into the information, its meanings, and its uses.

used as the basis for reports to inform agency leaders or constituents about progress toward goals. Simply reporting the information may be the extent of the agency's intentions; it can also be a first step toward more comprehensive assessment.

At the second level, the information that has been collected is compared with corresponding information so that changes can be identified and tracked. The comparison can be internal or external. Internal comparisons can be made to similar performance indicators or results achieved in different time periods or to levels of performance in other parts of the organization. This same information can also be compared externally with similar information that exists in other organizations in government or those in different sectors. Comparing information involves indexing the data within a context and using it to determine the current state of performance relative to the results achieved by others. It can be used to identify patterns and to chart and evaluate trends over time.

The third level, analyzing information, requires agencies to interpret the data and consider not only what the information means but also how it can be applied. At this stage, the agency uses the information not only to examine results and trends but also to analyze their significance. Agencies at this level begin to look at the underlying factors and processes that contribute to how those results are achieved. Leaders and managers must consider not only whether a program is doing well but whether changes are needed to enable improved performance. Through this type of analysis, agency leaders can consider not only the effectiveness or efficiency of a program or process but also its utility—that is, whether it is of use to the government agency providing it in meeting its goals and whether it remains an appropriate use of the funding and other resources available to it.

It is important to note that many government agencies do an excellent job of using data and information to analyze the performance of certain programs. The question is whether they are applying the same level of rigor to examining the internal processes of their agency. Many different assessment processes have been used in government agencies, and those processes are continually evolving to meet the increasing interest in assessment. The evidence indicates that government agencies at all levels are increasingly making better use of the information available to them, which results in more mature approaches to assessment.

Current State of Assessment in Government and How It Has Developed over Time

Government organizations have developed many different approaches, or methods, to study the workings of individual agencies or units and their resulting performance outcomes, including many ongoing processes as well as a number of tools, methods, and processes that are used by public sector agencies for self-assessment. The choice of which to use depends largely on the organization being assessed, the depth of analysis desired, and the time and resources available to conduct the process. These range from informal, less structured methods to more formalized, structured processes.

The Relationship among Assessment, Continuous Improvement, Performance Measurement, and Process Improvement

There are many different approaches to organizational improvement. What is the relationship among continuous improvement, process improvement, and performance measurement, and how do they relate to assessment? Often, these terms have been used interchangeably to refer to any process that assesses the need for change and recommends the type of change that should be made. While each term is a part of a common vocabulary, each has a different but important role to play:

- *Continuous improvement*, which has in many ways replaced the terminology of *quality improvement*, is an approach or philosophy that seeks to examine processes on an ongoing basis and to improve on the successes of the organization. Assessment is a methodology for examining the organization both to measure the success of continuous improvement efforts and to provide the impetus and support for continued efforts.
- *Performance measurement* is a system for identifying data to compare past and present performance. The process of using that information to monitor and adjust performance on a regular basis is called continuous improvement.
- *Process improvement* is a method of analysis that takes identified organizational processes and reengineers or changes them to increase efficiency and effectiveness. Over the years, a number of programs in the private and public sectors have been associated with process improvement,

including quality circles, total quality management (TQM), and reengineering. A more recent addition is Six Sigma, which uses data and statistical analysis to measure and improve performance by eliminating defects in manufacturing processes. While the names have changed, the concept remains the same: to involve those who are most knowledgeable about a process in the examination and revision of that process. While assessment helps to identify what processes need improving, process improvement asks what steps must be taken to successfully complete the reengineering effort.

In some organizations, certain types of performance assessment processes reside in units that already exist within the agency and are a normal part of day-to-day operations. Other organizations may use more formal processes, which are implemented on a periodic basis. Still others participate in external programs, such as regional, state, or national award programs. The Baldrige National Quality Award is perhaps the most well-known program for assessing the performance of any organization, but other efforts, both past and present, have been used to determine the effectiveness of government and its programs. Figure 3.2 shows some of the programs that have been used to assess the performance of government. The following examples describe how these practices have been applied in government agencies.

Audit and Accreditation Processes

    Internal Audits

    External Audit

    Accreditation Programs

Performance Measurement Processes

    Government Performance and Results Act (GPRA)

    Performance Assessment Rating Tool (PART)

Structured Self-Assessment Processes

    Accreditation Review Processes

    Balanced Scorecard

    Baldrige National Quality Award

    Baldrige-based Programs and Quality Award Processes

Figure 3.2   Types of assessment processes in government.

Internal and External Audit Functions

Many agencies are fortunate enough to have staff members who are already responsible, as their core work function, for examining processes, operations, outcomes, and results. One of the most available and readily accessible resources for conducting a review of the organization or of a specific program area is an internal audit function that reviews, on a periodic basis, the design, application, and outcomes of major organizational processes and programs.[2] Internal audit programs generally rotate their attention and examine different programs each year, so, while they may not provide an assessment of the entire organization, they can certainly be considered an input to the process. The review that they conduct of specific program areas can be thought of as an assessment process that is focused on that particular area.

Many states also have state auditors who are responsible for reviewing multiple agencies or programs. The federal government has the U.S. Government Accountability Office (GAO), an independent, nonpartisan organization whose mission is "to support the Congress in meeting its constitutional responsibilities and to help improve the performance and ensure the accountability of the federal government for the benefit of the American people."[3] One of the GAO's stated responsibilities is to ensure that government programs are accomplishing what they are supposed to be accomplishing. The GAO advises the various federal agencies about ways to "make government more efficient, effective, ethical, equitable and responsive."[4] In addition to internal audits, government agencies are often subject to external audits, often from other levels of government that have provided them with funding. This can include federal or state agencies that have made grants to states or municipalities.

> The mission of the Government Accounting Office is "to support the Congress in meeting its constitutional responsibilities and to help improve the performance and ensure the accountability of the federal government for the benefit of the American people."
>
> **—Website: Government Accountability Office**

Performance Measurement

One of the most widespread practices for addressing the need to quantify efficiency and effectiveness is through performance measurement. Berman and Wang (2000) describe the level of interest in using performance measures not only to improve performance but also to increase accountability. It is a form of assessment that relies on the development and analysis of data to determine the level of operation and achievement and to identify opportunities for improvement. Performance measurement is a critical function and one that is expected by the agencies themselves, their constituents, and legislators if agencies are to justify their methods, results, and progress. A great many government agencies have become very actively involved with performance measurement and proficient in the development of specific measures of program or project achievement. They are often key parts of the budget process and are important considerations in the allocation of funding. Performance measures can also be part of the decision-making process for distribution of state and federal grants, and state and local grant recipients must in return demonstrate compliance and performance. Most public sector agencies are quite adept at project-specific or technical performance measurement, but less effort has typically gone into determining the appropriate measures for more administrative areas.

Efficiency and effectiveness can be measured in both qualitative and quantitative terms. Some state, local, or federal agencies use quantitative measures of performance, an example of which might include financial outcomes such as total dollars spent per capita. Other agencies may measure the number of people reached by their programs or the processing times for certain transactions. Many others use increasingly more robust measures of performance. Some programs also require qualitative measures that can be equally important but are often more difficult to evaluate. The practice of measuring the performance of public sector organizations is not new, but performance measurement and program evaluation have become increasingly sophisticated.

Many government agencies have become very proficient in the use of performance measures. For those that have not yet reached that level or that wish to begin programs or to expand current efforts, many resources are available.

Examples of nationally recognized programs that assist agencies and promote the use of performance measurement to assess government include the following:

- The American Society for Public Administration's Center for Accountability and Performance, founded in 1996, offers training and resources to government practitioners, academics, and students in promoting performance-based, results-driven government. The resources offered by the center include training and a performance measurement workbook. The center maintains a series of case studies illustrating the use of performance measurement in various federal, state, and local government agencies.
- The National Center for Public Productivity at Rutgers University–Newark, established in 1972, has conducted extensive research into public performance measurement initiatives and provides resources and educational programs for municipalities and state and federal government agencies and nonprofit organizations. It offers a Web-based proficiency development program that results in a Certificate in Public Performance Measurement. The center also supports the New Jersey Municipal Performance Measurement System, with over 120 performance indicators.

■ The International City/County Management Association (ICMA) sponsors a Center for Performance Measurement, which includes a comprehensive program to collect information on performance measures. It began in 1994 as the Comparative Performance Measurement Consortium, a group of 44 city and county governments that identified a series of performance measures and coordinated that information through ICMA. Now called the Comparative Performance Measurement Program, it has expanded to include over 200 local governments that submit performance measurement data in 15 different service areas. In return, they can use the collective database of information for benchmarking. According to the ICMA website, members can customize their benchmarking "based on population, climate, urban density, method of service provision, community demographics" and other criteria.[5] In an article on the *Governing Magazine* website, the director of the ICMA program cited the ability to allow such comparisons as one of the reasons for its effectiveness.[6]

There is a continuing call for performance measures and metrics and a realization that the value of performance measurement has made it a required component in assessing government organizations. There is also a growing understanding by government that, in many cases, the availability of performance metrics is what constituents have come to expect.

The analysis of performance information also helps agencies respond to the question of whether a program or service—or even an entire agency—regardless of the level of its performance furthers the goals of government. In the budget narrative that introduced the federal Performance Assessment Rating Tool, its authors recognized that measuring performance was not enough. They acknowledged that a program could be very effective yet not be an appropriate role for government. The Government Performance and Results Act used performance information to ask not only whether government was doing well but also whether it was doing the right things.[6a]

The Government Performance and Results Act

The federal government has long played a role in measuring and improving the quality of government programs, and the approaches used have evolved to become more comprehensive over the last two decades. For example, Executive Order 12637, signed in 1988 by President Ronald Reagan, established the Productivity Improvement Program for the federal government, whose goal was to "improve the quality, timeliness, and efficiency of services provided by the Federal Government."[7] This executive order equated productivity with efficiency and proposed measuring a series of selected programs and requiring annual plans to improve productivity, including comparison with private business. The federal government has continued to follow the theme of improving its performance with subsequent initiatives.

One of the most extensive and well-known efforts at public sector performance evaluation is the Government Performance and Results Act (GPRA), signed in

1993 by President Bill Clinton and enacted by Congress to assess effectiveness and establish strategic planning and performance measurement practices in the federal government. It expanded previous federal government efforts at performance measurement by beginning to look at not only whether government was performing well but also whether it was providing the right set of services. Clinton's stated concept was to assess the basic effectiveness of government:

> We know we have to go beyond cutting, even beyond restructuring, to completely reevaluate what the federal government is doing. Are we doing it well? Should we be doing it at all? Should someone else be doing it? Are we being as innovative and flexible as the most creative private organizations in the country?[8]

The GPRA mandated the development of three document—a strategic plan, an annual performance plan, and an annual performance report—which would be used to link plans to measureable outcomes, to assess management practices, to involve internal and external stakeholders, and to support funding allocation through its links to the budgeting process (Long and Franklin, 2004; Dubnick, 2005). The GPRA also recognized formally the importance of constituents, and incorporated the concept of "customer focus" in its model.

Performance Assessment Rating Tool

In the fiscal year 2004 budget, the Federal Office of Management and Budget introduced the Program Assessment Rating Tool (PART) to help assess the management and performance of federal programs. PART is a question-based tool that reviews specific programs and identifies current strengths and weaknesses, using as its standard the motto, "Expect Federal Programs to Perform Well, and Better Every Year." It considers both outputs and outcomes. Its goal is to raise awareness by providing the public with information on how federal programs are performing. PART provides information to the public through its website, http://www.ExpectMore.gov, which was launched in 2006. It consists of what the website describes as 25 "common sense" questions about a program's performance and management, which examine four aspects of performance:

1. Programs and whether they are designed with a clear purpose.
2. Strategic planning and the availability of valid long-term and short-term goals.
3. Management, including financial responsibility and program improvement.
4. Results.

It tracks over 5,000 measures, and its website includes over 1,000 assessment summaries and performance improvement plans. The ratings are effective, moderately effective, adequate, inadequate, and results not demonstrated. The program's website states that it has assessed as much as 98% of all existing federal programs. In 2005 PART was awarded the Innovations in American Government Award from the Kennedy School of Government at Harvard University. The Government Innovators Network, in describing the award, said that "PART sets clear, achievable, and measureable purposes and goals for federal agencies to strive toward."[9] In November 2007, the program was supplemented by an executive order titled "Improving Government Performance Program" that required the head of each agency to appoint a "performance improvement officer" in each federal agency. It also required agency websites to include performance information and established a Performance Improvement Council within the Office of Management and Budget.

Over time, both GPRA and PART produced a great deal of performance-related information, but linking performance information to budget decisions remains a challenge (Dubnick, 2005).

Balanced Scorecard

A shift in thinking about organizational performance came about in 1992 with the introduction of the balanced scorecard model. Drs. Robert Kaplan and David Norton, of Harvard University, developed the balanced scorecard[10] as a performance management tool, and it has evolved into a strategic planning and management framework. Their self-described purpose was to add "strategic non-financial performance measures to existing financial metrics to give managers and executives a more balanced view of organizational performance."[11] They recognized that the traditional emphasis on measuring financial performance in the private sector did not present a complete picture that would account for the performance of excellent organizations. The balanced scorecard outlined areas besides financial metrics that must be considered and addressed to improve performance. The original model included four areas—financial, customer, internal business processes, and learning and growth—and businesses were challenged to select measures in each of these areas.

In 1996, the City of Charlotte, North Carolina, became the first municipality to use a balanced scorecard system to align its vision for the city with the roles and responsibilities of its government. It encourages people to look at organizations from four perspectives:

- Learning and growth.
- Internal business processes.
- Financial.
- Customers.

An article in *Government Finance Review* (Eagle, 2004) describes the evolution of Charlotte's system, which began with measuring outcomes and changed to a balanced scorecard approach. Charlotte was "ready to move beyond measuring mere outputs to a system that would provide actionable data on efficiency and effectiveness."[12] In a 2006 presentation available on the city's website, the city manager described the steps in their program. The city council translates the vision into a series of focus areas that form the basis for a corporate scorecard with 16 corporate objectives. Each of the city's business units links its efforts to those objectives, and each initiative has a target, or metrics, to measure progress toward the objectives.

The State of Utah introduced a balanced scorecard approach to performance management in 2006 in an effort to improve overall government performance. It uses outcome-based measures that tie into the state's strategic plan and allow each agency to track its performance against key performance indicators. The strategic plan is used to capture emerging issues statewide, which are then tracked through the balanced scorecard. This approach is also used at the agency level, where every state agency has a balanced scorecard that it uses as an internal management tool to provide feedback on internal business processes and external factors. Agencies submit department-level scorecards to the governor on a monthly basis for analysis. This is very much a partnership; feedback meetings are used to provide feedback. What is especially interesting about Utah's operation is that it applies this approach to a series of enterprise initiatives. One such issue is water—a critical issue in Utah. Rather than have each agency address its particular part of the problem individually, all the agencies that deal with water are brought together.

Utah's Enterprise Performance Approach

What makes Utah's approach successful? One factor is that its approach recognizes that government can't solve everything. It is strategic about the issues that it decides to take on, identifying a select number (currently less than 10) as enterprise initiatives. When multiple departments begin to identify the same issue, it becomes an enterprise issue. The agencies design metrics using a circle exercise that examines the issue from five perspectives, asking questions like, "What is it that you do? What does the customer want to know about what you do?" This has been so useful, they say, that the metrics "just fall out of it."

When the Governor's Office selects an issue to tackle, it identifies a champion that can "do it the right way." In the past, the governor would roll out a vision at a cabinet meeting, and a cabinet officer would offer to lead the charge on this new initiative. Group members would get back to the office, "realize they have a day job," and the initiative would stall. Now, the Governor's Office is careful to identify a champion for each initiative, which can sometimes involve partnering with private sector providers. As it enters into the process of designing a second round of initiatives, the process has changed to have the governor's staff members visit every agency and talk with each about emerging issues.

Utah's *Performance Elevated* website publishes performance data for the agencies. The agencies are required to report not only progress but also the reasoning associated with each measure: "Each department articulates why the measure is important and what the department does to influence the measure."[13]

Structured Self-Assessment Models

The introduction of assessment processes in many government agencies relies on performance measurement as a foundation and a critical input. The assessment process relies on outcomes and performance results, but attention is focused primarily on how the operation of the components and major functions of the organization take place. It attempts to determine whether agencies are operating in a way that will produce the best possible outcomes. Assessment asks not only whether the measures or results are positive but also whether the combination of processes, programs, and people used to achieve the results can or should be improved. There are several assessment models. What they have in common is that they provide a comprehensive examination of agency operations, although they may differ on which factors they emphasize.

Baldrige National Quality Award and Criteria for Performance Excellence

The Baldrige National Quality Award Program is one of the most comprehensive and most formal assessment programs and also the most widely used and recognizable self-assessment tool in the world today. It is acknowledged as a leader in defining quality. The program is administered by the U.S. Department of Commerce through the National Institute of Standards and Technology (NIST), with versions for business and nonprofit organizations, health care, and education. The Baldrige model is built around seven categories, as shown in Figure 3.3. Each of these categories contains a series of questions, which collectively make up the *Criteria for Performance Excellence*. A key philosophical component of the Baldrige Program is the presumption that these criteria identify the qualities associated with excellence

Leadership

Strategic Planning

Customer and Market Focus

Measurement, Analysis & Knowledge Management

Human Resources Focus

Process Management

Business Results

Figure 3.3   Baldrige Criteria for Performance Excellence—business and non-profit categories. (Baldrige National Quality Program, 2007a)

in organizations regardless of the type of organization in which they are found, and many research studies have demonstrated the validity of this approach.

The Baldrige model is used by organizations in two different ways. It is likely that the most well-known use of the Baldrige program is as an application process for the prestigious Malcolm Baldrige National Quality Award. Each year, companies, educational institutions, hospitals, and now government and nonprofit agencies go through the rigorous application process required to be considered for the Baldrige award. Organizations that complete the application process for the Malcolm Baldrige National Quality Award conduct an internal information-gathering process to obtain the detailed information needed to respond to the questions for each category that are necessary to construct the application.

Once submitted, the application is reviewed by specially trained members of the Baldrige Board of Examiners. From the many applicants, a limited number of applications are selected for site reviews, in which a panel of Baldrige examiners comes to the work site to observe and review in detail the actual processes underlying the submitted information. From those organizations selected to receive a site review, the national-level winners are selected. One of the most important benefits of the award process is that each organization submitting an application, regardless of whether it is selected to continue to the site visit or award phases, receives a feedback report containing applicant-specific information following the review process.

Basic organizational components, such as structure, communication, culture, and purpose, exist regardless of the type of business. This fundamental commonality describes why the Baldrige program can be applied to so many types and sizes of organizations. The Baldrige program has, in the past, adapted its own model to address the needs of other sectors. Its success and worldwide adoption in the for-profit business sector resulted in the development of customized versions for the health-care industry and for education. While they are built on the same basic model, each has some variations on the original wording of the criteria. This adaptation recognizes that each sector uses different language to describe its organizational components and processes.

The education version, introduced in 2001, adapted not only the questions and categories but also portions of the Baldrige statement of values. Rather than a focus on the business-version value of "customer-driven excellence," the education version talked about "learning-centered education" (Baldrige National Quality Program, 2007b). The education version was significantly different from the business version, which reflects the importance of language and culture. Even so, the continuing development of assessment processes in education illustrates that language and culture are important not just between the major organizational sectors but also within sectors. In the same way that the language of the private sector differs at some points from the language of education, there are differences within the education sector. The need to recognize the differences between prekindergarten to grade 12 education and institutions of higher education led to the development of *Excellence in Higher Education* (Ruben, 2007a). First published in 1995, this publication is significant because it demonstrated that it was possible to customize the Baldrige process not just to address the differences between sectors but also to meet the needs of specific, definable segments within sectors.

The first Baldrige award for health care was presented in 2002. In addition to an emphasis on patient-focused excellence, it also focused attention on the multilevel legal and regulatory environment that exists in the health-care industry. Interestingly enough, this version of the Baldrige award criteria, while reflecting the unique nature of the health-care sector, also provides concepts that translate well to the public sector. It addresses the need to consider not only current patients but also the need to anticipate future community health needs (Baldrige, 2007c), which is consistent with the community-based planning that takes place in government organizations. It also specifically addresses the idea that it is not possible that all patients will have the desired outcome; despite the best care, some patients will continue to have significant health-care problems. Similarly, some constituents in the public sector will also not have the desired outcomes. Government is placed in the spot of making decisions about actions in the best interests of society, even if those are not the outcomes desired by all. Consider as an example the issue of eminent domain, where government agencies take private property for a public good, such as school construction or community development.

Although the Baldrige National Quality Program was developed by government, it began only recently to include government agencies in its process. In 2007, the Baldrige program introduced a new version that adds the nonprofit sector to the existing Criteria for Performance Excellence designed for business, adjusting some of the language and descriptions to include concepts more familiar to the public sector. This new version permits charities, trade and professional associations, and government agencies to apply for a Baldrige award. That year, Coral Springs, Florida, became the first municipality to win the Baldrige award. The U.S. Army Armament Research, Development and Engineering Center (ARDEC) became the first federal agency to do so. ARDEC and Coral Springs have been sharing the story of their success across the country.[14]

The Baldrige National Quality Award Program

The Baldrige National Quality Award Program was created by Congress through the Malcolm Baldrige National Quality Improvement Act of 1987, Public Law 100-107, and signed into law by President Reagan on August 20, 1987. The Finding and Purposes of Public Law 100-107 recognize that the improvement of quality is relevant to all businesses, regardless of the size of the organization or its placement in the private or public sector. The genesis of this award program was a perception in the early 1980s that the competitive edge of the United States in business was slipping in relation to the rest of the global community. Other countries, which had adopted modern quality management practices, were perceived to have surpassed the United States, calling into question the ability of American companies to compete in the world market (DeCarlo and Sterett, 1995). Former secretary of commerce Malcolm Baldrige, who served in that position from 1981 until his death in 1987, was instrumental in developing the concept of an award to recognize and reward excellence in organizations and to create an incentive for improvement through a competitive process. Following his death, the pending legislation to establish the award was renamed for Baldrige in recognition of his contributions.

One of the most unique and valuable contributions of the Baldrige award is its educational component. Award winners are required to disseminate information about their successful practices to assist other organizations and thus to create a more widely based culture of quality improvement and sharing of successful programs and ideas. Through annual conferences sponsored by the Baldrige organization and other information-sharing opportunities, Baldrige award-winning organizations have given more than 30,000 presentations and have shared information with tens of thousands of organizations (Vokurka, 2001; Baldrige National Program website: www.quality.nist.gov).

Why is there so much emphasis on the Baldrige award as a model for organizational assessment practices? There is ample evidence that Baldrige-winning organizations outperform other organizations from a financial perspective. Until 2004, NIST annually tracked the "Baldrige Index," a hypothetical stock fund based on publicly traded Baldrige award winners. For eight straight years, the Baldrige Index outperformed the Standard & Poor 500 by as much as 6.5 to 1. NIST stopped the index in 2004 because a growing number of winners were from nonprofit health and educational organization winners. There is also evidence that these organizations excel in both growth and profits. A number of studies, including a 1993 report by the Conference Board, a business membership organization, have supported the idea that participation in a Baldrige assessment process can not only document but actually also can improve business performance. Similarly, a Government Accounting Office (Government Accounting Office, 1991) study of 20 companies that scored high in the Baldrige process showed positive results, including increased job satisfaction, improved attendance, reduced turnover, improved quality, reduced cost, increased reliability, increased on-time delivery, reduced errors, reduced order processing time, reduced product lead time, more rapid inventory turnover, improved customer satisfaction, reduced complaints, higher customer retention rate, improved market share, and improved financial indicators (Government Accounting Office, 1991; Heaphy and Gruska, 1995). Much of the emphasis in the Baldrige program is on business results. In fact, in the scoring system that is part of the Baldrige process, over half of the available points are allocated to results.

Whether an organization uses the Baldrige process with the goal of going beyond the initial assessment and application to compete for an award or solely as an internal process, it is still at its most fundamental a self-assessment process. Not all organizations that use the Baldrige assessment framework have ambitions to compete for or receive national award recognition. Many organizations participate in the assessment, review, and formal feedback phases without any expectation that they will contend for an award. Still others conduct a self-assessment as an internal activity using the Baldrige criteria and methodology, without ever submitting an application to the Baldrige organization. The NIST estimates that over two million forms have been distributed in response to requests since the program began, a number far in excess of the number of applications submitted (Baldrige National Quality Program website: www.quality.nist.gov).

Adapting the Baldrige Award Program

It is very clear that the Baldrige process has much to contribute to the assessment of government organizations. Paul Borawski, executive director and chief strategic officer of the American Society for Quality, describes the way that the Baldrige Award has contributed to quality in the public sector:

Quality has several definitions depending on the context of its use; two seem particularly fit when thinking of public service: quality is the least cost to society [and] quality is the systematic pursuit of excellence. They are complementary and supportive definitions. The first speaks of the "what." What a consumer (citizen) expects—that a company, or government, deliver its product/service at the lowest possible cost to society. This entails efficiency and effectiveness, the elimination of waste and considerations of the societal costs as well; sustainability and social responsibility. The second definition speaks of the "how." The only way an organization can make progress against the first definition is by adopting concepts, techniques, and tools that help turn their good intentions into actions and results. The Malcolm Baldrige National Quality Award provides a comprehensive model for any organization to use in determining their strengths and opportunities and examining the fundamentals of excellence. Award recipients provide evidence of the obtainments of "best practice" performance and models of success for others to emulate. Government recipients of a Baldrige award provide proof that the "best in government" equals the performance of the "best in business." Society is the benefactor.[15]

The Baldrige National Quality Award has been used as the model for various awards and assessment programs in the public sector at the state, local, and federal level. By 1991, over 25 different countries had used the Baldrige criteria as the basis for their own national awards (Przasnyski and Tai, 2002). Within the next decade, the number increased to over 60 national awards in other countries. The number of state, local, and regional award programs based on Baldrige increased from 8 programs in 1991 to 43 programs in 1999 (Vokurka, 2001).

Baldrige-Based State Award Programs

In 2007, 36 state awards programs were modeled after the Baldrige award and its criteria.[16] Using three of these state-level programs as examples illustrates the excellent support that they provide to multiple sectors, including both government and business, how they can be used as assessment processes, and some of the unique features that serve as educational mechanisms.

The Washington State Quality Award, established in 1994, is one such program (www.wsqa.net). It is administered by a not-for-profit organization that uses the Baldrige Award criteria to help organizations in the business, health care, education, and public and nonprofit sectors. The award process offers two types of applications: a full examination and a "light" examination. Like Baldrige, it requires an organizational profile and an application detailing responses to the criteria. Evaluation and scoring of applications is conducted by a Board of Examiners, and a feedback report is given to all organizations that apply. Organizations with high scores receive a site visit. The responsibility to share information and to create educational opportunities runs through many of the Baldrige-based programs, which the Washington State Quality Award Program does by hosting conferences and providing training opportunities.

In Florida, the Governor's Sterling Award and Sterling Management Model are also based on the Baldrige criteria (www.floridasterling.com). The Sterling Criteria for Organizational Performance Excellence are designed to be used in self-assessment, to receive valuable feedback and as an application for the Sterling Award, which is open to manufacturing, health care, service, education, and public sector organizations. The program offers three levels of assessment tools, the most basic of which is a survey-based evaluation tool; the highest level is a comprehensive assessment one. One particularly interesting and unique aspect of this program is that the beginning level of assessment, named the Navigator, includes a mentoring component for applicants. The City of Coral Springs applied for and won the Sterling Award prior to becoming a national Baldrige award winner.

Quality New Mexico (www.qualitynewmexico.org) represents one of the smaller states in terms of population but one of the largest in terms of the numbers of trained examiners and applicants for their New Mexico Quality Awards program. Like Washington and Florida, the program offers multiple levels of awards. The program is open to multiple sectors including government and is very sensitive to the needs of their stakeholders. A small business state, New Mexico interacts with many microbusinesses of five to six people for whom finding a way to participate is a challenge. Many organizations believe in the Baldrige criteria but do not have the time to devote to the process. One of the unique steps that Quality New Mexico has taken is to develop ways to help organizations complete their organizational profile. Jeff Weinrach, director of the awards program, has seen many applicants struggle with the organizational profile (Weinrach interview, Aug. 8, 2008). One of the most difficult aspects is reaching agreement on who their customers are and what they expect. He notes that the organizational profile is a major part of the Baldrige process but that examiners cannot provide direct feedback on what is submitted in the profile. How, he asks, would an organization know if it is supposed to do something to address or improve the profile? To address this, Quality New Mexico provides workshops and workbooks to assist organizations in completing their profile. Attending the workshop and receiving feedback on their profile can help them improve their performance.

Baldrige-Based Federal Award Programs

Another Baldrige-inspired assessment program was initiated by the U.S. Coast Guard. After having started out with a TQM program, it began using the Baldrige Criteria to assess its performance in 1996 by introducing the Commandant's Quality Award. The goals of the award program were (Irr, Kalnbach, and Smith, 2003):

- To educate the Coast Guard about the Baldrige criteria.
- To "encourage management excellence by providing a framework for assessing performance and sharing best practices."
- "To recognize the best and brightest practitioners, those who provided high quality services while maximizing taxpayer return on investment."
- To "publicize organizational achievements and successes."[17]

The Coast Guard subsequently changed its methodology for self-assessment twice to improve the process while reducing the resources required. The third version, called the Collaborative Assessment, combines a shortened assessment process with site visits by an examiner team. The resulting three-day process has been cited by those involved with it as a valuable tool both for organizational assessment and for teaching Coast Guard staff at all levels about the Baldrige criteria (Irr, Kalnbach, and Smith, 2003).

The President's Quality Award

The President's Quality Award, administered by the Office of Personnel Management, was initially established in 1988 to "recognize excellence in quality and productivity."[18] It originally included two awards, a Presidential Award for Quality and an Award for Quality Improvement, both of which were awarded on an annual basis. The award program used a set of performance excellence criteria that were based on and very similar to the Baldrige Award, with some modifications to make them more specific to the federal government. In addition to the criteria, the approach of the program echoed the Baldrige process. The guidelines from early program materials said that winners of the Presidential Award "demonstrate mature approaches to performance excellence that are well deployed throughout their organizations" (U.S. Office of Personnel Management Program guidelines). The guidelines also recognized sustained performance over several years as a point of recognition and called attention to the importance of quality programs and excellent customer service. Like Baldrige, the award criteria were promoted as a way to either apply for an award or to conduct a self-assessment.

The structure of the program was changed in 2002, when it was redesigned. Rather than using the Baldrige criteria and emphasizing overall excellence, it now recognized federal government agencies that achieve the objectives of the President's Management Agenda. The award is now based on performance excellence in some or all of the five categories that make up the President's Management Agenda, with a high priority on the use of technology in providing government services. In 2007, USA Services, an e-government initiative of the U.S. General Services Administration, won the award based on its contribution in the area of expanded electronic government. Former GSA administrator Lurita Doan said that the President's Management Agenda "challenged federal agencies to use technology to provide information from Washington when citizens want it, not just when Washington wants to give it to them…. Winning this award shows that we have met this challenge, led the way to simpler access to official information and services, and strengthened the bond between citizens and their government."[19]

> Winning this award shows that we have met this challenge, led the way to simpler access to official information from Washington when citizens want it, not just when Washington wants to give it to them."
>
> **Former GSA administrator Lurita Doan**

Federal agencies can apply in one of three award categories that make up this program:

- Overall management.
- Agency-wide performance in the government-wide management initiative.
- Innovative and exemplary practices.

These programs are representative of the many other assessment models that rely on a variation of the categories originally identified in the Baldrige program. Clearly, the Baldrige program has, more than any other process, established a model for assessment processes and influenced organizational assessment in government. However, opportunities still exist to further adapt the process to the structure and operations of government.

Adapting Existing Assessment Processes for the Public Sector Assessment

In Rogers's (1995) work on diffusion of innovation, he suggests that the likelihood that a new idea will be accepted depends on the degree to which the innovation meets certain qualities. Two of those qualities, compatibility and complexity, are particularly important in understanding the need to adapt assessment models to fit the public sector. Compatibility is defined by Rogers (1995) as the degree to which an idea fits with the values and experiences of those faced with a new idea. Complexity refers to the degree of perceived difficulty in understanding. Many government agencies, as previously discussed, have had a great deal of success in using the Baldrige Criteria for Performance Excellence. The question is the degree to which the language in the criteria reflects the values and experiences of the public sector, which would increase the likelihood of its acceptance. Using terminology and examples that reflect the experiences of public sector employees makes it more likely that an assessment model and process will meet the test of compatibility and complexity.

There are several aspects of government where a change in language from private sector practices and terminology that is used in the public sector could make it easier to conduct an assessment. One that comes readily to mind is the area of financial performance; another is in the area of human resource management. But nowhere is the issue of terminology more significant than in considering the approach government takes toward those for whom it provides service.

Customers and Constituents: A Lesson in Semantics

Much of the literature that has been written about assessment and continuous improvement focuses on the customer. It talks about the importance of identifying customers and determining their level of satisfaction. Is this applicable in the public sector? Certainly there are times when government agencies do not act as though customers must be considered. This partly reflects the difficulty public sector workers have in seeing those served by government as customers. While the concept of customers is, of course, very recognizable in private sector organizations, it has traditionally not been part of the culture of the public sector. For employees of government agencies, the idea of customers can sometimes be a tough sell, and this can start the conversation about assessment on a difficult note. There can be a strong negative reaction from staff members regarding the idea of customers. Although it may seem like a simple matter of semantics, it's not uncommon for disputes over such terminology to derail efforts toward assessment.

The word *customer* implies, to many, someone who desires the service or products that an organization provides. Customers are commonly defined as those people who can choose to select a company's product or to engage a service, choose to select the product or service made available by a competitor, or choose not to use that product or service at all. There are two problems with this approach in the public sector. First, many of the services provided in the public sector, such as tax collection, are not optional. Since people do not have a choice about whether to participate in this type of service, it is often difficult for public employees to regard them as customers. Second, it is often difficult to determine who should be considered the actual recipients of the services. When the New Jersey Department of Environmental Protection prepared its initial application for the Governor's Quality Award, it learned that many of its staff members identified the environment as its primary customer (Tucci, 2000). Similar organizations identify with the endangered species they are mandated to protect. In an assessment process conducted in a state Department of Transportation, an engineer described the federal *Manual on Uniform Traffic Control Devices* as his customer, since it was his responsibility to ensure the strict adherence to these regulations regardless of the wishes and concerns of contractors, property owners, or citizens (Immordino, 2006).

The word *customer* also has the connotation of a one-to-one relationship where the business is providing something that benefits an individual person. Consider how many motivational posters and books talk about providing excellent service "one customer at a time." There are many examples of individuals who benefit directly from a government provided service and many examples of one-to-one transactions in government. A person who receives a Social Security check or unemployment benefits can be described as an individual customer, as can a homeowner whose trash is picked up from the sidewalk in front of his or her house. However, government is more frequently thought of in terms of the broader level of services government agencies provide to everyone in their jurisdictions.

Generally speaking, it can be much more productive to encourage people to think in terms of beneficiaries and constituents. Beneficiaries are those who benefit from the services provided by government, whether or not they have directly sought those services. People can benefit either directly through the receipt of a specific service or by reaping the larger societal benefits of government services. Constituents can be defined as those who have an interest in the services provided by government, but in a broader role. This category can include, for example, the legislators who provide funding or the residents of an adjacent municipality who have an interest in what their neighboring community is doing.

Examining Results and Outcomes

Another aspect where existing assessment models may not match public sector practices is in the area of results. The use of financial measures in the private sector is not the same as in the public sector, and there are distinct differences in the relative importance of financial measures in the two sectors (Figure 3.4). For the most part, government does not use the same bottom-line, profit-oriented financial metrics. Although there are, increasingly, examples of entrepreneurial government, the majority of federal, state, and local agencies are not financially self-supporting. Younis (1997) describes the disincentives to financial responsibility that exist in many public agencies by pointing out, "The annual financing of public sector services produces a culture where it is prudent not to demonstrate savings but to emphasize lack of finances in the hope that more will be available next time."[20]

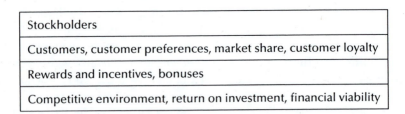

| Stockholders |
| Customers, customer preferences, market share, customer loyalty |
| Rewards and incentives, bonuses |
| Competitive environment, return on investment, financial viability |

Figure 3.4   Examples of private sector assessment terminology.

In agencies charged with distributing funds to communities or to other levels of government, success might be defined as having exhausted all available funding. A remaining balance at the end of the fiscal year is often interpreted to mean that the program had too much money to start with, and the result can often be a reduction in next year's allocation. Financial measures alone cannot explain the breadth of accomplishment in government. The need to provide services to society as a whole means that government will always have functions that will have difficulty being economically self-supporting, such as public transportation. Government also does not have the prerogative that the private sector does to eliminate unprofitable programs. What this means is that the results section of an assessment model needs to be structured in way that emphasizes factors other than financial measures as the primary methods of defining success.

Another area where the public and private sectors may differ in terminology is in human resources. Many government agencies work within merit systems and regulations that may preclude certain practices used in the private sector and whose limitations bring with them the need for different human resource models and practices. Although performance management is very important, pay for performance systems are difficult to implement in public agencies, as are bonuses and other types of financial rewards. Constituents are often critical of what they perceive to be excessive overtime payments, without completely understanding the need to provide some services without regard to staffing shortages.

At the same time, it is important to recognize that the public sector can often benefit from the practices of other sectors. As government becomes more entrepreneurial, it can benefit from the practices of other sectors. The implementation of Web-based services, acceptance of credit cards for constituent payments of services ranging from dog licenses to taxes, and the maintenance and operation of facilities are just a few examples of practices that can benefit from studying the operation of other sectors, including the way those processes or services are assessed. The key, then, is to assess the performance and operation of government in a way that uses common language when appropriate but that also recognizes the opportunities to speak specifically to the experiences of public employees.

For assessment to be effective and to gain the understanding and participation of the workforce, it must begin with a solid, proven framework and then be adapted—in terms of language, information, and key components—to government's unique needs. By making some simple changes in language and by adding different definitions of success, an assessment model is created that recognizes the realities of the public sector.

State Quality Awards

The following table shows the various state quality awards (as of 2008) that are open to applications from both private sector businesses and public sector organizations.[21]

State	Award Name
Alabama	Alabama Quality Award
Arkansas	Arkansas Institute for Performance Excellence Awards
Arizona	State Quality Award Showcase in Excellence Awards
California	California Awards for Performance Excellence
Colorado	Colorado Performance Excellence Award
Connecticut	Connecticut Quality Improvement Award
Delaware	Delaware Quality award
Florida	Governor's Sterling Award
Georgia	Georgia Oglethorpe Award
Hawaii	Hawaii State Award of Excellence
Illinois	The Lincoln Award for Excellence
Iowa	Iowa Recognition for Performance Excellence
Kansas	The Kansas Award for Excellence Recognition Program
Kentucky	Kentucky Center for Performance Excellence
Louisiana	Louisiana Performance Excellence Award Louisiana Environmental Management Award
Massachusetts	Massachusetts Performance Excellence Award
Maryland	U.S. Senate Productivity Awards Maryland Quality Awards
Michigan	Michigan Quality Leadership Award
Minnesota	Minnesota Quality Award
Missouri	Missouri Quality Award Governor's Quality Leadership Award
Nebraska	The Edgerton Quality Award
Nevada	Governor's Award for Performance Excellence
New Hampshire	Granite State Quality Award
New Mexico	New Mexico Quality Awards

State	Award Name
North Carolina	North Carolina Awards for Excellence
Ohio	The Ohio Award for Excellence
Oklahoma	Oklahoma Quality Award
South Carolina	South Carolina Governor's Quality Award
	South Carolina Governor's Explorer Assessment
Tennessee	Pyramid of Excellence Award
Texas	Texas Award for Performance Excellence
Vermont	Vermont Performance Excellence Award
Virginia	U.S. Senate Productivity and Quality Award for Virginia
Washington	Washington State Quality Award
Wisconsin	Wisconsin Forward Award

Summary

The use of data and information in the public sector exists on several levels: collecting information, comparing information internally or externally, and analyzing information to apply it to continuous improvement efforts. Government agencies are increasingly proactive in assessing the effectiveness of their programs and operations. Many are extremely skilled in the development of performance measures, a critical element in the ability of government to meet the needs of its constituents. A number of different programs have been designed to provide a comprehensive view of the overall performance of government agencies as organizations. Examples of these programs exist at all levels of government. Many of these programs are grounded in the Baldrige National Quality Award Program, the most well-known and often used programs for organizational assessment. The experience of the Baldrige organization in adapting the language of its model for use in the education and health-care industries has shown that this creates much more useful tools for organizational assessment. In the same way that the Baldrige program has been adapted for use in other sectors, continued opportunities exist to increase its usability in the public sector by integrating the language and culture of government into the basic assessment structure.

Notes

1. p. 390.

2. Not all public sector organizations have an internal audit function. It may depend on the size of the organization and its location in government. In some agencies, other areas have similar functions, with responsibility for conducting reviews. Some examples of these other areas include industrial engineering units, budget staff, or strategic planning offices. Oversight can also be provided by an agency such as a state auditor that has responsibility for a number of government agencies.
3. Government Accountability Office, http://www.gao.gov/about/index.html
4. ibid.
5. ICMA Center for Performance Management, http://www.icma.org/main/bc.asp?bcid =107&hsid=12&ssid1=2470&ssid2=2540
6. Walters (2006).
6a. FY2004 Budget Chapter Introducing the PART. www.gpoaccess.gov/usbudget/fy04/ pdf/budget/performance.pdf
7. Executive Order 12637, U.S. National Archives and Records Administration, http:// www.archives.gov/federal-register/codification/executive-order/12637.html
8. Gore (1995, p. 37).
9. Government Innovators Network, Harvard University, http://www.innovations.harvard. edu/
10. Kaplan and Norton (1992).
11. Balanced Scorecard Institute, http://www.balancedscorecard.org/
12. p. 19.
13. The information on Utah's balanced scorecard program is based on interviews with Michael Hanson, Office of the Governor. Utah's Performance Elevated, http://performance.utah.gov/performance-elevated.shtml
14. See Chapter 7 for more detailed descriptions of the award-winning performance of the City of Coral Springs and the Armament Research Development and Engineering Center.
15. E-mail communication from Paul Borawski, American Society for Quality (June 27, 2008).
16. Alliance for Performance Excellence, http://www.baldrigepe.org/alliance/who.aspx
17. p. 42.
18. U.S. Office of Personnel Management, http://www.opm.gov/pqa/
19. U.S. General Services Administration Press Release, December 7, 2007.
20. p. 123.
21. Adapted from the Quality Digest 2007 State Quality Awards Directory and the Quality Digest website listing of State Award programs (accessed February 1, 2009). http:// www.qualitydigest.com/mar07/articles/06_article.shtml

Chapter 4

The Public Sector Assessment and Improvement Model

Adapting the Baldrige process to government resulted in the creation of the Public Sector Assessment and Improvement model. This chapter looks at how it was adapted, including a discussion of the process model, the assessment categories, and their importance. By providing a model introducing continuous improvement processes in the daily operation of the organization, public sector leaders and managers can begin to create a culture of assessment. The present chapter illustrates the adaptation with examples of language and processes that are relevant to the public sector and can be understood by its members and constituents. It explains the model and discusses how it can be applied.

The Public Sector Assessment and Improvement model (PSAI) was designed specifically for use in the public sector, based on the understanding that the best assessment tool for government agencies is one that acknowledges the purposes, functions, culture, and language that is integral to the way they function. The PSAI model is based on the Baldrige Criteria for Performance Excellence (Baldrige, 2007a) and replicates its format of seven categories under which a series of questions (called the criteria) describe the information that will provide the inputs for assessing the organization. It also draws on other assessment models, particularly *Excellence in Higher Education* (Ruben, 2007a), which adapted the Baldrige criteria to the language and culture of higher education.[1]

As noted in Chapter 3, the Baldrige program has, in the past, adapted its own model to address the needs of other sectors by developing widely used versions for both education and health care. The Baldrige criteria have also been used by some government agencies either as an assessment tool or as the basis for many state and local awards programs that use both the criteria and model. In 2007, the Baldrige program expanded its existing business version to include an award in the nonprofit category, which was open to "local, state, and federal government agencies; trade associations; charitable organizations; social service agencies; credit unions, and professional societies" (Baldrige National Quality Program, 2007a).[2] The new 2007 criteria adjusted some of the language and descriptions to include concepts more familiar to the public sector. Even with the changes that were made, the broadened approach, and the focus of the new language, there remains a need for a framework that addresses the special challenges and needs of the public sector and, in particular, those of government. PSAI is directed specifically to government agencies at the local, state, and federal level, as well as authorities, commissions, and other similar government organizations, rather than to the overall nonprofit sector. While there are similarities between the public sector and the and nonprofit sector, there are also differences, such as in governance structures between the two, as well as the emphasis that nonprofit organizations must place on fundraising and development activities. A similar recognition—about the specialized needs of higher education compared with education as a whole—led to the development of *Excellence in Higher Education* (Ruben, 2007a) to address the specific concerns of higher education.

PSAI takes the business and nonprofit criteria and customizes them to the concerns of the public sector. It addresses the role that legislators and other levels of government play in the governance, financing, and evaluation of such agencies. Rather than using terminology such as *industries, market knowledge, customer loyalty,* and *globalization* (which are, without a doubt, appropriate for use in the business and nonprofit sectors), it speaks of constituent groups, elections, and offering a voice to those who must participate in government's services.

Structure

The PSAI model is made up of seven categories, each representing an area in which any public sector organization must demonstrate effectiveness. Combined, they provide a roadmap for achieving excellent performance. Each of the seven categories is significant, but the relationships between the categories also have implications for understanding the operation of government organizations. It is clear that the functions of all seven interact, but they can be further categorized into two major groups based on the most important features of the interaction.

The categories representing leadership, constituents, and the workforce are referred to as the Human Factors group, because they address the ways individuals think, act, communicate, and influence others to shape the behavior of the

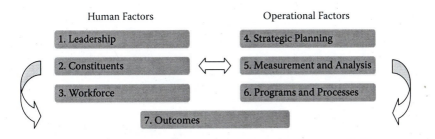

Figure 4.1   The Public Sector Assessment and Improvement Model (PSAI).

organization. Leaders make decisions and enact policies that influence the perceptions of employees about their mission, vision, values, and services. This directly impacts the way that the members of the workforce view their responsibilities toward the jurisdiction and the constituents that they serve. The constituents make up the third part of this triad, and their interaction with the workforce drives decisions about effectiveness. Factors in this area are affected by interpersonal relations, communication competency, and emotional intelligence.

The second set of three categories is called the Operational Factors group and includes the categories of strategic planning, measurement and analysis, and programs and processes. This group addresses the way the organization carries out its operations. Strategic planning is composed of the goals, objectives, and activities needed to direct the work of the agency. Programs and processes are the actions through which the work is carried out. Measurement and analysis drives strategic planning and provides a way of monitoring its effectiveness. The factors in this group are impacted by—and rely on—information, process documentation, and shared data.

As shown in the model in Figure 4.1, there is constant interaction between the two groups. Those on the Human Factors side of the equation continually make decisions or take actions that impact the Operational Factors, which in turn influence the decisions and actions of leaders, staff, and constituents. The interaction of the two groups enables the organization to function. Bridging these two groups is the seventh category, outcomes. This category represents the collective performance measurement outcomes that represent the results of the ways that the other six areas perform.

The ability to conduct an assessment of any government agency is contingent upon obtaining sufficient information about all of these areas to understand the way the agency currently functions. The process of assessing the performance and capability of the organization begins with collecting information that describes current practices and results. The questions presented in this chapter form an outline of the information participants will collect and use to assess the opportunities for improvement and design improvement initiatives to move forward.[3] The process of asking the questions in each of the seven categories and collecting the information required to answer them is both a research project and a learning process for those who take part. During the course of compiling and exchanging the

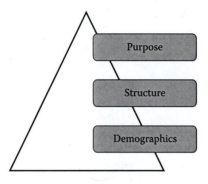

Figure 4.2 Organizational profile.

information, the participants will, without question, find that, while they know a lot about their agency, some of the assumptions and beliefs that they have about their workplace may not be completely accurate or may not reflect the whole story of the agency. They may begin to challenge some of their own beliefs or those of coworkers. Instead of relying on individual experiences alone, the assessment process allows them to compare their information with that provided by coparticipants and to mutually develop a more comprehensive and more accurate picture—which provides the basis for assessing the agency.[4]

The words *agency* or *organization* are used interchangeably throughout this section, but the questions can be applied to an entire agency or to any portion of an organization, such as a department, division, or work unit.

Organizational Profile

To be as effective as possible, the information collected for use in analyzing the categories must be put into the context of the organization's structure and workforce. For this reason, the PSAI model begins with the development of an organizational profile. This information can be used to construct a brief narrative description of the organization that can provide a context for groups or individuals throughout the process (Figure 4.2).

Organizational Purpose

1. What is the mission of the organization? What is the enabling legislation that establishes the organization and its purposes? What changes have been made to that legislation to expand or change those original purposes and responsibilities?
2. What jurisdiction does this organization represent? What are the demographic features of the jurisdiction?

Structure

1. How is the agency organized? Describe the structure including the levels of the organization, its divisions or subunits, and its links to other agencies such as commissions or boards that may fall under its jurisdiction.
2. What is the management structure?
3. Are there other levels of government to which this organization reports? What are they, and what are the primary points of contact? What degree of autonomy exists between these levels of government?
4. Where is the organization located, including its primary location or headquarters and other major facilities including regional locations and points of service?

Demographics

1. How many employees are in this organization? How has this number changed over time?
2. What are the major job categories and the number of people currently assigned to each?
3. Who are the labor representatives?

The Human Factor Group: Interpersonal and Communication Competence

Category 1: Leadership

Leadership is the art of accomplishing more than the science of management says is possible.

—Colin Powell (Powell and Persico, 1996)

Leaders in government organizations face an interesting set of challenges. At best, they have the potential to shape entire societies through their actions. At worst, they are charged with leading organizations whose missions may be determined by people outside their organization to provide services people do not always want to people who have no choice but to use them. In government, leaders may be elected or appointed to their positions, or they may be career employees who have risen to leadership positions. When we think of leaders, we tend to think of the formal leaders at the top of the agency, although there can be leaders at many levels throughout the organizational structure. While the mix of responsibilities may differ, senior administrators in organizations have these leadership duties, as do directors, managers, bureau chiefs, committee or task force chairpersons, team leaders, and project coordinators.

One of the best descriptions of the trust that society places in the leaders of government organizations and the responsibility that goes with it is the Athenian Oath, which historians tell us was taken by the young men of the City of Athens when they reached the age of 17. While there are some variations in translation, one passage appears consistently: the commitment that "we will transmit this City, not only not less, but greater and more beautiful than it was transmitted to us."[4]

The Athenian Oath

We will never bring disgrace on this our City by an act of dishonesty or cowardice.

We will fight for the ideas and Sacred things of the City both alone and with many.

We will revere and obey the City's laws, and will do our best to incite a like reverence and respect in those above us who are prone to annul them or set them at naught.

We will strive increasingly to quicken the public's sense of civic duty.

Thus in all ways we will transmit this City, not only not less, but greater and more beautiful than it was transmitted to us.

There are as many definitions of leadership as there are books and articles on the subject. A recent search of online library resources for the word *leadership* turned up nearly 45,000 entries. However, certain aspects of leadership are commonly used to represent some of the key elements for success in individual and organizational leadership in the public sector, including the following:

- Focusing the attention and energy of the workforce on the organization's mission, vision, values, plans, and goals.
- Educating staff about the opportunities and challenges facing public sector organizations and supporting the need for both performance measurement and continuous improvement.
- Motivating staff and promoting teamwork and collaborative problem solving.
- Creating a sense of urgency about the need to take those actions critical to securing the welfare of the public.
- Demonstrating a respect for constituents and beneficiaries and supporting the role that these groups play in the formation of public policy.

Key to the success of organizational leaders is the need to synchronize what they say with what they do. By exemplifying organizational values and principles in their actions, they model the behavior they wish to inspire in the remainder of the organization. Responsible conduct is particularly important in government. Leaders in the public sector must demonstrate the highest levels of ethical and socially responsible behavior. Acting ethically in one's personal behavior is only one aspect of this requirement. Leaders must be alert for ethical challenges—particularly conflicts of interest—that face the organization as a whole and should take steps to establish a clear expectation of ethical behavior among everyone in the workforce. Leaders must demonstrate socially responsible behavior, which considers the impacts caused by the operation of the organization: those things (ranging from, e.g., pollution risks from salt storage or waste facility locations to safe driving by employees) that either allow or prevent being a "good neighbor" and a responsible presence in the local community.

This category covers the actions of leaders in directing the day-to-day and long-term operations of the agency, maintaining a clear focus on the mission, supporting the workforce in accomplishing its goals, and establishing ways to incorporate and address the needs and expectations of the constituents and beneficiaries they serve.

Leadership Elements (Figure 4.3)

Leadership Structure and Practices

- What is the leadership structure? Who is included when we talk about leaders?
- What actions do leaders take to communicate and build a commitment to the mission across the organization?
- What steps do leaders take to define their priorities and make sure they are clear and understood across the organization?
- How do leaders review and monitor performance and progress on plans and goals?
- How do leaders promote a focus on the needs of beneficiaries and constituents: the people for whom you provide services

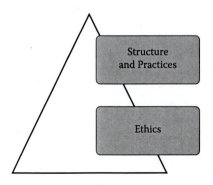

Figure 4.3   Leadership.

- How do senior leaders build public and legislative support for the organization's priorities and plans? How successful are these efforts?
- In what ways are leaders visible to and accessible to employees?
- What steps do leaders take to advocate for the agency and its needs?
- How do leaders at all levels of the organization share their expertise and experience with the organization?

Ethical Leadership

- What do leaders do to emphasize the importance of integrity and ethical behavior across the agency?
- What actions do leaders take to demonstrate their personal integrity and to promote ethical behavior? How do they model ethical behavior?
- What are the areas of potential ethical concern for the organization (e.g., conflicts of interest, bidding processes, nepotism, inappropriate influence)? What mechanisms are in place to address each of these areas?
- What impact do the agency's operations have on the community in which it is located? What impact do they have on the environment? How are these addressed in a proactive manner?
- What are the legal and regulatory requirements that pertain to the organization's operations, and how are these requirements and associated standards met? How is this information made known throughout the organization?

Category 2: Constituents

This category, which represents the second leg of the Human Factor triangle, looks at how the agency identifies the needs, expectations, perspectives, and satisfaction level of the agency's constituents: the individuals, groups, publics, and organizations for which you provide programs or services. The term *constituents* refers to those inside or outside the organization who benefit from its services or programs or those who have an interest or stake in how it functions. They may also be referred to as beneficiaries, although this generally implies those who receive a direct benefit from the agency. The term constituents can include the following:

- Those who benefit—either individually, as part of a larger constituency, or as members of society as a whole—from the agency's programs and services.
- A small organization that is part of the agency under consideration, for example, a division or unit.
- A different government office or program that is dependent on the programs, services, regulation, or funding provided by another government agency.
- Those who provide support and funding for programs or services, including taxpayers, legislators, other levels of government, or organizations that provide grants.

■ Those who provide materials, contracted services, or expertise that is essential to accomplishing the work.[5]

For technical or program units, the list of constituents may include the public at large, schools, businesses, travelers through or visitors to the jurisdiction, state and federal funding agencies, advisory boards, local, state, and federal government, regulatory agencies, the citizens or other residents of a community or state, the media, and other groups. For example, if the organization under consideration is an entire agency—such as a department of state government, a whole municipality, or a federal agency—the list of constituents would include the residents of the state or community, members of the business community, educational institutions, advisory or governing boards, other local, state, and federal governments, regulatory agencies, the media, external groups that enable the agency to accomplish its work, such as suppliers, consultants, and contractors, and others. If the organization being considered is a public works division with a mission involving construction and maintenance of municipal infrastructure, the list would likely include community residents, state government, procurement offices or funding agencies, members of engineering or public works firms, and other municipal departments it works with on a daily or a project-specific basis.

The concept of constituent focus is equally important for administrative departments that provide programs and services within the agency, such as human resources, budget and accounting, information technology, equipment or fleet maintenance, or other similar services. For these units, the constituents would typically be the technical or program departments for which they provide services. For a facilities department, for example, the list of constituents would include departments or offices for which custodial, maintenance, or construction services are provided, as well as vendors and suppliers that are needed to provide these services.

In government organizations, the need to address the perspective of constituents or beneficiaries is often overlooked. Those who work in government often have a difficult time thinking of people and groups who benefit from their services as "customers" since this implies that they are "shopping" or making a choice to engage in business with that agency. Many government agencies provide services to groups that have no choice about taking advantage of the services. For example, individuals cannot decide to "opt out" of the tax collection activities of the federal, state, or municipal government. External groups and individuals may also have no choice when it comes to who provides a service—an individual who wants to receive a check for unemployment benefits cannot go to another "vendor" besides a public agency to receive the service. Nor are services restricted to a particular group of "customers." In government—perhaps more than in any other sector—the societal nature of the work means that people are likely to be beneficiaries of an agency's services even if they are not direct "customers" or consumers of those services. Some government agencies are more constituent focused than others. An example might be a municipal recreation department that offers programs tailored to the interests of the community at large or specific youth programs. End-user interest is a key to success in this instance. The programs must appeal to the potential participants to get them to participate. This in turn provides sustained revenue levels.

Input from constituents is essential to determine whether the goals of efficiency and effectiveness in programs and services are being realized. To be successful in developing and maintaining good working relationships with constituents, effort must be directed to learning about the perspectives, needs, and expectations of these individuals, groups, and organizations. Information from constituents and beneficiaries can be used to evaluate current programs and services, to identify needed improvements in communication about existing programs and services, or to create new programs and services.

This information is also needed to identify and address constituent dissatisfaction, which can result from differences between the expected and the actual level of service, gaps in service or in populations served, or lack of access (physical or electronic) to services. Many constituent groups make assessments of the work being performed by public sector organizations, and all of these judgments have an important impact on the agency's credibility, which in turn affects the ability to accomplish the mission. The manner in which a government agency responds to individuals who need financial assistance, housing, or road reconstruction following a natural disaster such as a hurricane can translate into trust that engenders the support of the community during normal work operations. Once lost, such credibility and respect are difficult to regain. Failure to listen to constituents can translate into dissatisfied citizens who can lobby against and delay projects, invoke media support, and engage in legal challenges that tie the hands of a government agency. Moreover, external judgments about the quality of a state, local, or federal government agency or program can translate into financial support, in terms of the allocation of often limited funding streams that is critical to the work and well-being of the agency.

Constituent Elements (Figure 4.4)

Identifying Constituents

- What major constituent groups benefit from the work of the organization?
- What are the primary programs and services provided to each group?
- What other constituents groups have an interest in the services provided, even if they are not direct beneficiaries? (See Figure 4.4.)
- How are these groups changing? What constituent groups have been added or are anticipated to change in the next two years?

Assessing Constituent Needs, Expectations, and Satisfaction

- What information is collected on a regular basis about the needs and priorities of each of these groups? How is it collected, and how often is it collected?

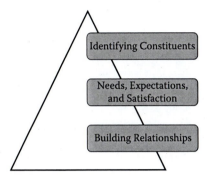

Figure 4.4   Constituents.

- How is this information used to anticipate future needs?
- How do you determine current satisfaction levels of individuals, groups, and organizations with the services provided?
- What are the most critical needs and expectations of each constituent group?
- What changes are anticipated in the critical needs and expectations of these groups over the next one to five years?
- How, and to what degree, does the organization seek diversity in the participation of constituents—that is, drawing participation from many groups that may have different viewpoints rather than only those that have the same policy perspective?

Building Constituent Relationships

- What actions are taken to include constituent needs, expectations, perspectives, and satisfaction levels in project planning?
- How do you incorporate this information in performance measures and standards, such as standards regarding waiting times, telephone call-back response time, and responding to letters of complaint or in terms of expectations for service?
- How is information about programs and services in general and about specific projects made available to constituents (e.g., public forums, newsletters, websites)?
- What staff groups have regular and significant contact with members of constituent groups? How does this contact take place, and how is the quality of the interaction monitored?
- What steps are taken to ensure that people have access to programs or services at times and places that are convenient and appropriate to their needs?
- What methods are used to identify and assist people who need special assistance or accommodations to enable them to use the agency's services?
- What processes are in place for people to provide feedback about programs and services?

Category 3: Workforce

This category focuses on the agency's most valuable resource: its people. It considers how the agency manages, supports, and develops the workforce so it can use its full potential to support the mission, vision, and plans. Excellence in the public sector depends on the ability of staff members to deliver services in a competent, effective, and efficient way. The Agency relies on staff knowledge and expertise combined with the ability and desire to work collectively for the public good. Therefore, it is important to create an organizational culture that encourages high-quality practices and that both enables and motivates people to achieve high performance levels. The organization has to build and maintain a climate that values excellence, diversity, collaboration, learning, and personal and professional development. Just as importantly, workplaces must provide environmentally safe work locations and practices as well as workplaces that safeguard the security of the workforce.

There is often a disconnect between the public perception of the government workforce and the reality of the excellent level of public service provided. From the perspective of government employees, they believe the public does not understand the challenges of public service or the complexity of their jobs. Nor does the public understand or appreciate the inherent dangers in many public sector jobs. In 2006, public sector jobs accounted for nearly 1 of every 10 occupational fatalities.[6]

Creating an effective public sector workplace requires supportive leadership, effective management practices, attention to workforce planning and the organizational culture, recognition, and appropriate professional developmental opportunities. The work systems and practices implemented by the organization must promote effectiveness and efficiency while taking into account the needs of the workforce. Government faces some unique challenges compared with the other sectors. Recruitment can be inherently more difficult for government organizations where civil service regulations, designed to create a level playing field, instead result in very generic job categories that hamper recruitment by making it difficult to obtain needed skill sets or when complex recruitment procedures take so long to implement that qualified candidates are lost to jobs in other sectors. Restructuring jobs or revising job descriptions to match a rapidly changing external environment is often a slow process that results in a mismatch between the skills needed and the skills recruited. Compensation is subject to public scrutiny, and the types of financial incentives or rewards that might be available in business, such as bonuses, incentive pay, or pay for performance, are not often available.

A systematic method for identifying staff expectations, perspectives, priorities, and satisfaction or dissatisfaction is needed, along with a process for responding to concerns as they are identified. In this atmosphere, employee development becomes one of the primary tools to accomplish the work of the agency. The focus on employee development must include all staff groups, including the front-line employees who play a crucial role. Their behavior enables the organization to deliver services and accomplish its goals, while their interactions with constituents form the basis of public impressions. These impressions have a major impact on the perceived credibility of the organization and the satisfaction of groups served, which, in turn, impacts the availability of human and financial resources. Government organizations can be hampered by a reluctance to invest in workforce development. They often hesitate to spend public funds on staff development, the concern being a perception by leaders and by constituents that such expenditures take funding away from the programs that constitute their "real business."

The need for strong leaders at all levels of government organizations, in both technical and administrative areas, is clear if government is to address the challenges it faces. However, many government agencies have been slow to adopt workforce initiatives such as succession planning, workforce planning, and structured leadership development. Professional development, including leadership development, has long been neglected in the public sector, and expenditures for training generally fall far behind those of the private sector. Instead, the tendency is to promote those who have excelled in technical areas higher and higher up the chain of command. This approach can be short-sighted: although there are exceptions, the best technicians do not always make the best leaders. When dealing with an extremely stable workforce and human resource practices shaped by the requirements of civil service systems, combined with limited incentives and disincentives related to performance, a lack of commitment to professional development can be a real problem. The skills and knowledge required to lead people, to set forth a vision and goals, to manage effectively, and to inspire people to achieve the goals and priorities of the organization may already exist to some degree, but they can always be improved through education. A more desirable approach is to define the desired competencies for managers and leaders and then to provide the kind of development opportunities that will identify and develop individuals to become effective leaders.

Workforce Focus Elements (Figure 4.5)

Workforce Planning

- What process is used to identify current and future workforce needs? How frequently are anticipated workforce needs reviewed?
- What are the critical jobs in your organization without which the work of the organization could not be done?
- What functions if any are currently outsourced?
- What are the core competencies and skills for each major employee group or job category? What steps are taken to anticipate new skills that will be needed in the future?
- How are current skill sets and competencies assessed?
- What processes are in place to ensure that new employees are recruited in a manner that recognizes and supports diversity?

Figure 4.5   Workforce focus.

- What formal processes are in place to address succession planning and retention of organizational knowledge?
- Are career development processes in place, including career counseling and mentoring? How accessible are these processes to the workforce as a whole?
- How are collaborative work practices including cross-training, cross-organizational teams, and task forces used to increase employee knowledge and abilities?
- How is demographic information tracked and used in workforce planning?

Performance Assessment and Recognition

- What systems are in place to review performance and to provide feedback? How do these systems encourage outstanding performance?
- Do performance review systems encourage excellence in both individual performance and team performance and collaboration?
- How are individual and team excellence recognized and reinforced?

Learning and Professional Development

- How are new knowledge, skills, and capabilities needed by staff identified?
- What methods (e.g., classroom, online, webcasts, subject matter experts, on-the-job training, contracted training, tuition reimbursement) are used to make training and professional development available and accessible to employees?
- What standards or goals exist for the amount of training made available to all employees?
- How are professional development programs evaluated?
- What are the major subject areas or categories of training and professional development available to staff?

Workplace Climate

- What processes are in place to assess and improve workplace health, safety, and ergonomics?
- What procedures are in place to ensure a secure workplace where employees will be free from harm?
- How does the agency ensure that the workplace is free from discrimination and harassment?
- How does the agency ensure that the workplace is prepared for emergencies, natural, health, or environmental disasters, and security emergencies? What plans exist, and how are they communicated to staff and reinforced?
- What is the relationship between organizational leaders and employee representatives, such as unions or associations? How are communications between the organization and these groups maintained?
- What methods (e.g., surveys, interviews, exit interviews, measures of staff retention, absenteeism, and productivity) are used to assess the workplace climate and staff satisfaction levels? How and how often is this satisfaction and climate information gathered?

The Operational Factors: Enabling the Work of the Organization

The second set of categories in the PSAI model involves the Operational factors. These categories—strategic planning, measurement and information, and programs and processes—describe the way the work of the organization is accomplished.

Category 4: Strategic Planning

Strategic planning is one of the foremost tools available to government organizations in creating and maintaining alignment between human and financial resources and the goals to be achieved at each level. It provides a way for agencies to translate the mission, as explained in its legislative mandate or enabling regulations, into direction and priorities. A strategic plan can serve as a compass that guides staff members in decision making. It provides a way for leaders to communicate the mission throughout the organization.

As important as strategic planning is, it can be overlooked in the press of day-to-day work operations. Many people believe that strategic planning is a time-consuming process that results in a document that will "sit on a shelf" or that it is necessary only to meet budget requirements. Instead, a well-constructed strategic plan will identify the most critical opportunities facing the organization. It validates the investment of resources into those programs and services. At the same time, strategic planning enables leaders to identify functions that are no longer linked to accomplishing the core mission and sets the stage for shifting resources away from functions that the agency may be used to performing but that no longer add value.

Creating an actionable plan is the measure of an effective strategic planning process. Although it can require an investment of time, strategic planning can return that time tenfold by focusing attention on the most important functions of the agency. The challenge for government leaders is to construct a strategic plan that:

■ Identifies the "critical few"—the most important goals of the organization.
■ Identifies strategies to transform the agency to meet upcoming priorities and future challenges.
■ Aligns functions and resources (financial, human, technological) with goals.
■ Appropriately allocates resources among competing priorities.
■ Translates priorities into action plans.
■ Contains processes to measure progress and to make adjustments as needed.

This category looks at the manner in which the mission is translated into a set of goals and how the agency develops and implements short- and long-term plans and strategies to advance those goals. It also reviews how these plans and goals are disseminated throughout the organization and how progress on plans and goals is assessed. In addition to goals and plans, this category also looks at the values of the organization, which might be defined as the attributes that employees can expect from their coworkers as they perform their jobs.

Strategic Planning Elements (Figure 4.6)

Strategic Plan Development

■ Is there a formal, adopted statement of the organization's mission and vision?
■ To what extent is the mission defined by law or regulation? What are the applicable laws and regulations, and how is this information made known to employees?

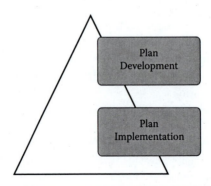

Figure 4.6 Strategic Planning.

- Has the organization identified its core values and communicated them to employees?
- How does the organization translate the mission and vision into plans and goals?
- Is there a formal, documented strategic planning process? If so, what are the major steps in the process? Does it take place on a regularly scheduled basis?
- Does the planning process include an analysis of the current environment (strengths, weaknesses, opportunities, and threats) as well as information from any previous organizational assessments, self-studies, and internal or external audits or reviews?
- How are staff members involved in the planning process? How is staff input and feedback encouraged and incorporated in the planning process?
- How are goals, strategies, and action plans determined for all levels of the organization?
- How does the planning process incorporate information about the following:
  - Trends in the jurisdiction (e.g., the city, district, county, or state)?
  - Funding issues and resources (both current and anticipated)?
  - Legislative environment and pending or proposed legislation?
  - Organizational capabilities?
  - Information on needs and expectations of constituents?
  - Human, fiscal, and other resources needed to accomplish the mission?
- How does the planning process align human and fiscal resources with identified goals?
- How are goals, strategies, and action steps established?
- What actions are taken to ensure that plans throughout the organization are aligned with the larger organizational goals and plans?

Implementing the Strategic Plan

- What steps are taken to communicate the plan to all employees and to build commitment for the plan throughout the organization?
- What steps are taken to ensure that people have a clear understanding of the goals, strategies, and actions to be taken?
- How is the plan implemented? Who is responsible for its implementation?
- How is progress toward goals, objectives, strategies, and actions monitored?
- What processes are in place to adapt the plan for changes in available fiscal and human resources, organizational capabilities, and unanticipated obstacles, challenges, and opportunities?
- What performance measures or key performance indicators are used to measure progress toward goals, strategies, and action plans?
- What steps are taken to ensure that organizational decision making at all levels is guided by the strategic plan?

Category 5: Measurement and Analysis

The availability and effective use of information is critical to all components of organizational excellence. A fundamental use of data and information is to measure or assess organizational performance. Such information may be used to evaluate the quality of programs and services and the organization's relationships with the groups it serves as well as such internal factors as the workplace climate, level of staff satisfaction, and operational effectiveness. One of the major benefits of developing integrated measures of performance is that it helps the organization define excellence and create a common understanding among the leadership, employees, and constituents of how performance will be assessed.

Agencies develop performance indicators, or measures, to translate the mission, vision, values, plans, and goals into metrics that can be used to evaluate how well they are doing. The Center for Accountability and Performance, part of the American Society for Public Administration, encourages the development of performance measures as a way for government "to move to performance-based, results-driven management."[7] Measures can be developed for every category in the PSAI model. In this category, organizations are asked to examine how they decide—from all the possible measures available—which performance measures are important. They are also asked how they identify the information needed, whether it is available, and how to collect the necessary data.

Performance measures are used to monitor progress on plans and goals and to compare current results to the accomplishments from previous years. They can also be used to draw comparisons between outcomes in one organization and those in another. By comparing measurement and performance data, agencies can learn from other public sector organizations and, where appropriate, from organizations in other sectors as well. This process of comparing processes and outcomes against those of other organizations is called benchmarking.[8] Comparisons may be with similar government organizations in other geographic locations or with other types of organizations that have comparable processes or activities to those of your unit. For example, for a state government agency, facilities or purchasing processes may be compared with similar processes at peer organizations in another state or with organizations in other sectors. Comparisons with recognized leaders in government or with leaders in business, health care, or higher education can provide a basis for setting goals for the organization.

This category also examines how the agency shares and uses information, knowledge, and expertise internally and externally. The question becomes what—and how much—information to share to convey a sense of the current status without overwhelming people with data that is so extensive as to be meaningless. Many organizations identify a small set of core measures that are vital to accomplishing the mission of the organization or key to identifying and communicating the success of a particular program.

Ideally, the performance measures selected should:

- Reflect the mission, goals, plans, and priorities of the agency, department, or program.
- Measure factors that influence the decision making of constituents, including those for whom services or programs are provided and those who determine the scope and funding of the agency's activities.
- Provide a sense of accountability.
- Be widely accessible and easy to understand.
- Meet external reporting requirements.
- Involve members of the organization in determining what to measure and why.

Performance measures for programs, services, and activities should indicate progress toward achieving performance goals or meeting target levels of service provided, as well as quality, effectiveness, and efficiency. Performance indicators that measure the quality of relationships with constituents should include factors that are important to the groups and organizations served. These indicators might be based on results of surveys or focus groups with constituents or legislators. Also potentially useful are indirect measures such as complaints or suggestion received or positive or negative media attention. Indicators of human resource/staff satisfaction and workplace climate might include the results of surveys or interviews, retention, turnover rates, absenteeism, or analysis of exit interviews.

Dashboards

Once these measures are defined and the information is collected, they can be communicated to those responsible for improvement in that area and also shared with employees and with constituents as part of an annual performance review or as part of an assessment process.

One example of how to communicate performance information related to the core mission of an organization is the use of "dashboard indicators." Organizational dashboard indicators provide a visual representation of the status of selected core measures in a way that can be easily understood. Dashboard indicators can be helpful in the same way that the gauges of an automobile's dashboard provide information on the car's important functions. Is the organization achieving its mission, providing effective and efficient programs and services, progressing toward its vision, and achieving its plans and goals? The example in Figure 4.7, which comes from the Virginia Department of Transportation (DOT), shows a very effective use of dashboard indicators to display the status of core, mission-critical activities. Each element of the Web-based Virginia DOT dashboard links to expanded information about that category. Since Virginia DOT makes this information available on its website, it offers not only employees but also constituents of all kinds the ability to review its performance in key areas.

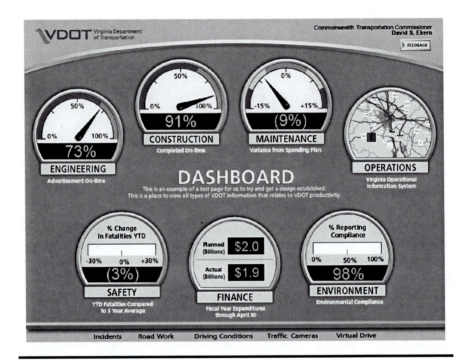

Figure 4.7 Virginia Department of Transportation Dashboard. (From Virginia Department of Transportation. With permission.)

Measurement and Analysis Elements (Figure 4.8)

Information

- What information is collected about major work programs and processes?
- How is information collected and disseminated so it is available for use?
- What information is required by regulatory or other external agencies?

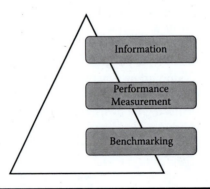

Figure 4.8 Measurement and Analysis.

- Are information systems user-friendly?
- What actions are taken to ensure the integrity, reliability, accuracy, timeliness, and security of data and information?
- What safeguards are in place to protect data security and employee/constituent privacy considerations?

Performance Measurement

- What performance measures are used to determine the organization's performance against the mission, plans, and goals?
- How are performance measures or indicators developed?
- How are performance indicators reported throughout your organization?
- How does the agency review performance measures to make sure that they reflect current priorities?

Benchmarking

- How does the agency use data and information to compare current outcomes and measures with the outcomes from previous years?
- How does the agency compare its information with that of other organizations to evaluate outcomes and achievements? What organizations are currently used for benchmarking, and why were they selected? Do the organizations chosen reflect government agencies at the same or other levels of government or those in other sectors?

Category 6: Programs and Processes

Every government organization carries out its mission through its programs and services. This category looks at the programs administered by the agency to provide the services required to serve its constituents and the processes through which those programs are carried out. The missions assigned to government agencies have grown—sometimes incrementally, through the addition of programs, services, or constituents, and sometimes through significant transformation, such as combining departments or consolidating jurisdictions to address resources issues or to increase efficiency. Such changes require that agencies rethink the mission and identify what changes in priorities, structure, programs, and processes must be made within the agency to carry out the mission. They must also consider whether the core programs are valid and whether the processes through which they are enacted are still effective.

Every organization has a set of programs that are essential to accomplishing the mission. These programs are referred to as *core programs*. Programs are carried out through processes, which can be defined as a sequence of action steps that constitute a work activity. The processes that are directly responsible for carrying

Office of Workforce Development Core Processes	Office of Child Assistance Core Processes	Support Processes
Unemployment Claim intake	Request for child assistance intake	Recruiting and hiring staff
Determining eligibility for unemployment	Case worker assignment and investigations	Processing accounts receivable and paying bills
Conducting safety inspections	Support for foster home placements and tracking	Providing and maintaining technology equipment
Providing reemployment services and job counseling	Facilitating adoption processes	Maintaining facilities

Figure 4.9 Examples of core processes and support processes in government agencies.

out the core programs of the organization are called *core processes*. Core processes are those for which the organization has particular expertise. For technical units, core work processes typically include activities directly associated with the specific discipline of the agency, such as planning, engineering, social work, health care, or workforce development.

Organizations also have administrative functions that support the accomplishment of core programs and that are necessary to the effective and efficient operation of the organization. The processes through which these functions are carried out are called *support processes*. Often, these processes are invisible to external groups. Examples of operational support processes would include recruiting and hiring, conducting performance reviews, training, purchasing equipment and supplies, coordinating repairs and maintenance, scheduling for the facility, preparing work materials, and scheduling and conducting meetings. Financial support processes might include fiscal management, budget development, grants development, and grants management.

Figure 4.9 shows what the core processes might be in a workforce development agency and in a child welfare agency and the support processes that would be common to both of them. Leaders and managers must ensure that the staff members who are charged with implementing the core and support programs and processes maintain a focus on the organization's goals and the needs of constituents. It is very common for individual staff members to be knowledgeable only about their own job and to feel detached from the overall purposes of their department or the agency. When this happens, the individuals tend to focus only on the part of the process they perform instead of looking at the whole process from start to finish. More often than not, core and major processes involve the work of individuals in more than one department or program. The interdepartmental—or, as it is often termed, cross-functional—nature of work is apparent even in many basic activities.

Take, for example, the sequence of events in recruiting, hiring, and orienting new staff. The recruitment–hiring–orientation process—at a minimum—involves the department that has a vacancy to fill and the human resources department. It could also involve the Equal Employment Opportunity Office and the finance/budget department as well as leaders who might have to approve the hiring. Add to that the support areas that need to identify office space and order and to install computers.

Processes can be documented and analyzed to identify the specific steps involved, the sequence in which they are performed, and the people or departments responsible for each activity to determine how it might be improved. A focus on processes and outcomes, instead of on individual job duties, helps to overcome the tendency to look at the organization in "silos."

In some cases, organizational programs and processes require collaboration with external groups and organizations. Depending on the mission of the agency, examples might include collaborative relationships with other government organizations, universities, or communities. Examples of collaborative programs might include health initiatives between a state health department and a community hospital or a recruiting partnership between a government agency and a local high school, community college, or university.

The emphasis in this category is on how these programs are designed and how their corresponding processes are standardized, documented, monitored, and continually improved to achieve the highest possible levels of effectiveness and efficiency and to meet the needs and expectations of the groups being served.

Programs and Processes (Figure 4.10)

Core Programs, Services, and Processes

- What are the organization's core programs and services?
- What are the major processes associated with each core program or service?
- What constituent groups are served by each program or service?
- How are new programs or services developed?
- What steps are taken to ensure that core processes are appropriately standardized, documented, and monitored?
- How do you ensure that new and existing processes make the best use of available technology?
- What performance measures or indicators are used to assess the effectiveness and efficiency of core processes?
- How often are core processes reviewed and (if needed) redesigned?

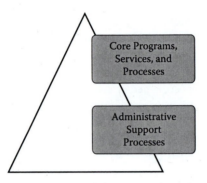

Figure 4.10   Programs and Processes.

Administrative Support Processes

- What are the organization's most important administrative support processes?
- What steps are taken to ensure that administrative support processes are appropriately standardized, documented, and monitored?
- How do you ensure that new and existing administrative support processes make the best use of available technology?
- What performance measures or indicators are used to assess the effectiveness and efficiency of administrative support processes?
- How often are support processes reviewed and (if needed) redesigned?

Category 7: Results

The goal for any government agency is to fulfill its core mission and to serve its constituents effectively and efficiently. In government, where the decision to add, eliminate, or expand programs is not based on profit or loss statements, organizations must still measure their accomplishments against the mission, vision, plans, and goals to determine whether a level of organizational excellence is being achieved. Category 6 (Measurement and Analysis) focused on identifying the key measures, or indicators, of organizational performance and effectiveness and asked what should be measured. In Category 7, the actual information collected for each of those measures or indicators is examined. This data, referred to here as "outcomes," is compared with outcomes for other time periods or from other agencies to determine the level of organizational performance. Both current outcomes and outcomes over time can be examined (see Figure 4.11).

This category does not consider how the work is done or how the mission and goals are carried out. Instead, the results category asks *what* the results were: *How well* was the work accomplished? Essentially, it asks what was found when the measures were taken. It includes results that document outcomes and achievements in each of the first six categories: leadership, constituents, workplace, strategic planning, programs and processes, and measurement and analysis. Documentation on results in each of these areas is needed for organizational self-assessment, planning, goal setting, and process improvement. It is also extremely valuable for communicating the accomplishments of the organization to internal and external constituencies. Presenting results and outcomes is a good way to "tell the story" of an agency and its accomplishments, which can in turn generate support and additional resources.

This information can be used to improve the organization by:

■ Comparing results against goals established in the planning process to assess progress and to plan improvements.
■ Comparing results with previous years to determine trends.
■ Comparing results with other government organizations.

Results

Performance Measures and Results

For each of the other six categories:

■ What are the results associated with each measure of organizational performance?
■ How do these outcomes compare with information from the previous years?
■ How do these outcomes compare with established targets or goals?

Strategic Planning	Progress toward goals
	Implementation of action plans
Constituents	Improved constituent satisfaction levels
	Reduced cycle times for processing actions
Workplace	Decreased absenteeism
	Reduction in turnover
	Improved staff satisfaction levels
Programs and Processes	Percent of constituents served and/or increases in service levels over previous years

Figure 4.11 Examples of outcome measures.

- Stage 1: Understanding the current state of the organization
    - Information collection and exchange
- Stage 2: Visioning and Gap Analysis
    - Identifying strengths and opportunities for improvement
- Stage 3: Improvement Planning and Prioritization
    - Prioritizing the opportunities for improvement
    - Developing improvement plans
- Stage 4: Outcomes and feedback
    - Communicating assessment outcomes
    - Implementing improvement priorities

Figure 4.12   The stages of the assessment process.

Assessment: Applying the Information Learned

It is important to remember that information, by itself, is not assessment. A review of the assessment process shown in Chapter 1 shows that it includes four stages, illustrated in Figure 4.12. Information collection and exchange represents Stage 1.

Stage 1

The information collection and exchange process produces the input for an evaluation of the agency's operations in each of the seven categories. This evaluation asks those in the organization to consider three points, based on the available information:

- Does the organization have a positive approach to all the issues covered by the questions contained in this category?
- Does the approach extend to all areas of the organization, or is it limited to only some areas?
- Do the available results indicate that the organization is improving in each of the categories?

The worksheets shown in Figure 4.13 can be used to complete this evaluation. By determining the answers to those three questions a comparison of the relative strength of the agency in each category can be made. This can be a useful tool in setting priorities for further action.

Stage 2

The Information Collection and Exchange stage results in a picture of the current state of the organization. The next stage—Visioning and Gap Analysis—calls for an analysis of the agency. This is done by mining the information to identify both

Category Name:		
Rating	*Approach/Implementation/Outcomes*	*Assessment*
Excellent	All areas of the category are addressed A systematic approach to assessment and improvement is in place in all parts of the organization There is a pattern of excellent performance results over time Recognized as a government leader in the category	
Very Good	Most of the areas of the category are addressed A systematic approach to assessment and improvement process is in place throughout most of the organization There is a pattern of very good outcomes and positive trends which compare favorably to other organizations Recognized as a government leader in some aspects of the category	
Good	Many of the areas of the category are addressed A systematic approach to assessment and improvement is in place in many areas, although there are some gaps There is a pattern of good to very good current outcomes, including good comparisons to other organizations	
Fair	Some of the areas of the category are addressed A systematic approach to assessment and improvement is in place in some areas, although there are major gaps There are positive current outcomes, and the beginning of a program to track trends or benchmark other organizations	
Preliminary	Few of the areas of this category are addressed, or the category criteria are addressed in only a few programs, services, or processes The beginning of a systematic approach to assessing and improving effectiveness and efficiency in some areas Some positive outcomes, but little or no comparisons to others	
No positive approach	No systematic approach to category Only anecdotal information on approach and implementation No documented results No documented comparisons	

Figure 4.13   Assessment worksheet. Assessing the approach, performance, and outcomes in each category allows the participants and leaders alike to determine the extent to which effective, documented practices and positive outcomes exist throughout the organization and in various areas. For each category, check the description that best matches the current state of the agency.

the strengths that currently exist and the potential opportunities for improvement for each of the seven categories.

Stage 3

Once a list of prospective opportunities for improvement has been created, the relative priority of those opportunities must be determined. Taking into account the relative strength of the organization in each category, the strategic plans, the available resources, and any other pertinent factors, the opportunities can be grouped into priority categories (highest/lowest) or ranked. An option is to use negotiation and consensus-building to reach agreement. When this has been accomplished, the next step is to begin the project planning process for the highest-priority projects.

Stage 4

The final stage completes the cycle of assessment and improvement. The outcomes of the assessment process, including the prioritized opportunities for improvement, are communicated to the organization as a whole, and the improvement plans developed in Stage 3 are implemented.

Notes

1. The Excellence in Higher Education (EHE) model was developed by Dr. Brent Ruben, director of the Center for Organizational Development and Leadership at Rutgers University. The EHE program materials and workshop guide are available through the National Association of College and University Business Administrators. A parallel workshop guide for public sector organizations titled *Excellence in the Public Sector* (Ruben and Immordino, 2006) is available through the Center for Organizational Development and Leadership at Rutgers.
2. p. 61.
3. In addition to the information in this chapter, Appendix A contains the PSAI model and questions. Appendix B contains a short form of the model that can also be used for assessment purposes.
4. Process note: the stages of assessment. Looking back to the stages of assessment in Chapter 1, the categories in the PSAI model represent Stage 1: Understanding the Current State of the Organization.
5. http://www.essentia.com. The oath also appears on the websites of many government offices at all levels and was used by New York mayor Rudolph Guiliani at his swearing in and the rededication of Central Park. At the New Jersey Department of Transportation, a framed copy of the oath is "handed down" to each new commissioner on his or her first day on the job. The Athenian Oath and its relevance for government are also discussed by Holzer and Callahan (1998).
6. Adapted from *Excellence in Higher Education* (Ruben, 2007a).
7. http://stats.bls.gov/news.release/cfoi.nr0.htm
8. American Society for Public Administration, http://www.aspanet.org.
9. Adapted from *Excellence in Higher Education* (Ruben, 2007a).

Chapter 5

Implementing a Self-Assessment Program

This chapter presents recommendations for organizations that would like to conduct a self-assessment process, based on the best practices of those that have already undertaken assessment processes. It discusses the differences between short-term assessments and long-term planning processes. It provides a description of how to create a culture of assessment. An area of emphasis is the flexibility organizations have in examining component parts of organizations or overall assessments. It includes a discussion of the importance of benchmarking for public sector organizations and how benchmarking can take place both within government and with other sectors.

An organizational assessment is an excellent starting point for any public sector agency looking to evaluate and improve the way it functions. It provides a way to designate the staff members of an agency as the lead researchers in developing and documenting information and in recommending options for future direction. The shared knowledge produced by the assessment can have a very powerful effect on the way people perceive things by making them aware of strengths and opportunities for improvement previously unknown to them. Research on assessment has documented that the participants can learn—sometimes a great deal—about their organization through active engagement in an assessment process. As a result, this tool has the potential to tremendously impact the workforce and its operations. While this is a strong incentive for proceeding, it is important to remember that the process requires an investment of time, energy, and resources. Therefore,

Step 1: Planning for the assessment

Step 2: Conducting the assessment

Step 3: Following through on outcomes

Figure 5.1 Major steps in the implementation process.

government agencies should approach the decision to implement an assessment the same way that they would any other major project. This means doing a careful job of planning the implementation by identifying the steps to be taken and the key decisions to be made (Figure 5.1).

Step 1: Preparing for an Assessment

The suggestion to undertake an organizational assessment can originate from any number of sources, both internal and external to the agency. It can come from the top down, from a newly appointed organizational leader seeking a way to learn about the organization's level of effectiveness or efficiency, or from an existing leader, manager, or program director who wants to enhance the quality of programs and services. The idea can "bubble up"—being generated from within any administrative or technical/program area. External forces, including constituents, beneficiaries, or advocacy or regulatory groups, can also initiate an assessment process as a way to address concerns over program quality or service delivery.

The motivation for initiating an assessment process can range from the desire to be proactive, such as looking to improve the organization or to achieve recognition for outstanding programs and services, to being reactive, for example, recognizing that there has been a crisis in agency performance and using the assessment to plan a response. Some other possible reasons for undertaking this type of process can include the following:

- To set the stage for a strategic planning initiative.
- To provide new leaders with an understanding of the agency.
- To improve communication across and among the agency's leaders and major work areas.
- In response to an identified problem.
- To determine the best possible use of an infusion of resources.
- To determine how to reallocate reduced resources.

Regardless of where the idea originates, the person or agency responsible must be clear about the reason why an assessment is being proposed. Although it might seem obvious—to evaluate the current performance of the agency—there can be many different perspectives among different staff and constituent groups on why an assessment is needed and what an assessment can accomplish. These perspectives can translate into different expectations. It is important that everyone involved starts with a clear understanding of the goals for the assessment and a clear sense of what the agency hopes to achieve. Leaders must also consider whether they are willing to learning about the good news and the bad news—both the strengths and the obstacles that face them.

Determining Readiness for Assessment

Having the political will to undertake an assessment does not guarantee that the organization is ready to do so. Before beginning the process, those involved in planning the assessment must evaluate whether the agency is ready to engage in an assessment process. Berman and Wang (2000) studied the need for government organizations implementing performance measurement systems to first ensure that they had the capacity, which includes having management support, along with the ability to collect information, to analyze the resulting data, and to apply the information to operations. The same is true in designing and implementing assessment processes. The purpose of this first step in planning is to decide whether the time and resources that must be invested in the process are available and whether the agency is willing to commit to them. Determining organizational readiness for an assessment involves, at a minimum, considering each of the following factors:

- The level of leadership support.
- The current workforce climate.
- Timing and agency priorities.

Leadership Support

The support of the agency head—whether it is a commissioner or secretary in federal or state government or a mayor, city manager, or township administrator in local government—can be invaluable in implementing an assessment process. The same is true for the support of the senior leadership team of the agency. Whether the senior leaders are the ones who initiate the process, their support opens many internal and external doors. Their open or implied endorsement provides a go-ahead signal to the agency as a whole that encourages participation and enables access to information that exists in all parts and all levels of the organization. It can also serve an important purpose by providing access to various external constituent groups and sending a formal signal that their participation is both requested and welcomed. The support of agency leaders often provides a bridge to the political leaders associated with the jurisdiction. Leadership support indicates willingness to make the organization's resources available. It can foster a comfort level throughout the organization by sanctioning the process through communication with employees and constituents (Figure 5.2).

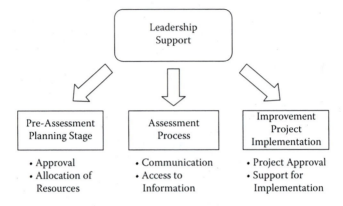

Figure 5.2   Key leadership support roles.

The need for leadership support extends throughout the assessment process and beyond, as the assessment outcomes are put to use. One of the most important areas of concern for participants and staff in general is the level of commitment the agency leaders make to the project planning and improvement phase and to the implementation of the identified improvement projects. Prior to deciding whether to undertake an assessment process, it is important to determine whether senior leaders are committed not just to taking action but also to implementing at least some of the recommendations for improvements that develop from this process. There is nothing more frustrating in an assessment process than for employees to invest their time and energy in producing an analysis and recommendations, only to realize that the action plans will not be enacted. In addition to being counter-productive, it makes it much less likely that employee participation will take place willingly during any future assessment efforts.

Workforce Climate

Those planning the implementation must consider what the potential response of the agency's workforce might be. Therefore, a second consideration in planning is to determine the prevailing workforce climate, which can have either a positive or negative impact on the response of the staff (both participants and nonparticipants) to an assessment process. Workforce climate can represent several different dimensions, including the following:

■ Openness to change.
■ Willingness to participate.
■ Support for the open exchange of information.

Although the information developed during an assessment can be used to try to correct or rebalance a negative organizational climate, the success of the initiative relies in large part on the willingness of the staff to participate by providing the information needed, serving as active participants in the process, and accepting and implementing the outcomes. If the organizational climate is negative, it may be difficult to encourage people to participate in the assessment process or at least to provide the needed information about their particular area of responsibility. A positive workforce climate makes it more likely that people would be more willing to participate. Their willingness to participate can also be affected by the degree to which they believe that management is committed to the process and is willing to listen to the outcomes.

Timing and Agency Priorities

A third factor to consider in planning an assessment process is timing, particularly as it relates to other priorities in the organization. In other words, what else may be going on in the organization that will compete for the available resources at the point in time when the assessment would take place? Will the staff and leadership be able to devote both attention and resources to the process?

Just as there is no "best" time to undertake many types of projects, there is no one best time to schedule an assessment. It depends on the core processes and the demands on a particular agency and must balance the need for assessment against the available resources. There are certain times during the annual cycle when the work of the agency makes it predictable that the needed level of attention would not be available. During those time frames, it would be less advantageous to schedule an assessment. Consider these examples:

- An oceanfront community with publicly maintained beaches relies heavily on tourism as a funding source. They would most likely have less success if they schedule an assessment during the summer season when the attention of the staff must be focused on tourism as a critical function. The likelihood of success would be much higher if staff members would instead use the winter as a time when they would be more available and have more "down time."
- An agency considering conducting an assessment wants to include its financial staff as participants in the process, since management believes that this unit is one of several "priorities" to be looked at in the assessment. The time period being considered for the assessment is the same block of time devoted each year to preparing the annual budget. It would be advantageous to schedule the assessment for a time after the budget process is completed.

The Election Cycle

Another event that can impact the timing of an assessment is the election cycle. Since it is probable that the organization will have new leadership as a result of an election, it is generally counterproductive to be in the middle of an assessment process during an administration change. There are two options for timing. The first is to schedule the assessment process such that the current administration has the ability to support the process and enact at least some of its recommendations. The second is to complete an assessment immediately prior to the arrival of a new administration. The information from an assessment could potentially be very helpful in the transition from one administration to the next, for their use in learning the organization and setting priorities. However, the potential usefulness should be balanced against the possibility that the organization is investing time and energy and that the information may not be welcomed or used.

The important thing in scheduling an assessment is to carefully consider the timing and to make a conscious decision based on the best possible time frame.

Another input in determining organizational readiness can be an estimation of the sense that leaders, managers, and staff have about leadership, workforce climate, and timing. This information can be developed through discussions or focus groups or by using a series of questions related to each of these factors. The sample Assessment Readiness Checklist shown in Figure 5.3 is a tool that can be used to gain some basic insight into the feelings of those surveyed and allows the planners to evaluate how much agreement there is on the answers.

Planning the Implementation

Once a decision has been made that the organization is ready to undertake an assessment, the next step is to plan the implementation. This includes defining the scope of the process, identifying an individual or team to lead the efforts, selecting an assessment model and a method for applying it, and identifying and preparing the people who will participate. The designation of an individual or a team sets the stage for the needed preparations. Assessments can vary in scope and depth, depending on the needs of the organization and the level of involvement of the workforce. The less formal methods of assessment rely on collecting and reporting input from employees, leaders, and constituents. A simple assessment might involve a brief survey of employees or customers/constituents, interviews, focus groups, or a strengths, weaknesses, opportunities, and threats (SWOT) analysis. There are also more formally structured and comprehensive assessment methods, which include specific processes to direct the type of information to be collected and the manner in which it is obtained and applied. A very detailed organizational assessment can involve potentially hundreds of employees and take a year or more to complete.

Indicate your level of agreement with each of the following statements:				
Leadership	*Strongly Disagree*	*Disagree*	*Agree*	*Strongly Agree*
Senior leaders are interested in determining the current level of performance				
Senior leaders are willing to support an assessment process				
Senior leaders are willing to make the results of the process available throughout the organization				
Senior leaders are willing to act on the results of the process and implement improvement recommendations				
Workforce Climate				
Staff members are willing to contribute time and energy to this process				
Staff members are willing to contribute information				
It would not be difficult to get volunteer employee participants				
Managers are willing to allow their staff to participate				
Timing				
There are no major events or agency commitments which would prohibit an assessment at this time				
Resources are currently available, including the time and energy of the staff, to allow an assessment to take place				

Figure 5.3   Assessment readiness checklist.

Identify the Scope of the Assessment

The first step is to define what the scope of the assessment will be or, in other words, what part of the organization will be covered by the assessment. Is the intention to assess the entire organization or to limit the process to a section of the organization, like a division, office, or a center? The greatest potential benefit comes from assessing the whole organization in one process, because you gain an agency-wide perspective on core work processes and also because of the potential to create new linkages and new knowledge. It allows you to look at the organization as a whole and to consider the impact each part of the operation has on the others—as well as the impact that any improvements will have on the organization.

While this may be ideal, it may not realistically be possible or practical at a given point in time. Timing is one factor that has already been discussed, but other reasons an agency may consider limiting the scope of the assessment to a portion rather than an entire agency include the following:

- The agency has geographically dispersed offices. Depending on the format chosen for the assessment, the process may require frequent meetings at central locations. If that is the case, then an organization with multiple offices that are not within a reasonable distance of each other to find it difficult to provide access to the process to all employees and can allow staff from all locations to be active participants. While this is not insurmountable, it could provide a reason to initially limit an assessment process to particular geographic locations. It could also be an issue if the staff members at different locations deal with significantly different activities or constituent groups.
- Different parts of the organization have different peak activity seasons. This goes back to the question of timing but recognizes that availability differs for different parts of the agency. For example, in a public works area, the summer may be the most active time for those involved in construction, while participation during the winter might be impractical for those involved in snow removal.
- The level of management support may differ from area to area. Is there consistent management support for the idea of an assessment across the entire organization? If not, is there a higher level of support in one or more areas? When assessing readiness for participation, it may become clear that one part of the organization is prepared to engage in this type of self-consideration, where others are not. In this case, it may be best to use one area as a pilot group to test out the assessment process and to provide positive feedback on the experience to other areas.

Whatever the reason, the inability to assess the entire organization at one time should not preclude the managers of divisions, offices, or other units from undertaking their own assessment process.

Another decision to be made when considering the scope of the assessment is whether it will cover all the potential categories of things to be assessed. For all the same reasons that an organization might decide to assess only certain areas, it might also decide to perform an assessment on only a limited number (one or more) of the categories. If the agency determines that there is insufficient time or resources available to complete a full assessment, it might instead focus on one or two categories that appear most important or most in need of evaluation. The agency may, for example, decide to focus on the workforce, if employee morale is perceived to need attention. Strategic planning might be selected if there is a problem with having common goals. In such a case, the organization can follow up at a later time with the remainder of the categories—one at a time, or together. A small agency might decide to implement assessment by reviewing and focusing attention on one category each year.

Overcoming Obstacles to Participation

If the organization includes multiple geographic locations, both the method chosen and technology can help foster across the board participation. Rather than use a workshop format where people might have to travel to a central location, it might be more practical to use a team-based format where people from each office collect information about their location and forward it to a central team for consolidation. Another option might be to use technology, such as teleconferencing, to permit people from various locations to be part of the discussion, negotiation, and consensus-building stages. If consistent management support is an issue, a smaller unit can be used as a pilot to demonstrate the process and benefits to the remaining parts of the organization.

Select a Model

While the overall goal of identifying the strengths and areas for improvement may remain the same, many different process models are available for assessment. They range from very basic, less structured models to others that are more formally structured. Each model differs somewhat in the factors, or topics, it considers and the specific questions to be asked. Three examples of available models are as follows:

■ SWOT analysis: Probably the most basic assessment model is the SWOT analysis, which consists of identifying factors that fall into each of those four areas. The SWOT analysis is not generally limited to any particular categories but instead considers information about any process, anticipated event or situation, workforce issue, or other information perceived as fitting into one of those areas.

■ Baldrige National Quality Award: The Baldrige National Quality Award is a model that specifies a set of seven categories, each of which contains a list of questions ("criteria") to be addressed. The Baldrige criteria provide a structure for collecting information and considering strengths and opportunities and are used not only for the Baldrige award process but also in a number of different state and local government assessment processes.

■ Public Sector Assessment and Improvement Model (PSAI): This model is discussed in detail in Chapter 4 and is based on the Baldrige categories but is adapted to the language and culture of the public sector.

Any model chosen can be adapted to meet the specific needs of an organization. An agency can begin with any available model and can change or customize it to meet its needs.

Choosing an Implementation Method

Selecting an implementation method for an assessment is not the same as identifying which model to use. While the choice of model influences what questions are used for collecting information, the word *method* refers to the way the actual assessment process is conducted: how the information is collected, by whom, and how it is used. Although there may be other considerations, the choice of a method depends in large part on two factors: (1) the length of time available to conduct an assessment; and (2) the human resources, or the number of people available and willing to serve as participants in the process. The decision depends to a large degree on how the overall effort is envisioned. Is this intended to be a short-term (or one-time) effort or a long-term effort? Is the goal to produce general awareness of the workings of the organization or to create a document for review and distribution? At one end of a possible continuum of options are efforts where a few people conduct an extensive data-gathering effort, study the information, and write a report for use by a leadership group. At the other end of the continuum are retreat efforts where the emphasis is on engagement and increased self-awareness rather than documentation. Most efforts fall somewhere between the two, but all these factors influence the method of assessment selected.

Balancing the Available Time Frame with the Available Resources

Realistically, any assessment process will involve an investment of time and human resources. The required amount can vary, which impacts the depth and thoroughness of the effort. Determining the available time frame differs from identifying

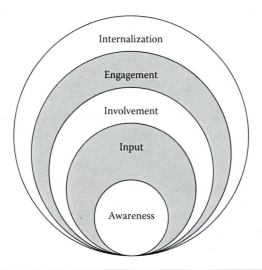

Figure 5.4   Levels of staff involvement.

whether a particular point in time is feasible. The available time frame is the length of time for which the resources of the agency can be devoted to assessment, a judgment based on the amount of time organizational leaders are willing to have those resources diverted. The time frame for an assessment process can span days, weeks, or months. A short, focused assessment process may take no longer than a day. An in-depth, extensive process can take much longer, sometimes as much as a year or more.

Generally speaking, most of the cost associated with the process is in staff time.[1] In reality, the investment of staff time and energy is the biggest resource needed. One major factor in choosing a model is to determine the desired level of employee involvement in the process. There are five levels of employee involvement, as shown in Figure 5.4:

- Level 1: Awareness. Staff members are introduced to and made aware of the concept of assessment but are not, generally speaking, actively involved in the process.
- Level 2: Input. Staff members are asked to provide available data and information for use in the assessment. This may take place through a single-directional tool, like a survey or through focus groups. While they may be subsequently advised of the outcome, either at intervals or at the completion, they are not active participants in the analysis and application of the information.
- Level 3: Involvement. Staff members are given the opportunity to actively participate in the process by researching assessment questions for which the answers may not be readily available. They not only contribute information but also engage in the analysis and interpretation of the information. They

may have input into how the information will be used and help determine the assessment outcomes.

- Level 4: Engagement. Staff members are active participants in the process of assessment, seeking out, collecting, interpreting, and applying the information. They are actively involved in decisions about the progress of the assessment process. More than just participating, staff members at this level are actively creating new information and determining outcomes and priorities.
- Level 5: Internalization. At this level, assessment becomes part of the workforce culture. Assessment and improvement become part of the consideration for every workplace decision. The ability to assess the organization and its processes becomes a core competency for employees and a valued trait for leadership.

The first two levels (awareness and input) are called passive involvement, whereas the next three levels (involvement, engagement, and internalization) reflect active involvement.

Selecting an appropriate assessment model also requires that leaders understand and respect the time and human resources available. Balancing available time against available staff members is a "chicken and egg" question. If there are a limited number of available participants, it would not be a good idea to select a more complex or extensive method that requires the participation of a large number of people. This is a particularly difficult issue in many organizations, such as corrections or social work agencies that may be chronically short-staffed and do not have what would be considered down time. The time available to participate might vary by program area or by occupational group. It becomes a question of who has the time to participate and the perceived importance of including different groups and levels. The people at the highest levels may have the least available time, yet their participation can be critical to a successful process. If an active participation model is used and there are a number of groups with significant time limitations, it may be possible to incorporate passive participation from those groups as part of the overall process.

The decision of an assessment model also depends on the level of organizational commitment for the process. If there is limited commitment, then it is unlikely that resources will be available for an extensive assessment process. In this situation, a simpler method of assessment will provide at least some information. If this process is well received, it can serve as a starting point for more in-depth assessment later on.

Comparison of Methods

There may be as many different methods of assessment as there are government agencies willing to try them. However, four primary methods can be adapted for use in any organization. They represent various combinations of time and resource needs, and the decision of which one to use must be made by each agency based on their circumstances at that time. Simply stated, the best process at any given time

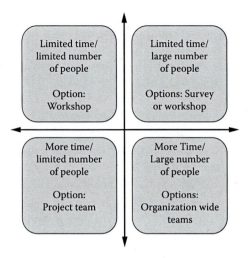

Figure 5.5   Methodology options based on available resources.

balances the improvement needs of the organization with the available resources (Figure 5.5). The four methods discussed are the use of surveys, workshops, project teams, and organization-wide teams.

Survey

A simple way to conduct a very basic assessment is to survey employees. Using a paper or Web-based survey tool, staff members can be asked to identify the perceived strengths and opportunities for improvement—either in the organization as a whole, the section in which they work, or both. A well-designed survey with an appropriate distribution method can provide access to the entire organization and, as a result, can collect information from all program areas and demographic groups.

One consideration, though, is that since completion of a workplace survey is generally not mandatory, the response rate can vary widely from area to area and group to group. This can impact whether the information received reflects the views of a true cross-section and, accordingly, can impact the applicability of the information across the organization. Surveys can also be distributed to a random sample of employees, which might again impact the information that can be obtained. Surveys can also be used to collect similar information from beneficiaries and constituents. Once the information is collected and the results are compiled, the information can be used, most likely by management, to develop action plans and priorities for improvement.

The main drawback to using surveys as an assessment tool is that while they have the potential for agency-wide involvement, they do not provide an opportunity for interaction, including information exchange, negotiation, and consensus-building. It may not be feasible to engage survey participants in setting priorities for identified improvement opportunities, although this can be done by means of a follow-up survey in which they could rank identified areas for improvement.

The advantage of using surveys is that they enable the organization to get information from a broader group of participants than could physically be incorporated into the process. In an agency of 5,000 people it is not likely that everyone can or will want to be involved. This becomes a way to engage people who might not otherwise express interest in participation. A survey can also be a first step in a more structured assessment process as a means to gather information. It can be used to gather preliminary information; for example, in a large organization, a survey can be used to find out what the commonly held beliefs are about the need for improvement so that subsequent efforts can be more focused.

Workshop

A facilitated workshop is a popular method of conducting an organizational assessment. Generally lasting from one to two full days, a workshop allows an assessment process to take place with a relatively small, focused investment of time and resources. A workshop often uses trained facilitators, drawn either from inside or outside the agency, to guide participants through a review of the categories or topics to be assessed. After each category, the participants exchange the information that they bring from their personal experience and organizational knowledge and then develop a list of the strengths and areas for improvement in each category. The last step in the workshop process is to prioritize the areas for improvement and to select projects for future action. The disadvantage of the workshop method is that the participants may not have all the information needed to fully respond to the questions in each category. Because of the time allowed and the structure of the workshop, there is no opportunity in this model for participants to seek out or research additional information. The time frame also limits the amount of time to discuss and review the information.

The extent to which the staff and leaders can participate in this process depends largely on the size of the organization. This concentrated model is often a good way for a small agency or unit to include the entire staff. Workshops can include as few as 10 or as many as 100 people. One benefit for smaller agencies is that by including everyone in a single workshop, the information is shared with all staff members at the same time, and everyone becomes part of the assessment process. In larger agencies, the size limitations may require the use of a representative group of people to provide information from different areas. Alternatively, multiple workshops can be held to include a larger proportion of the workforce.

Project Team

A project team is a limited number of employee participants who are chosen or who volunteer to undertake the assessment process on behalf of the agency. The project team can be any size but should be representative of the different employee groups or areas to be assessed. Those identified as team members are responsible for managing the overall project, which includes identifying how and from whom information is collected. Project teams typically meet on a predetermined schedule and establish a time frame for the expected duration of the process. An advantage that a project team has over either surveys or workshops is that it is not limited to the existing information each member possesses nor to asking just once for that information. Project teams can collect and compare information, evaluate it, conduct additional research as needed, and tap multiple sources. A potential disadvantage of a project team is that the process might be seen as "belonging" to those individuals and not the workforce as a whole. To counteract this, the project team needs to employ various communication strategies to keep the workforce as a whole involved and engaged in the process and to build interest in the assessment outcomes.

Organization-Wide Team Processes

This method has, for larger agencies in particular, the broadest possible level of participation of those presented here. It involves selecting a project coordinator or coordinating team, which then creates a large team of participants, representative of each area and discipline in the agency. The participants are divided into smaller teams, with each team assigned to one of the assessment categories. Each team is charged with collecting the information on its category from across the organization and, like project teams, has the ability to conduct research to get the best possible information from a wide number of perspectives concerning its category. The team can then take the information and develop a list of the strengths and opportunities for improvement and can prepare an analysis to be shared with the other teams.

A potential problem with the use of organization-wide teams is that they may overlap in their information-seeking process and may ask the same people for information. A more serious concern would be that teams assigned to each assessment category may have less of an opportunity to gain an overall sense of the assessment-wide information, since they are focused on only one aspect. However, these potential limitations are really dependent on how the process is conducted, and a good project coordinator or coordinating team can find ways to integrate the information and to include all the category-based teams in the review of all the material. As shown in Figure 5.6, each of these methods varies in the level of involvement in the stages of the assessment process.

Decide Whether and How to Use Facilitators

Many organizations use professionally trained facilitators to conduct an assessment process. They can come from inside the agency or can be external consultants or organizational development professionals. The decision to use facilitators is based,

Method	Information Collection	Information Exchange	Negotiation and Consensus	Improvement Plan Development	Agency-Wide Involvement
Survey	Medium	Low	Low	Low	High
Workshop	Medium	High	High	High	High-Low
Project Team	High	High	High	High	Low
Organization-Wide Team	High	High	High	High	Medium-High

Figure 5.6 Comparison of the level of involvement for each method based on the stages of assessment.

in large part, on the assessment method and model. If the method selected for the process involves work in teams, either as an ongoing process or as a workshop, then it makes sense to have someone facilitate the workshop or meetings so that they do not get bogged down in particular areas and to ensure that every area gets similar consideration. Organization staff members who are going to be in charge of teams could also benefit from training as facilitators.

What is the role of a facilitator? The facilitator in an assessment has several very important roles.

First, the facilitator serves as an educator by:

- Educating the participants about the chosen assessment model and how it is used.
- Explaining the terminology of assessment and creating a common vocabulary.
- Providing information about the purpose of assessment and the specific goals for the process.

Second, the facilitator serves as a moderator by:

- Ensuring that all participants have the opportunity and a process through which they can contribute.
- Challenging participants to develop information to support their perceptions.
- Making sure that all categories to be assessed and all areas under assessment receive appropriate attention.

Identify and Train the Participants

The next step is to identify the people who will participate in the process. There are several ways to approach selecting the participants. The assessment method chosen will determine, to a large degree, the number of participants who will be required. But who should be included? Every question about participation has two sides that must be evaluated. The first question to ask is whether leaders—organizational leaders or the directors or managers of specific areas—will be included in the process. People at this level have broad knowledge of the organization and should be able to contribute a different perspective. The benefit of tapping their knowledge must be balanced against the possibility that their participation can have a chilling effect on the candor of the discussion of those who work for them. Whether to include leaders and managers in the process is up to the individual agency, as long as the advantages and the consequences of the decision are understood.

The next question is whether to integrate participation as part of the normal work performed or whether it becomes a full-time assignment. Some organizations set up organizational assessment or strategic planning offices as full-time assignments. That may work well in some agencies, but it can also create a sense of distance from the process and lack of buy-in as opposed to the sense of ownership that comes from involving people across the organization. A middle ground for a project team or organization-wide project team is to temporarily assign people to teams on a full- or part-time basis.

Once participants are selected, it is important that they be given all the information necessary to ensure their success. For many people, it will be the first time that they have participated in this type of process, which may introduce several unfamiliar concepts related to assessment. One way to address this is to provide, prior to beginning the assessment, training to participants that does the following:

- Explains the process to be used and reviews the categories and the questions that will form the framework of the assessment.
- Introduces assessment and continuous improvement terminology.
- Discusses the expectations of both management and the participants for the process and outcomes, including the amount of work, how the material will be presented, and the associated time frames.
- Identifies the resources that will be available to the participants.

Taking steps to prepare people in advance maximizes the time that they have available to spend working as a team.

Communicate the Plans for the Assessment

Sharing information about the assessment process is a theme that runs through all stages, methods, and models, beginning with the planning process. It serves a very important purpose in preparing the organization for the assessment. Candid and ongoing communication provides a way to engage people who may not actually participate in the process. The messages that go out to staff members—by e-mail, memo, or in person through meetings and discussions—should inform people about what will happen and what they should expect to see. Address the motivations of the agency up front; if the goal is to improve the way services are provided to constituents, say so. This will reduce speculation that it is being done in anticipation of downsizing or solely for the purpose of reorganization.

Keys to Success

Get People to Believe in the Concept and Process, Not the Label or Name

In the early stages of introducing an assessment process, people will sometimes focus on the name or label that they believe goes with it. They may express skepticism, saying, "We've already done quality—we've been through quality circles and total quality management." Communicate to participants and nonparticipants that this is not the newest flavor of the month but is instead a concept that focuses on collecting information and making fact-based determinations without being limited to a specific method. The focus should be on mutual agreement to study and improve the organization, not on a label.

Create Realistic Expectations

It is important to be aware of the expectations that introducing an assessment process creates. Assessment leaders must be careful not to lead people to think that every opportunity for improvement will be accomplished or even that every improvement plan will be completely followed out. They must communicate in a way that is realistic about the amount of change that can take place. One of the issues in any kind of organizational intervention, not just assessment processes, is that it creates an expectation that things are going to change. For example, an agency may be located in a less than adequate facility, and it is reasonable to assume that one of the "opportunities" with which participants will identify is to relocate to another building. Unfortunately, the control of building leases may rest with another agency, and it may not be possible to make a change for a long time, or not at all. Be clear that an assessment process does not change the fact that certain factors are outside the control of the agency.

Find a Champion

Try to identify at least one high-level leader who will support the process—vocally and, when possible, visibly—by attending briefings, sending encouraging notes, or addressing team members.

Pay Attention to Participant Demographics

The best possible information is obtained when the knowledge and perspectives of all groups are considered and included. Therefore, it is extremely important to make sure that the participants match the demographics of the organization—in terms of major job category, union and management, ethnic and gender, seniority/ length of time with the organization, and education.

Use This as an Opportunity for Political and Career Staff to Learn from Each Other

The tendency in identifying or selecting assessment participants is to think of this as a process that is most applicable and of most interest to career employees. However, politically appointed staff will have a different perspective on constituents and priorities. Involving both groups provides an opportunity for both groups to learn from each other.

Step 2: Conducting the Assessment Process

Compiling an Organizational Profile

One of the first steps in many of the more structured assessment processes, such as the Baldrige process or the PSAI model, is to create an organizational profile, which is a brief overview of basic information describing the agency. It may at first thought seem superfluous to have the agency members develop a profile of their own agency, but many times people have only limited knowledge of the organizational structure and demographics or understand only their part of the organization without knowing how the pieces fit together. The idea is to capture as broad a description as possible and to use it as a framework or context for how the information in the assessment can be understood. The organizational profile can be developed by the group, or, alternatively, it can be prepared by an individual or team and presented to the group as part of their resource material.

The following categories of information should be part of an organizational profile.

Structure

- A formal mission statement, if available, or a description of the agency's purpose.
- A description of the governance structure, which could, for example, in local government include the administrative management as well as the elected or appointed officials. Boards and commissions that are part of larger state agencies would describe how they are linked and the required approval structure, for example, if the minutes of board meetings must be approved by the governor to be official.
- A list of the major groups of beneficiaries and constituents.
- The geographic location, including all field offices, and regional locations. In a Parks and Recreational department this could include a list of all the neighborhood parks and facilities available in which staff members are located or conduct programs. In a public works or transportation agency, it could include all the district or regional maintenance headquarters and yards. At the federal level, it could include regional or state-based offices.
- Regulatory environment. All organizations are subject to certain regulatory requirements, such as federal or state employment laws that would pertain to any business in any sector. Other regulations apply only to certain industries. What are these in your case?

Staffing

- A description of the major job categories. What are the critical jobs that serve the core purpose of the organization without which you could not function?

- Employee representatives, including unions and associations.
- Demographics, including age, ethnic, and gender representation. It may be important to capture the educational level. What percent of the staff members are within five years of retirement?

Select Appropriate Benchmarking Partners

Part of the process of information gathering is the identification of appropriate benchmarking targets, that is, the organizations within or outside government that will be used for comparisons. Folz (2004) conducted a study of benchmarking in municipalities, in which he concludes that successful benchmarking requires the selection of comparable organizations and that the likelihood of success can be improved if the organizations selected for benchmarking are performing at the level that the organization wishes to achieve and that constituents are willing to support. He suggests that it is important to focus not just on the highest performers but also those with comparable citizen expectations. Folz says that the community's challenge is to find "benchmarking partners that provide the service at the desired level of quality and to identify the best practices that explain why that partner is able to provide the service at a higher level of efficiency and effectiveness."[2]

Communicate Progress

Throughout the process, communicate the progress being made to the rest of the employees. This is especially important if team-based processes are being used, where people may contribute information but not see results for some time. Communication can include, where appropriate, newsletters or other bulletins outlining progress to date and expected completion dates.

Keys to Success

Capture Organizational Stories

Look for opportunities throughout the process to listen to and to capture organizational "stories." Do people tell stories that describe the essence of what the organization is all about? These can be positive stories about, for example, how employees felt they were supported on an important issue or how the organization celebrated a big success. They can also be negative stories, which describe behaviors or values not considered part of the organization's culture. Such stories can be used both in the assessment process and outside of it to build organizational identification and to solidify the organizational identity.

Create an Environment Where There Is a Willingness to Challenge Information

An important part of the assessment process is to bring together information from various sources and perspectives, which means that not all the information will line up—in other words, there will be different interpretations based on the workforce experiences of the participants. The assessment process needs to allow people to challenge information and beliefs they believe are not accurate or do not correctly explain the workings of the agency so that they can reach agreement on the best possible explanation. To create a realistic awareness of the strengths and opportunities for improvement, participants must feel that challenging information is not only appropriate but also welcomed.

Do Not Lose Sight of the Positive

It is easy for an assessment process to become a complaint session for everything that is wrong. Instead of focusing on the opportunities, it is also easy to turn this into an analysis of "why we are the way we are." An example could be the tendency of some people to focus on the dysfunctional leader—who left years ago. It is important to remind them that history cannot be undone but that the process can accomplish the most by focusing on the positive steps that can be taken to move forward. Incorporate the concept of appreciative inquiry, an approach to evaluation and assessment that asks people to focus on instances where the organization has performed especially well and to identify the factors that made it work so successfully.

Use Participants as Ambassadors for What You Are Doing

Participants can be the best source of information about the potential of an assessment process to create positive change. Since communication is so important, encourage them talk to others about the process, the information and how it is being obtained, and the results. This can dispel concerns and helps spread the information needed to bring about change.

Step 3: Following Through on Outcomes

Like so many other projects in government, the work is not done when the assessment process has been completed. To ensure the success of the efforts, it is critical that those involved follow through on the work that has been accomplished.

Identify Steps for Further Action

A critical part of any assessment process is to identify the opportunities for improvement and to develop implementation or action plans. While it is certainly important to determine the highest-priority "items" for action, also consider selecting some low-hanging fruit—that is, some easily implemented and recognizable improvement opportunities. This demonstrates to the rest of the workforce that the process will result, as they were originally told, in some level of improvement. Small successes build support for the more difficult, and perhaps more important and long-lasting, changes that will also result from the process.

In developing action plans, it is important to assign reasonable time frames for completion of projects, identify processes and mechanisms for reporting progress, and name the responsible parties. This is the step where it is easiest for improvement processes to fall apart. Whether the process has taken a few days or several months or even a year or more, it is normal for people go back to their regular work lives, at which point the improvement projects become of secondary importance compared with the everyday need to accomplish the regular mission of the organization. This includes also communicating to all employees the steps taken and the accomplishments achieved.

Follow-Up Interviews

It is possible to add to the benefits of assessment and to create an opportunity for increased organizational learning by incorporating a feedback loop. Adding follow-up interviews that assess the satisfaction of participants, nonparticipants, and organizational leaders with the assessment process itself provides an opportunity for double-loop learning as people learn how to improve the process.

Plan to Repeat the Process

Even if the time frame is one or more years away, plant the idea that assessment is an ongoing process that will be conducted at regular intervals.

Keys to Success

Make Use of Process Experts

The New Jersey Department of Environmental Protection, after the completion of a site visit by examiners for the New Jersey Quality Award, invited the lead examiner to come back and give a presentation to any interested agency employees to explain what they were looking for and what they found. Using a process expert to help explain the process and outcomes can add credibility and help people grasp the most important aspects of the assessment and its outcomes.

Share and Educate

Do not think of the information gained in an assessment as proprietary. The two winners of the first Baldrige awards for government (the U.S. Army Armament Research, Development and Engineering Center [ARDEC] and Coral Springs, Florida) are fulfilling the requirements of the educational component of that process by participating in seminars being sponsored around the country by the Baldrige organization. They were also willing to share their experiences for this book and other educational purposes. Sharing information with other jurisdictions builds relationships that can be drawn upon in the future. Similarly, be certain to brief incoming leaders about how assessment has become part of the organizational culture.

Summary

An organizational assessment can be tremendously beneficial to any government agency, but it is important to remember that it is a process and requires planning and forethought. To conduct an assessment but to still meet the ongoing work requirements of the organization, careful thought must be given to the existing workplace climate, the current demand for services, and the available resources. Communication and visible leadership support are two areas that can make or break this effort. Keeping those things in mind, agencies can benefit from the best practices of other government agencies. Organizations that have successfully implemented self-assessments have found that a number of factors can have a positive influence on the process and the outcomes achieved, including the following:

- Understanding the level of organizational support.
- Conducting up-front planning.
- Finding an optimal time to conduct the assessment.
- Selecting a model and a method that are compatible with the available resources.
- Being clear about expectations.
- Following through on outcomes.

The best practices described in this chapter can support the organization's efforts to implement a successful assessment process. Planning and project management can contribute to increased organizational involvement and the engagement and buy-in of all those involved, from the leaders who sanction the process to every staff member regardless of his or her ability to participate.

Notes

1. While the cost of an assessment process is primarily staff time, there can be additional costs if external consultants or facilitators are used. The decision to use or not use facilitators is based in large part on the method selected for the assessment and the level of expertise within the organization for assessment or facilitation.
2. p. 211.

Chapter 6

Assessment, Improvement, and the Process of Organizational Change

Completing the cycle of assessment and improvement, which an organization must do to fully realize the benefits of the process, requires the organization to apply the information obtained. This chapter examines the way an assessment process, by examining the organization, its people, and practices, provides both the information needed and the motivation to initiate the change necessary to carry out improvement efforts. It looks at the way assessment can support both an internal and an external case for change and why both perspectives are necessary. It discusses how organizational change takes place and the role of individuals and teams in change processes. Examining concepts such as organizational identity and organizational identification, and the link between change and organizational and individual learning, it emphasizes the importance of participation by an agency workforce in both understanding the issues and developing changes.

An organizational assessment process can be a powerful tool, not only for identifying the current state of an agency but also for initiating improvement. Assessments can vary in depth and scope; while the most basic process involves simply taking the temperature of an organization, the full benefit lies in completing the cycle by using the information obtained to bring about improvement. Because of this, assessment, improvement, and change are invariably linked. Going back again to the model, we can see that not only does an assessment process result in the collection of information, but it also provides a mechanism for identifying the gaps between an agency's current ability to provide programs and services and the level of performance needed to fully achieve its mission. One of the major goals of assessment is to determine what changes are needed to improve the agency's effectiveness, its efficiency, and its overall ability to serve its constituents. Once the process has helped determine what improvements are needed, the prioritization and project planning stages help set a path for how change can take place. The decision as to which improvements can and will be made and what actions will be implemented to close those gaps remains with the agency under assessment.

The first three stages of assessment produce a series of useful outcomes: information about the current state of the organization, identification of and consensus about the gaps between its current and desired states and the corresponding opportunities for improvement, and the establishment of a sense of the relative priority of those opportunities. The fourth stage of assessment is the implementation of the desired improvements, which—no matter the size and scope of those efforts—means introducing an element of change in the organization. Many times, the perception by those inside or outside the organization that some kind of change is needed is the catalyst that initiates interest in organizational assessment. A critical function of assessment is to support and enable such change, not only by providing the information that leads to identifying the improvements to be made but also by using the process to build an understanding across the agency, among participants and nonparticipants, that change is needed. The question becomes how best to:

- Determine what improvements are needed, desired, and achievable.
- Identify the changes needed to implement the improvements.
- Foster an internal and external awareness of the importance of change.
- Take systematic steps to bring about the desired change.

Understanding the way an assessment process can facilitate change starts with understanding the theory and the dynamics of organizational change. Because change can be a complex and difficult undertaking, the success of implementing the desired improvements can hinge on the ability of the organization's leaders to understand the theories and practices that influence the way change takes place and to use that information to anticipate the obstacles and challenges they will encounter along the way.

Change Efforts in the Public Sector

Organizational change is a process that affects people, processes, and relationships. Van de Ven and Pool (1995) describe change as a process that results in an observable difference in the structure, processes, practices, or performance of an organization over time. It can also be described as a process through which an organization identifies and implements improvements with the goal of reaching its best or optimal state of operation at a particular point in time (Purser and Petranker, 2005). While we may not stop to consider, in the midst of day-to-day operations, about how change takes place, it can generally be said that the process of change is initiated when there is a difference between the current organization and its desired or planned condition or, as Weisbord (1987) describes it, when there is "an incongruity between what they want or need and what they have."[1] The emphasis in both academic and popular management literature has not been on **whether** organizations need to change but instead on **how** they change—understanding the reasons for change and the way it is designed, introduced, and implemented.

Anyone who has tried to initiate change in government knows that it is not always an easy thing to accomplish, despite the strength of the perceived need or the best intentions. Government agencies are generally highly structured, regulated, and bureaucratic, which can make it difficult to gain consensus on new directions. The change process can be slow, which makes it difficult to meet public expectations for the speed of change. It is also highly dependent on the perspective and priorities of agency leaders. Boyne (2006) points out that there is relatively little documentation of successful change processes in public sector organizations when compared with the amount of information available for private sector organizations (Figure 6.1).

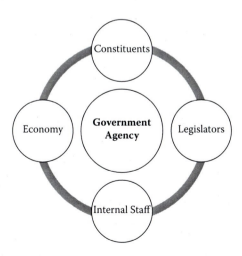

Figure 6.1   Interactions that influence change in government agencies.

Identifying Barriers to Change

Change is a complex process, and there are many potential barriers to change in public sector organizations. Identifying those barriers and examining them in the context of how change takes place can help agencies anticipate the challenges and incorporate the information into planning for change initiatives.

Individual Resistance to Change

Despite any differences between them, every model of organizational change recognizes that involving the members of the organization in the change process is a critical component for success. The inherent resistance of individuals to change is a commonly accepted belief in the field of organizational development and change management. Many people resent or even fear change because they are unsure about the impact on their immediate work processes, their jobs, and the organization as a whole. Uncertainty about what will happen can be a powerful obstacle in implementing organizational change. Many people do not think about their work as a series of processes and relationships that are constantly evolving. When proposed change is introduced, it can cause a great deal of discomfort. People can be very reluctant to consider how the places, people, and process that form their daily routine could change, and it is often very difficult to get them out of this comfort zone. Instead of accepting the idea that change will be a positive experience, they may view it as a threat. As Mark Tucci of the New Jersey Department of Environmental Protection put it:

> Middle managers don't like you to tamper with their world. They've learned how to manage the status quo.[2]

Anderson and Anderson (2001) believe that overcoming employee resistance is one of the major factors in organizational change. Many managers have tried to initiate change only to meet resistance they did not anticipate in their planning process. In response, some may take the approach of mandating change in what they believe to be the best interests of the organization. Change can certainly be imposed, but that often does not bring about the kind of acceptance or buy-in from employees that will tip the scales toward success.

Seeing Agencies as Systems

To begin, we need to think of government agencies not just as collections of independent programs or offices but also as systems, made up of many interdependent processes. Those outside the agency see the external services and programs provided—those visible to and directly beneficial to the public. But providing those services and programs also requires an internal infrastructure of support services.

Because of this essential interdependence, changes made to any one part of the organization will affect, to a greater or lesser degree, all the other parts. Take, for example, a strategic decision by a transportation agency to shift from its current practice of contracting out engineering design services to moving 50% of the service back "in house" over a 12-month period. Some of the changes required to implement this change are readily apparent, such as the need to increase the internal design staff. What may be less obvious, at least initially, are the impacts throughout the rest of the organization. The need to increase staff in a relatively short period of time means that the capability of human resources to handle the recruiting effort must be considered, as well as the need to provide professional development for newly hired staff. Is there adequate office space, furniture, and information technology equipment to support the staff? What internal changes in review and approval processes will be required? What impact will there be on constituent relations, including with the engineering firms that previously handled this work? Does the change from external to internal service provision decrease the workload of accounting staff and increase the work of the payroll staff?

Looking at it from this perspective, it becomes apparent that there are very few, if any, "small" changes. A change in an organization has a ripple effect that reaches much farther than its origination point.

External Drivers of Change in Government

While the primary focus in looking at organizational assessment is the internal development of improvement opportunities, many of the change "initiators" in government are external. What are some of the forces that bring government agencies to the point where change becomes recognized as necessary and achievable? The impetus can come from any numbers of sources or events, but the following examples represent some of the major external drivers of change in government agencies.

Change in Administration

One constant in government is that there will be transitions in leadership following every election. Even when current leaders or legislators (regardless of the level of government) are returned to office, there are invariably new approaches, commitments, and ideas to be implemented. More often than not these days, a theme in campaigns is a commitment to "change government." Administrations come in expecting that they will have to do things differently and face an expectation that the changes will take place in a way that is very visible to the public. The impact of transitions in leadership is not limited to the immediate level of government in which an election or the appointment of a public official takes place. New leadership at the state level can create changes to programs and funding that affect local governments, and similarly, a new federal government administration brings new priorities that will cascade down to both state and local levels. Transitions can influence the timing of change efforts. Political leaders and those they appoint to lead agencies have a limited amount of time to accomplish their goals and priorities, so the pace of change is accelerated. This can create a focus on short-term benefits rather than thinking about or planning for the long term.

New Mandates

The emergence of different needs and priorities can bring with it new mandates for programs and services, often enacted through the promulgation of legislation or regulations. New legislation, in and of itself, suggests a change in priorities and a decision to commit resources to it. Sometimes an agency can initiate new legislation as a result of issues that arise during its normal operations and can work with legislators to craft appropriate language and provisions. Other times, legislation is initiated outside the agency and may or may not reflect what the staff believes is most important or effective. Anytime new legislation is passed or new regulations are written to enact legislation, a need for new or revised processes can be generated.

External or Constituent Advocacy

Advocacy efforts ranging from grassroots efforts to media campaigns are increasingly effective in changing the agenda of government. Increased advocacy by constituent groups has assured them access to the process of government decision making. As proof of this, consider the tremendous impact that environmental organizations have had on government policies, programs, and priorities over the last 30 years. In addition to reordering priorities, external forces and constituents can also push for improvements in how government works. The availability and evolution of technology has shifted people's expectations for the way services will be provided and the speed at which they will be delivered and has, in turn, accelerated the pace of change. The move to providing government services electronically has grown many times over in the last several years, in large part because the public has developed an expectation that e-government should be the norm for conducting business.

Crises and Emergencies

Crises can be critical learning experiences. They engage the public and foster discussion about needed changes in response and responders. They can bring about changes in government priorities and drive the reallocation of resources by focusing public opinion on specific problems or incidents. Consider the devastating impact of Hurricane Katrina on New Orleans and the resulting backlash against the leadership and response of the Federal Emergency Management Agency (FEMA) and the levee-monitoring efforts of the U.S. Army Corps of Engineers. The tragic 2007 bridge collapse in Minnesota created widespread public awareness of the state of the nation's infrastructure. It brought demands from legislative leaders and constituents for immediate and extensive bridge inspections, despite the many state and local bridge inspection programs regularly conducted across the country, and generated calls for increased funding and priority shifting to enable investment in bridges and infrastructure. Emergencies can call priorities into questions and can create new roles and responsibilities, such as the importance of emergency management as a major function of government and the need to position governments to be as prepared as possible in responding. Emergency management and response has become a critical field of study for government administrators, with over 142 colleges and universities now offering programs in emergency management.[3]

The Process of Organizational Change

To initiate and carry out the changes necessary to implement the improvement efforts resulting from an assessment, government leaders and administrators require an understanding of how change takes place. While there are many models of organizational change, one of the most widely known is that developed by Kurt Lewin, whose model theorizes that change takes place by following a prescribed sequence of events (Lewin, 1951). It describes change efforts as a three-step process in which the members of the organization engage in a sequence he terms *unfreezing, moving,* and *refreezing* (Figure 6.2). The first step, unfreezing, is based on the idea that organizations at any point in time are locked into or "frozen" in a pattern of behavior, conducting their operations in a particular way. For change to occur, the organization must let go of its current way of doing business and think about what it could do differently. It recognizes that people become set in and comfortable with the everyday routines of their work and that organizations similarly become comfortable with the way they conduct their operations. The unfreezing phase requires a decision by the organization to let go of its existing stability and to consider other possibilities for accomplishing their mission. Once this first step has been taken,

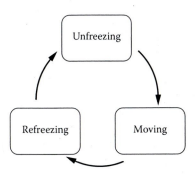

Figure 6.2   Lewin's model of organizational change.

the specific changes needed to bridge the gap can be identified and decisions can be made about how to implement them.

The next stage in Lewin's model is moving. An organization "moves" by acting on the identified improvement plans and putting in place new ways of doing business. The moving phase is a time of transition when new ideas and processes are being introduced and integrated into the existing work operations of the organization. This can be the most difficult part of the process, as anyone who has ever tried to implement change knows. Understanding and accepting the idea that the organization will be doing things differently can be very difficult for people and may result in reactions ranging from the well-known calls of, "We've always done it this way," to outright refusal. Therefore, in addition to determining what to change and how to change it, leaders and managers must be able to understand the importance of overcoming the inherent organizational forces pushing for the status quo.

The third stage in this model is called refreezing. Having made some form of change, the next step for the organization is to restabilize by incorporating the changes, including new processes, ideas, and ways of thinking, into the daily life of the organization.

More recently, some researchers have suggested a new way of interpreting Lewin's model by reinterpreting and renaming the stages to reflect the idea that organizations are in constant motion. Instead of unfreezing, moving, and refreezing, current literature (Higgs and Rowland, 2005; Purser and Petranker, 2005) suggests that the stages might better be viewed as *freezing*, or stopping the organization in its tracks (figuratively speaking); *rebalancing*, a transition from the way things currently exist to a new way of operating; and then *unfreezing*, or letting go and permitting the members of the organization to continue to move toward future change.

Others disagree with the idea that change is a linear process. They believe that organizations are constantly in the process of changing, involved in multiple change efforts of various sizes and at all levels at any given time with some of the changes so small that they are not readily observable to most of the people who work there (Kanter, 1991a). Van de Ven and Poole (1995) support the idea that an organization, having changed, cannot maintain the perceived equilibrium that results. Collins and Porras (1994), the authors of *Built to Last*, believe that successful organizations must continually work to balance change and stability. As a result, organizations are constantly fighting to achieve some level of operational stability. Because of the multitude of external and internal influences that impact organizations, it is not realistic to think that they can stay the same for more than the briefest periods of time. As soon as that state of stability is achieved, new forces begin the process of change all over again. This sense of continual change can be difficult to accept. Constant change can be difficult and often frustrating to leaders and staff alike. This can lead to the tendency at many levels throughout the organization to regard any new program or improvement initiative as the "flavor of the month." The idea that a government agency will always be changing is in sharp contrast to the beliefs of many managers and employees who think that if they can just get through implementing the current change initiative, things will get "back to normal." The difficult reality is that change is, in many ways, the normal condition of the agency.

Understanding the Scope of Change

In addition to understanding the process through which change takes place, a plan to implement improvement opportunities requires an understanding of the way that staff members will view the level of personal, professional, and organizational risk associated with the change. This sense of risk can be directly influenced by the breadth or perceived significance of a particular change. Organizational changes can be considered in terms of the extent of the prospective impact on people, processes, and workplaces. Management theorists divide the level of impact into two categories. Although different models of change may use different terminology, they are generally referred to as incremental change and transformational change.

The term *incremental change* is used to describe the improvement of existing programs, routines, or processes. Anderson and Anderson (2001), in their book *Beyond Change Management,* refer to this as developmental change. During this type of change process, the organization as a whole stays fundamentally the same but makes incremental changes to existing operations in a predetermined direction. This type of change can take place at any level in an organization. Much of it takes place at lower levels as a practical response to a perceived need to do things differently. Kanter (1991a) writes that much of the incremental change in organizations takes place at this grassroots level before it ever rises to the level where organizational leaders recognize it as a formal organizational change process. Incremental change can also be viewed as a planned sequence of small changes, which eventually result in a much larger overall change.

A simple example of incremental change is adapting an existing work process to incorporate a new requirement, such as adding an internal review and approval step to an existing process for reserving the use of a public park. The first actions taken might include examining the current process and determining how it could be adapted to incorporate the new requirements. New or different steps might be written into existing policies and procedures and shared with everyone in the organization. Employees could be trained in the new way of operating and then could incorporate the change into their daily work.

Incremental or developmental change can be successful because it presents a relatively low level of uncertainty for participants. Because these changes adjust or build on the existing systems and processes of the organization, people can "see" what is coming. This type of change is less threatening, because it can be recognized as an adaptation of what employees know and has a specific direction and projected outcome, which is generally known in advance (Figure 6.3).

Figure 6.3   An example of incremental change: revising an existing procedure.

But what if the type of change the agency is contemplating exceeds the scope of this description? There are times when the planned improvement requires change in an organizational structure or represents a way of operating that is fundamentally different from what currently exists. This level of impact is referred to as *transformational change*. In government, examples of transformational change would include major changes in organizational structure, such as a reorganization of major units or the elimination or consolidation of agencies and programs. It could include the introduction of a completely new service or the addition of responsibility for a population that was previously not served. Transformational change is often more difficult to enact because it is less predictable for staff members. It can represent a significant difference from what people know and expect from their workplace. They may not, for example, be able to anticipate what the "new" organization will look like. People may be required to let go of their existing beliefs about the organization, its mission, or its core values. This level of change can create a great deal of anxiety, because it does not guarantee that the existing organization will continue to look or behave the same way. (For more information, see "Organizational Identity" on page 137.) At the same time, transformational change has the potential to significantly improve the organization (Figure 6.4).

These two categories of change are not mutually exclusive. Many change initiatives simultaneously include elements of incremental change and transformational change. Take, for example, a state-level economic development agency that

Incremental Change	Transformational Change
• Improvement of existing processes	• Fundamental change to what currently exists
• Organization remains essentially the same	• Less predictable for organization members
• Predetermined direction	• May impact structure, mission, or core values
• Can take place at any level; often at lower levels	• Can significantly improve the capability of the organization
• Low levels of uncertainty	

Figure 6.4   Comparison of incremental and transformational change.

identified a lack of systematic strategic planning as an opportunity for improvement following an assessment process. In response, the agency is implementing a formal strategic planning process. For those in the agency who already engage in some elements of strategic planning (e.g., through the budget process or a performance measurement effort), part of this implementation could be considered an incremental change that enhances some of the things they already do to improve the operation of the organization in the short run. However, if a new Office of Strategic Planning is created and puts into place a significant change in how data and information are obtained, considered, and acted upon, this could be considered a major change that "transforms" the agency.

How People "See" the Agency: The Role of Organizational Identity

The success of incremental and transformation change can be tied to how much the outcome differs from the way an individual "sees" the organization. When people consider proposed changes, they will do so in the context of what they perceive to be the *identity* of the organization. An organization's identity, as described by Albert and Whetten (1985), is what the people who work in an organization see as its underlying purpose and central focus—what they believe makes it distinct from other similar organizations. People have a personal understanding of how they think the organization will behave in certain situations based on what they perceive to be its core values. Dutton and Dukerich (1991) suggest that this perception of organizational identity influences both the way that people interpret information they receive and how they think about approaching and solving questions or issues. Organizational identity is created and reinforced every day through the interaction that people have with coworkers, supervisors, and leaders and through their experiences at work.

In practical terms, this means that one factor that should be considered in approaching improvement initiatives and change is whether the proposed outcomes will be in accordance or in conflict with what employees see as the identity of the organization. If they believe that the proposed changes are consistent with the agency's identity, they may be more willing to accept it. On the other hand, if they believe that a proposed change does not fit with the agency's identity, they may be less willing to support it and make the necessary adjustments— or they may actively opposed to it. For example, government commonly uses the term *mission creep* to describe a type of incremental change in which the mission of the agency is gradually expanded to include functions that were not originally seen as part of their core purpose. If these gradual changes have resulted in a significant difference from where the mission started, people may believe that those changes do not fit the agency's identity. If so, they are less likely to accept them even if the leaders believe the new functions are appropriate. From looking at the potential reaction to incremental change, it is easy to see that transformational change could certainly impact organizational identity.

The assessment process provides a way to get people to think about their perception of the organization's identity and the compatibility of proposed improvements. The information that is provided and the interactions that take place can result in changes in the perceptions of the participants. The process can be an opportunity to surface and share enough information about the organization as a whole—some of which was most certainly not previously available to employees—to influence what they believe to be the organization's identity. The organizational and personal learning that takes place during an assessment process may significantly impact the individual definitions that people have of the organization's identity.

Why is this important? People who differ in their perception of the organization's identity may also differ, perhaps significantly, on what issues and challenges face the organization. They may be very sincere and well-meaning in their efforts to do their job but may be working at different or cross-purposes because they perceive the issues and priorities differently. A study conducted at the New Jersey Department of Transportation (Immordino, 2006) demonstrated that participation in a self-assessment can increase the amount of consensus on organizational identity. Reaching consensus on the identity of the organization can also help to create agreement on the strengths, issues, and challenges the agency faces. As part of an assessment, an agency may identify a large number of opportunities for improvement—more than can reasonably be addressed—and must narrow them down to a smaller, more achievable set of opportunities that will form the basis for improvement plans. If the participants are in agreement on the challenges and opportunities, the agreement facilitates the selection of priorities for improvement and helps the organization to focus improvement efforts where they are most beneficial.

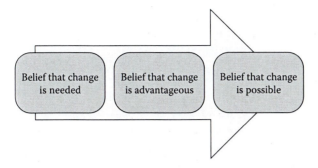

Figure 6.5   Requirements for change.

Organizational Learning and Personal Learning: Creating an Internal Case for Change

Understanding the complexity of change, what are some of the critical considerations for implementing improvement initiatives? One of the most fundamental ways to approach and overcome resistance to change is by presenting people with sufficient credible information about the organization to enable them to see why the change is being enacted and why it is beneficial. The process of successful organizational change has several key components (Figure 6.5). It requires that people:

- Believe that there are things that need to be changed, possibly because they have seen problems that occur time after time.
- Believe that there is an advantage to changing and that moving forward will be better than maintaining the status quo.
- Believe that change is possible within their organization (Pace and Faules, 1993; Witherspoon, 1997).

When we examine these requirements for change, it becomes clear that the common supporting factor for all three is that some type of learning must take place: the acquisition of information and an increase in knowledge. The ability of the organization to learn is widely recognized as a critical factor in organizational change theory, but organizational learning cannot take place without personal learning by the members of the organization (Ruben, 2005). Learning, in this case, does not just mean understanding a new way of doing things. It also requires "unlearning," which can be defined as recognizing and letting go of the established way of doing business. This concept is consistent with the work of Schein (1980) and Lewin (1951), who both describe learning and unlearning as the key components in creating change in organizations. Lewin's model of change is grounded in the idea that people need to learn and understand the issues facing the organization to unfreeze or open themselves to the possibility of change. Similarly, studies by Jick (1995) show that change in organizations takes place when organization members unlearn patterns of behavior and routines. Frohman (1997) conducted a study of people who were successful in bringing about change, and his results suggest that organizational learning occurs when individuals see a problem or opportunity and self-educate to bring about change. Witherspoon (1997) refers to this as reframing, or establishing new perspectives.

Assessment plays a critical role in enabling such organizational and personal learning. W. Edward Deming, who is regarded by many as the father of the quality movement, believed that one of the key benefits of using any type of quality improvement methodology was that it had the ability to bring about changes in thinking by the members of the organization. Ruben (2005) describes the relationship between learning and change in organizations as a series of stages: first, defining a standard of excellence and determining where you stand, followed by a commitment to action, and then by a change stage that involves developing a strategic plan for action and following through.

Using a self-assessment process to increase the organizational knowledge available to participants also reflects basic learning theory, which shows that people learn most effectively when they learn the information for themselves rather than when they are given the information (Hart and Bogan, 1992). The process makes them active contributors in organizational learning.

The influence of assessment on organizational learning is not limited to a particular "instance" of assessment. Literature in the field of organizational development, which describes methods of facilitating change, suggests that people in organizations can actually "learn to learn." They can learn to see the disconnect between where they are and where they want to be (Burke, 1982; Weisbord, 1987). The long-term effect of assessment processes on organizational learning is to create what Argyris (1992) calls double-loop learning. The participants in an assessment learn not only a way to address their immediate concerns but also the assessment process itself, which provides them with a problem-solving methodology that they can apply at other times and for other purposes (Burke, 1982). Jick (1982) also believes that that a deeper level of change—change in the organizational culture—takes place when people learn new ways of behaving and thinking.

How People Approach Decision Making: The Role of Organizational Identification

The way staff members approach change is also impacted by the level of identification each individual feels with the agency. Organizational identification can be defined as the way the individual views his or her personal connection to the characteristics that make up the organization's identity. People vary in the strength of identification they have with their workplace, and the level of identification with the organization can impact the way people behave in the workplace and the way they make workplace decisions. Staff members can have multiple points of identification, and people may identify more with their immediate workgroup or with their profession (e.g., engineers, human resource professionals) than they do with their organization as a whole (Scott and Lane, 2000). Cheney (1983) believes that a person with a strong sense of organizational identification will evaluate choices and make decisions based on what he or she perceives to be in the best interests of the organization. An increase in identification with a group brings with it increased motivation to reach group goals rather than ones that represent the self-interest of the individual (Scott and Lane, 2000). Therefore, a self-assessment process that increases organizational identification may be of value to the organization because it increases individual motivation toward the goals that are of importance to the organization.

An assessment process can also impact the level of organizational identification in other ways. Research has also demonstrated that the more interactions people have with others in the organization, the more likely it is that their identification with the organization will increase (Scott and Lane, 2000). Therefore, an organizational assessment can strengthen identification levels by facilitating interaction with staff members from areas with which they may not interact on a day-to-day basis. Access to information may be limited as a result of social divisions in the workplace. Managers, professionals, laborers, technicians, and clerical staff have different levels of access to the decision-making process (Deetz, 1995). They may not have common views of the organization since they do not have the same information on which to base their conclusions. By bringing people together, assessment processes can help break down the barriers between those who normally have access to information and those who do not. Those who have the opportunity to participate in an assessment process may be very different from those who normally make decisions.

Cheney (1983) believed that participation in decision making is one of the processes that organizations use to foster a sense of identity in their members. In his study of organizational identification, he describes how one employee felt a stronger level of identification with the whole organization after having the chance to work in several different areas and to see how the overall operations work. Assessment, therefore, can also provide a broader view of operations across the organization, bringing a richer perspective to participants and, at the same time, increasing their level of identification.

The Role of Organizational and Personal Learning in Communicating the Need for Change

One of the problems in change initiatives is an assumption by organizational leaders that staff members understand the reasons for change, yet this may not be true. These people may not have access to the same information as the decision makers and, therefore, may not perceive the underlying reasons for the change. They may not be aware of threats or opportunities that are driving the change effort. If people do not understand why change is taking place they will be much less likely to accept it. Instead, acceptance of the need for change is created by educating people. The assessment process can help overcome resistance by providing an opportunity to both identify the issues and develop the changes to be implemented. Research has documented that participation in an assessment process can shift the way people think about the things they believe are priorities. In a study conducted through Rutgers University (Immordino, 2006), participants in an assessment process in a major department of state government were surveyed to determine what they believed were the most significant challenges facing their agency. After participating in an assessment process, they were surveyed again, and there were significant changes in what they saw as the organization's priorities compared with what they believed was important prior to participating. Employees who participate in a self-assessment are given the opportunity to see the organization in a different way and to learn firsthand what change is needed. The process in which people work together to collect and share the information required during the assessment process facilitates learning, as does the role of participants in identifying the existing strengths and the opportunities for improvement. This learning process continues through the selection of priorities for improvement and the development of implementation plans. Al Brenner, director of Support Services at the NJDOT (New Jersey Department of Transportation), was one of the participants when his division completed an assessment, which gave him the opportunity to observe the learning process as it took place. Brenner says:

> The process gave people direction on areas to be improved and an awareness of what to focus on…. Participants were more in agreement on challenges facing the division, because they represented every unit in the division so people became more aware of what every individual unit faces. People had a better understanding of why decisions were made.[4]

The involvement of employees at this stage is particularly important in terms of implementing improvements through a change process. This can be especially true when cross-organizational teams are used in the assessment process because it increases the likelihood that people will bring different types of information to the table [5] Lewin (1951) believed that people were more likely to accept change when they have a role in developing the solutions.

Lewin's study of group dynamics and Senge's (1990) disciplines for creating a learning organization both suggest that using a team or group is significantly more effective than appealing to individuals in creating support for organizational change (Raven, 1995). Ruben (2005) describes it this way:

> The problems that matter to colleagues will be the ones they define as critical, and these may not be the same ones that preoccupy you or the administrators who created your program.[6]

Creating an External Case for Change: Constituent Involvement

A key factor in the success of any quality effort that involves the evaluation of constituent satisfaction is the involvement of the professional staff of government in recognizing the right of constituents to have a seat at the table. This translates into the need for an assessment process that includes beneficiaries and constituents as a focus. If constituents feel that they can actively participate in government by providing input for programs and services, the next logical step is to include them in the assessment of the organization. To do this, government's perceptions of constituents must recognize that this input can provide a more complete picture of how an agency functions and can create opportunities for improvement. Government often has difficulty in both identifying its constituents and establishing methods for their participation.

While we have spent some time discussing the benefits to be gained by involving the members of an organization in the change efforts that facilitate organizational improvement, a significant challenge in moving forward is whether and how to involve government's constituents in the process. Unfortunately, in the past many government agencies have conducted themselves as though constituents and beneficiaries did not need to be part of that process. Kaifeng and Callahan (2007) note, "Many public officials are reluctant to include citizens in decision making, or if they do, they typically involve citizens after the issues have been frames and decisions have been made," which can cause frustration on the part of those constituents.[8] The benefits of including constituents apply to both specific programs (projects) and policy decisions. Constituents are increasingly seeking to be part of that conversation, both in terms of the services being offered and the way they are provided. Constituents can be allies in establishing the need for change, especially in terms of obtaining funding. Constituents have the ability to delay or derail any program or project if they are not supportive or if their concerns are not adequately addressed. They also have the ability to influence the assignment of resources and priorities. In the same way that instituting change relies on the ability of the organization and its members to learn new ways of looking at how they do business, government must develop the ability to assess the expectation levels of constituents and to find ways to educate them about the challenges the agency faces.

A study by Younis (1997) of the Brighton, Colorado, police department examined the department's policy decision to increase the amount of citizen involvement in its processes to improve the level of satisfaction with services. The study describes how the department was subsequently transformed from a bureaucratic culture to one that welcomed citizen involvement in continuous improvement. The result was a significant increase in constituent satisfaction. One way for agencies to engage their primary constituents is to invite them into the process and to translate processes into terminology that is readily understood by constituents and that respects their ability to be part of the conversation. Doing so creates a sense of ownership. Long and Franklin (2004) describe the extent and quality of the outreach process as one of the independent variables influencing the success of policy implementation, which is partially measured by whether agencies reach out to the "usual suspects" or coordinate a more far-reaching approach to collect information from multiple constituent groups. They describe the potential benefits of such outreach:

> [Constituent involvement] focuses resources on key concerns of those the organization serves, and improves the likelihood of successful implementation because stakeholders perceive that they have "ownership" of a policy or program.[9]

The response of these groups, whether cooperative, differentiated, adversarial, or disinterested, provides valuable information to the agency about the effectiveness of its efforts to involve constituents.

An Example of Constituent Involvement: Context Sensitive Design

The New Jersey Department of Transportation is responsible for thousands of miles of state and interstate highways and bridges. Like many similar transportation agencies, its organizational culture was heavily focused on the technical expertise of its engineers. This culture believed that engineering expertise was the most important—and sometimes the only—factor of importance in decision making. This did not stem from any intention to exclude constituent input. In fact, the department had an excellent community relations staff and a track record of meeting all federal requirements for citizen involvement. Simply put, many staff people sincerely believed that, essentially, "They're our roads, and we know best what to do with them." Still, the department's leaders recognized the need to more proactively incorporate constituents and other levels of government in their process.

In 1999, the department formally incorporated the concept of context sensitive design (CSD), which they describe as an "approach to planning and designing transportation projects based on active and early partnerships with communities" (www.state.nj.us/dot). CSD recognizes that a state highway can be, at the same time, someone else's "Main Street," especially in a state like New Jersey with high traffic volumes and population density. The department undertook an extensive multi-year training program that included not only NJDOT engineers, planners, project managers, and community relations representatives but also consultants, legislators, government administrators, and community leaders. The training program included many techniques of CSD, including flexible design, respectful communication, consensus-building and community participation, negotiation, and conflict resolution.

Having this shared knowledge between the department and its constituents allowed the department to engage people in participation and decision making in a way that balances local priorities with the need to solve transportation problems. The outcome is a much richer level of constituent involvement than what had previously been available and a shared sense of responsibility and collaboration.[10]

Using Assessment Outcomes to Implement Improvement

Assessment can be looked at as a type of action research, where organizational change becomes a planned activity based on the data and information rather than just a reaction to the internal or external environment.

Argyris's (1992) model of organizational development specifies three conditions that must be met as the basis for creating change:

- Making available valid and useful information that describes the factors and their relationships.

Assessment facilitates organizational change by:

- Determining the current state of the organization
- Identifying the gaps between the present and the desired state
- Providing the supporting information on which decisions can be based
- Engaging employees so that they understand the need for change
- Providing a baseline for measuring the impacts of change

Figure 6.6 The role of assessment processes in organizational change.

- Allowing the client the choice of alternatives for action in response to the information.
- Having the organizational members make the choice of action and bear the responsibility for implementing it.

The process of organizational assessment contains each of the conditions described in this model. In terms of information, the process requires information about not only the current state of the organization but also the relationship among the major operating processes. For example, the knowledge developed during an assessment can establish the groundwork for change by providing the supporting information on which decisions can be made. Why is this so critical? Initiating change without a firm understanding of an organization's current capabilities and resources can result in false starts and wasted resources and can jeopardize support for change in the future. The process also creates a baseline against which the effects of change on the organization's future performance can be compared (Figure 6.6).

Summary

Public sector organizations are under continual pressure to improve their operations. Organizational change is the term used to describe the complex process through which current operations are modified to create a different and presumably more effective way of doing things. Change can be limited to a single area or can affect an entire organization. It can be incremental, taking place in small, planned steps, or transformational—substantially changing processes, structure, or the organization itself. No matter what the scope, change can be difficult because it requires employees to let go of what is familiar, to adjust to a new situation, and then to integrate the changes into their work.

For any change process to be successful, it has to involve the members of the organization by providing them with the information they need to understand the reasons for change, to believe that change is possible, and to feel that the change will improve the organization. The key to providing this information to employees is through personal and organizational learning; assessment processes are a valuable tool for learning. The assessment process, through its emphasis on information collection and employee participation, enables leaders to build a knowledge base throughout the organization on which they can draw to act on the priorities for change. The process can facilitate change by reframing the way individuals and groups think about their work. It enables them to recognize different sets of priorities than they might otherwise consider. Assessment can also create agreement on the organization's identity, which is the way that the members define the most important characteristics and purposes of the organization; perceived organizational identity can also influence the way staff view change initiatives.

The process of change is always challenging, and government agencies face a number of barriers to change—some that are common to all agencies, such as employee resistance, and some that are specific to the public sector. By recognizing that these barriers exist, organizational leaders can plan for them and incorporate them into the learning that takes place during an assessment.

Notes

1. p. 229.
2. Interview with Mark Tucci, March 17, 2008.
3. Federal Emergency Management Agency, http://www.fema.gov/
4. Al Brenner, interview June 25, 2008.
5. Cross-functional team can be horizontal, drawing together people at comparable levels from diverse parts of the organization. They can also be vertical, incorporating people at different levels.
6. p. 384.
7. p. 11.
8. p. 249.
9. p. 313.
10. New Jersey Department of Transportation, http://www.state.nj.us/dot

Chapter 7

Case Studies and Best Practices in Assessing Public Sector Organizations

> This chapter presents descriptions and case studies of organizations at the federal, state, and local government level that have engaged in organizational self-assessment. It includes both award winners and those who have done so as an internal organizational development practice. By examining the best practices used by these organizations, as well as things that could be improved, those who are new to assessment can gain insight into the process of conducting assessment.

The use of organizational assessment processes in public sector organizations is not a recent phenomenon. Some government agencies have years of experience in assessment, improvement, and organizational quality practices. The models have evolved over the years, but the interest in understanding operations to improve performance is engrained in public service. The range of available examples is impressive. Many government organizations have successfully undertaken and completed formal assessment processes. It is not unusual to find that these organizations have made formal applications to one or more of the various state, federal, or local award and assessment programs. Many others have conducted information assessments.

The models used vary from agency to agency. As described in earlier chapters, many government organizations have employed the Baldrige Criteria for

Performance Excellence as the basis for an assessment using the business criteria or, more recently, the additional language for nonprofit organizations. Others have developed unique processes that align with the needs of their organizations. The Public Sector Assessment and Improvement (PSAI) model integrates the Baldrige model with the practices and culture of government. A common feature that runs throughout these models is an expectation that participants will share information about their experiences. Government may have a distinct advantage over business in this area because of the lack of market competition between similar programs. The nature of government service encourages the sharing of best practices with peer organizations. It is very important that agencies that have conducted assessment processes serve as models and provide an opportunity for those interested in assessment to examine how assessment processes can be applied. Reviewing the processes used and the lessons learned by agencies that have implemented assessment can be an effective learning tool for other government agencies. Learning from their experiences provides an insight into some of the challenges and the rewards of self-assessment.

The experiences of three government agencies are presented here. They have agreed to share not only their assessment processes but also how the use of assessment processes came about and how they impacted the agency. The following case studies represent the three primary levels of government: federal, state, and local. They include both national- and state-level award processes and internal processes. The federal government and local government are represented by the first two public sector winners of the Baldrige Award: The U.S. Army Armament Research, Development and Engineering Center (ARDEC) and the City of Coral Springs, Florida. The state level is represented by the New Jersey Department of Environmental Protection (NJDEP), winner of the New Jersey Quality Award and the National Public Service Award. All three illustrate the process and the benefits that can be derived through assessment.

The case studies include the following elements:

- The assessment model and processes used.
- The role of the participants.
- The outcomes.
- The impact of management support.
- Issues faced and lessons learned.

Case Studies

Federal Government: U.S. Army Armament Research, Development and Engineering Center

- 2007 Malcolm Baldrige National Quality Award (MBNQA) Recipient

- 2007 American Society for Training and Development (ASTD) Best Award for Workplace Learning and Performance
- Top 5 Department of Defense Program Awards (2004, 2007, 2008)
- U.S. Army Research and Development (R&D) Collaboration Awards (2005, 2007, 2008)
- 2007 Recognized as the Lean Six Sigma Center of Excellence by RDECOM Headquarters
- 2006 CMMI Maturity Level 5 Certification: Software Engineering, Systems Engineering, Supplier Sourcing (Armament Software Engineering Center)
- 2006 Army Performance Excellence Award—Gold
- Army Large Development R&D Laboratory of the Year Awards (2004, 2006, 2008)
- 2002–2008: 17 of the Army's Greatest Inventions of the Year Awards (as selected by soldiers)

ARDEC

- Strategic objectives.
- Leader in armaments technology innovation.
- Exceptional customer satisfaction through execution of the life-cycle mission.
- Continuous improvement through innovative business initiatives.
- Pioneering facilities and knowledge management systems supporting a flexible, agile, innovative, and diverse workforce.

ARDEC is headquartered at Picatinny Arsenal, a 6,500-acre military installation in New Jersey with locations at Benet Labs in Watervliet, New York, and Rock Island, Illinois. ARDEC's mission is to develop and maintain a world-class workforce and to execute and manage integrated life-cycle engineering processes required for the research, development, production, field support, and demilitarization of munitions, weapons, fire control, and associated items. ARDEC's vision is "Innovative Armaments Solutions for Today and Tomorrow."[1] It is a unique organization that can trace its history back to the time when it made cannonballs for George Washington's army. Today, the purpose of ARDEC is the advancement of armaments technology and engineering innovation. ARDEC provides research, development, and engineering for a wide range of armaments technologies and products for use by the military and the Department of Homeland Security. It has no single counterpart in the world and provides the research, development, and engineering for 90% of the Army's suite of armaments.

ARDEC has a well-defined focus on its products' end users, who are warfighters—primarily ground-combat soldiers, marines, and special operations forces. The ARDEC workforce is driven by two of the Department of the Army objectives: (1) to provide the latest available technology to today's warfighter; and, simultaneously, (2) to support a complete transformation of future forces. ARDEC engages in public–private partnerships and has been successful in transferring some of the technology to create nonmilitary applications. To accomplish this mission, ARDEC employs over 3,300 civilian scientists, engineers, technical specialists, business and administrative personnel, and contractors.

ARDEC has a long history of engaging in quality practices and can trace its quality journey back to the introduction of quality circles in 1984 and the establishment of a total quality management (TQM) council. However, its interest in the Baldrige criteria began with what ARDEC calls a "significant emotional event"—a challenge to its existence when in the 1990s an ARDEC commander asked for a formal survey of ARDEC's customers.[2] He expected a positive response, but instead the response from the customers was that ARDEC was expensive and did not listen to them. One ARDEC official described his reaction to this information, saying, "This was a shock—to learn we were not as indispensable as we thought we were."[3]

The organization, faced with feedback from the external environment telling it to improve, decided on a course of action. ARDEC had a visionary leader, military commander General James Boddie, who moved them in the right direction by saying he wanted them to be "like Jiffy Lube—tell customers what you will do, tell them how long it will take, and how much it will cost."[4]

By the early 1990s, the organization had put process teams in place and had created a quality management board. ARDEC officials describe the period from 1995 to 2002 as its "transformational years" and during that time adopted the Baldrige criteria as the agency's quality management framework. They downsized the management structure and initiated a cultural change to a team-based, customer-focused organization. They also began to engage in formal benchmarking and replaced their existing dashboard system with a balanced scorecard approach that focused on 15 organizational objectives using approximately 30 measures (Figure 7.1).[5]

In 2003, ARDEC reorganized from an autonomous set of sometimes competing business units to an enterprise competency-based structure. As part of the reorganization, managers had to reapply for their jobs, explaining why they wanted to do that job in the new organization. This was followed in 2005 by a model that incorporated and linked a series of quality "best practices" including ISO 9001, Capability Maturity Model Integration, Voice of the Customer, Lean Six Sigma, and Baldrige under a single business initiative called Enterprise Excellence.

Since 1995, ARDEC has applied for recognition and validation through a variety of different award processes, including state-, Army, and national-level competitions, as a way to get feedback. Management applied the information received from those competitions as a catalyst to systematically generate improvement and innovation ideas and used the identified opportunities for improvement to stretch

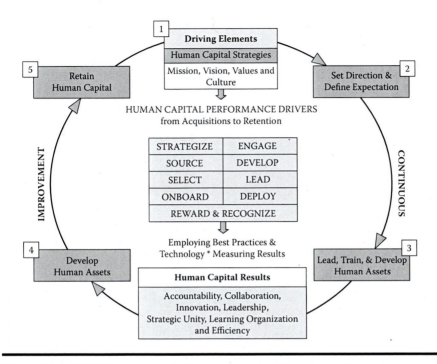

Figure 7.1 ARDEC human capital improvement and performance system.

forward as an organization. ARDEC was able to build each year on the work that had been done in previous assessments and applications. It also participated in other government (Army) award processes as a way of benchmarking itself to similar organizations. It won a string of significant quality awards, beginning with the President's Council for Management Improvement Award in 1991 and the Vice President's National Performance Review "Hammer" Award. In 1994, it competed for the Army Center of Excellence Award, which used the Baldrige framework to stimulate continuous improvement in Army organizations and to improve operations on Army bases. In 2004, ARDEC applied for the New Jersey State Quality Award and the Army Performance Excellence Award.

In November 2004 it was recognized by *Time Magazine* for its innovative technology. Over a four-year period, ARDEC won over a quarter of the Army's 10 Greatest Inventions of the Year Awards and a number of Baldrige-based awards at the state, federal, Department of Defense, and Department of the Army levels. The Army Audit Agency identified ARDEC as a benchmark organization for Technology Transition in 2006. ARDEC established a pattern of organizational improvement. Each even-numbered year it would apply for an award and then evaluate the feedback and gaps and spend the odd-numbered years implementing improvements.

ARDEC continued to use the Baldrige criteria as a management framework, and when the Baldrige organization announced a pilot program to include nonprofit organizations in its award process, the decision was made to apply. Despite ARDEC's experience with the criteria, it was not selected for a site visit. However, the top leadership of the organization made the decision to apply again the following year, when nonprofits would be an official category in the Baldrige National Quality Award process. Dr. Joseph A. Lannon, director of ARDEC, in commenting on the decision to apply again, felt that "win or lose the Warfighter is the winner."[6]

ARDEC approached the preparation of its Baldrige application as an employee-led, participative effort using an organization-wide team approach. The application process was treated as a formal project, with a project leader, timeline, and reporting requirements. Donelle Denery, who served as ARDEC's project officer for Baldrige and organizational development, was also a team leader, an MBNQA examiner, and a judge for Pennsylvania's state Baldrige-based competition. A dedicated team of 10 people was assigned to this effort for a period of four months. A champion was assigned to each of the seven criteria categories, normally a senior-level leader. These leaders of the organization took on the responsibility of being the champions for the categories of leadership, strategic planning, customer focus, measurement, analysis and knowledge management, human capital, and process management. Each category also had a writing team, generally made up of three people who normally perform the type of work covered by that category. For example, the lead person for ARDEC's strategic planning efforts served as the lead writer for the strategic planning category, and the head of the Business Interface Office served as the lead writer for the customer focus category. Section 7, results, incorporated information from each of the other groups. External consultants were used to assist with critiques and conducted mock interviews. The champions for each category worked with their team to review feedback received and to assess the strengths and opportunities for improvement and were responsible for driving performance improvement.

The process included a communication plan designed to reach every employee. The first step was to talk to staff members about the process, to provide them with some information about Baldrige-based improvement initiatives, and to ask them to think about how they fit in the organization. As the time for the site visit drew closer, ARDEC implemented a second level of more targeted staff training, which gave more detail about what Baldrige is and provided process information, such as what to do if you are asked questions by an examiner. The third phase was an additional level of training for those who were most likely, because of their role, to be talked to by an examiner. They also conducted a mock site visit, using an independent expert who came in and acted like an examiner to help people understand what it would be like.

After submitting its second application, ARDEC was selected by the Baldrige organization for a site visit. The same teams that served as writers for the application were responsible for preparing for the site visit and escorting the Baldrige examiners as they reviewed the organization and interviewed over 300 ARDEC employees at three locations. Following the completion of the site visit phase, the secretary of commerce announced that ARDEC had become the first federal government agency to receive the Malcolm Baldrige National Quality Award.

Beginning with the first phone call informing ARDEC that it was a recipient and that it would be announced on the national news that evening, there was a conscious effort to include every employee in the celebration that followed. Dr. Lannon sent a broadcast message to the entire workforce about the Baldrige journey to put the organization's efforts into perspective. A bus full of staff members went to Washington, D.C., to attend the award ceremony. The ceremony itself was recorded and subsequently broadcast on the agency's computers so that all employees were able to see it. Brad Sampson was part of the core team for the Baldrige application and was responsible for writing the results section of the application. He described ARDEC's employees as proud and excited, saying, "It broke the paradigm that government employees can't do anything…. We showed that a Department of Defense organization is top quality."[7]

In his speech at the Baldrige Award presentation, Dr. Lannon credited the organization's "hard work and an unbelievably strong commitment to our customer." He credited four basic components that shaped ARDEC:

> Innovation in both product and process; persistence in the pursuit of excellence; external evaluation and continuous learning to accelerate improvement; and a culture that thinks like a "for profit" great business with a bottom line…. Instead of pockets of isolated improvement, the framework helps us ensure we have integrated and aligned performance excellence across ARDEC.[8]

Moving forward, ARDEC continues to use a team concept to implement improvement. Each identified opportunity for improvement is evaluated in terms of its cost–benefit, and opportunities judged to have the highest potential return on investment are piloted. The results of the pilots are evaluated and improved and implemented more widely. Meetings are held every two weeks to review the efforts, and a key element of deploying these projects is celebrating the successes. The areas that were identified in the assessment process as strengths are also reviewed regularly to evaluate how the organization can sustain them (Figure 7.2).

ARDEC realizes that being a recipient of the Baldrige award presents a different type of challenge. The new challenge is "finding a way to keep sharp" and to keep positive tension in the organization. ARDEC leaders are considering what to do next. Since the organization cannot apply for the Baldrige award for five years after being a recipient, it has discussed the idea of applying for other different awards and prizes. It recently applied for the Global Six Sigma CEO of the Year award, coming in third in the world and won the U.S. Army Large Development Laboratory of the Year Award for the third time in five years.

In looking back over the process, Sampson believes that they would not have done anything differently. The key, as he sees it, is to be prepared, noting, "We had

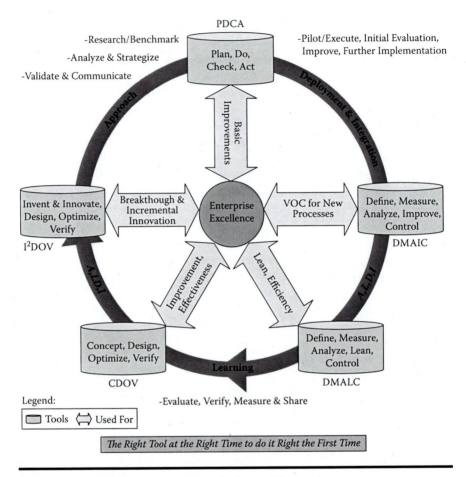

Figure 7.2 ARDEC process/product design and improvement system.

done it since 1994, so we had practice.... We had the process issues worked out."[9] While he did not think that language was a problem, there were some places in the Baldrige criteria where they had to "look out for new definitions of key terms in the criteria each year as they applied the concepts to their organization. ARDEC's internal process evolved over the years, as did the people who were involved. The Baldrige Opportunities for Improvement provided a roadmap to the path for Excellence."[10]

State Government: The New Jersey Department of Environmental Protection

- Bronze-level winner, 2000 New Jersey Governor's Award
- Winner, 2002 National Public Service Excellence Award

NJDEP was established in 1970 and is responsible for "formulating comprehensive policies for the conservation of the state's natural resources, the promotion of environmental protection and the prevention of pollution in the environment."[11] As a regulatory agency, its mission requires it to deal effectively with the challenge of balancing the needs of its constituents while maintaining the integrity of its regulatory requirements. By the early 1990s, as the agency matured, it took a proactive approach to creating a focus on continuous improvement, instituting a results-based management system, and adopting the Baldrige Award framework as a process to examine and change its operations. As a result of its efforts, the department took the bronze-level award in the 2000 New Jersey Governor's Award program and subsequently won the 2002 National Public Service Excellence Award.

The process of applying for the award was grounded in a proactive approach to quality. Beginning three years earlier, in 1997, NJDEP (an organization of 3,300 employees at that time) began to implement an organization-wide quality improvement effort. After the appointment of Commissioner Robert Shinn in 1994, NJDEP began to look for ways to change the organization's "fundamental business approaches to environmental regulation and business management."[12] In 1996, it began an organization-wide effort to introduce strategic planning and quality processes into the organization by creating a strategic planning process team to establish a framework, followed the next year by the appointment of a strategic planning group that created a four-year plan. NJDEP also established a two-year Performance Partnership Agreement with the U.S. Environmental Protection Agency as part of the National Environmental Performance Partnership System (NEPPS). The NEPPS model stressed the use of outcome-based measures such as air quality rather than activity-based measures of performance such as counting the number of permits issued. In 1999, NJDEP deployed its results-based management system, which provided the data necessary for detailed analyses of programs and operations and periodic reviews of the alignment among organizational goals, objectives, and resource allocation. The system was implemented department-wide, with annual goal briefings provided by the assistant commissioner for each area—first to the management team and then to all staff.

In 1999, senior administrators started to explore how they could enhance the use of quality practices in the organization and considered the potential of using the Baldrige process to help the organization achieve higher levels of performance excellence. The effort to institute quality processes was championed at the senior leadership level by Ronald Tuminski, assistant commissioner for management and budget. Leaders enacted a strategic plan with five environmental goals and one business goal, "Open and Effective Government," and used the Baldrige criteria as their definition of open and effective government. Working in partnership with Quality New Jersey, an organization dedicated to promoting and recognizing quality practices in the state, NJDEP set a goal of applying for the Governor's Award, a Baldrige-based award program for New Jersey organizations in the business, education, health-care, and government sectors. NJDEP established a core team made up of 20 people representing all areas of the department, including people from both program and administrative areas. In 1999, administrators hired Mark Tucci, a certified examiner for Quality New Jersey, to be the coordinator for the core team. Joe Genovay, one of the original core team members, described the initial efforts as "confused, until Mark focused them.... He gave everyone confidence that they could move forward." NJDEP used the Baldrige criteria as a way to create a common focus in the organization. Baldrige, says Genovay, "became one big thing we could focus on."[13] When Tucci was hired, it was initially suggested to him that the department should be prepared to submit an application later that year. Tucci had previous experience with the Baldrige criteria in other organizations and through his work with Quality New Jersey. Knowing the extent of what would be involved, he responded that the time frame might not be feasible. In the end, it took almost another year—until fall 2000—before the organization was ready to apply.

NJDEP set a department-wide focus on Baldrige as a business model and prepared to submit an application to Quality New Jersey for the 2000 Governor's Award. Tuminski gave the core team members total discretion on how to implement quality processes, allowing them to adapt the process based on the needs of the individuals involved. The core team went through Baldrige training and then formed work groups around each of the seven criteria. Members met regularly to discuss the award criteria and how NJDEP could meet them. Tucci describes it as an "awareness-building process" where people began to see how NJDEP operations fit into the process. The role of each work team was to collect and analyze information.[14] Teams were charged with crafting responses to the category questions and had to be able to support their responses with data. Team leaders were empowered to meet with whomever they needed to in the organization and collected data in partnership with their staff. They collected information through surveys and personal contacts. They wanted to capture success stories reflecting what the department was doing well. The reporting system was used to identify successful areas and annual progress reports reviewed to point to those who should be interviewed. Focus groups were used to get information about the issues. The work teams would report back to the core team, whose role was to discuss the information and reach consensus. In addition to collecting information, team members played an important role in disseminating information about the process itself, serving as ambassadors for the effort throughout the organization.

The department's management team, composed of the senior leaders of the agency, served as the Quality Council. Its role was to "review key performance data linked to the Department's strategic priorities with a constant focus on strategic adjustments to ensure continuous improvement."[15] Tucci, as head of the core team, reported to the assistant commissioner for management and budget, and the team functioned as a Quality Advisory Board. NJDEP was also a member of Quality New Jersey, where employees served on its boards and as examiners.

The application NJDEP submitted for the 2000 Governor's Award articulated its vision statement: "Making New Jersey a Better Place to Live, Work, and Raise a Family." NJDEP knew that it was among the first state agencies in New Jersey to apply for the Governor's Award. It achieved bronze-level status, which made it the first government agency in New Jersey to win the Governor's Award at any level.

Communication throughout the organization played a critical role in the application process as well as in building credibility and using the information to support further change in the agency. After the results were announced, copies of the application were sent out to everyone in the agency. The significance of this achievement was well noted, and the agency, as part of its celebration, took out an ad in the local newspaper thanking employees for their efforts. NJDEP also invited the lead examiner from Quality New Jersey to come to the department and explain to employees what the site visit team had found and what it meant. Tucci describes the reaction as a real "wow" factor: Employees could see that their agency had a great story to tell. Many employees, however, were unaware of the scope of NJDEP's activities and asked, literally, "Do we really do all these things?" In an atmosphere where "everything is a priority," many staff members knew only the part of NJDEP's functions in which they were personally involved and did not have the opportunity to see or understand the whole organization. People "don't hear the whole story—just what they are doing."[16] Genovay says that the benefit of the process for individuals and the team is that "you learn so much about the organization—you find out that you are doing a lot and doing it well."[17] In discussing what constituted the most difficult part of the process, Tucci said that it was getting hundreds of pages of good news about NJDEP's work and achievements edited down to the maximum-allowed 50 pages for the application. Doing so required asking what constitutes the essence of the information and reaching consensus on the story to be told.

Despite NJDEP's success in the Governor's Award program, the election of a new governor and the transition of administration to a newly appointed NJDEP commissioner resulted in dramatic changes for the program. The new NJDEP administration specifically rejected the use of the Baldrige process, terming it an initiative of the "other party." Despite the lack of formal support, those who had been most involved with it remained committed. Even though NJDEP did not formally continue the program as it had originally existed, those who had been part of the process continued to work toward implementing the identified opportunities for improvement. These same people also made the decision to follow through with plans to apply for a national-level award. The same core team developed an application for the National Public Service Excellence Award and essentially continued the assessment process, using the common language that was developed in earlier processes. As a result of the team's efforts, NJDEP was presented with that award in 2002. It was the organization's last application to date for quality recognition.

While NJDEP continues to be an outstanding organization with a strong core mission and commitment to the environment, there has been no formal department-wide organizational assessment process since 2002. The core team no longer exists, and the results-based management system was also discontinued. The department's organizational development area continues to support continuous improvement, has developed a set of formalized core skills for managers and staff, and created a leadership training academy based on those core skills as part of developing a succession planning program.

A few years later, the experience of the Quality New Jersey program also served to illustrate the value of management support. In a difficult state budget situation, the Annual Best Practices in Government Conference sponsored by Quality New Jersey was canceled after four successful years. Similarly, without high-profile support in government, the Governors Award program ended in 2007.

Challenges Faced

NJDEP understood that the organizational assessment process it undertook was not common for public agencies. It noted in its Governor's Award application, "This organization-wide improvement initiative represents a very innovative approach for any entity, particularly for a regulatory government agency which has undertaken this on a voluntary basis, without a political or legislative mandate."[18] There were several challenges NJDEP faced:

- Adapting to an external model. The difficulty in getting people to understand and accept a new business model should not be underestimated. This was compounded for NJDEP by the challenge of applying an external model like Baldrige to what you already do. Leaders must recognize that implementation of an assessment program such as this requires an understanding of cultural change in organizations. It must be approached not just as a discrete project but also as a long-term process. To be successful, organizations must be prepared to teach people not only the model and process but also the skills necessary for them to become adept at change.

- Recognizing the unique role of managers in the process. It is important to realize the difference that managers can make and the importance of obtaining the support of all levels of management. Tucci believed that upper management and line employees "get it," but the difficult sell is middle management. He believes that middle managers "don't like you to tamper with their world. They have learned how to maintain the status quo" and when faced with organizational assessments often fall back on the statement that they "have real work to get done."[19] NJDEP communicated the outcomes of the process to managers at all levels and involved them in plans for moving forward. A copy of the written feedback report was given to all managers, and they had the opportunity to question the Quality New Jersey examiner. The management team was empowered to select what opportunities for improvement would go forward and developed an improvement plan, based on what it judged would be realistic and practical.

- Overcoming the perception that this was "just a fad." When NJDEP approached staff members about participation, people expressed concerns about investing their time and energy in an effort that was not guaranteed to be successful. The larger, and perhaps unanticipated, cultural issue was their desire to know what the impact would be on them professionally if they were associated with an unsuccessful effort. Tucci believed it was critically important that people bought into the integrity of the process and understood that it was not about making the administration look good. It needed to be perceived as both a safe and a serious process.

Lessons Learned

One of the most important lessons learned was appreciating the value of the interaction the process facilitates among the staff members and between the various units in the organization. Tucci says that while it was possible for the organization to put a price on the time, in terms of calculating salaries and hours spent, the positive value to NJDEP of the time spent could not be calculated.

Other factors were as follows:

■ Ensure that you have access to essential participants. Success depends on the ability to draw in whoever you think is important to the process. This includes having access to the people who have the information needed for the assessment as well having the right participants involved in the teams. While it is important to make sure that all employee and organizational groups are represented, it is also important to have people with the skills needed to perform the work. Genovay says, "What we didn't do was look at the functions of the teams and bring in people who had the needed skills—we worried instead about whether every area had a representative."[20] While having representation from across the organization helped create buy-in, he believes that team functioning could have been more effective and the teams could have performed better.

■ Keep the goal of the process in front of people. It is important to remind people that the concept of quality improvement is important, not the label of the individual process used. Instead of focusing on Baldrige, the core team focused on the concept of improvement when talking to staff members. The team's goal was to convey the message that what is important is gauging how you are delivering services, no matter what you call the process.

■ Understand the difficulty staff members may have with customer terminology. There was a cultural hurdle in terms of the Baldrige and Quality New Jersey focus on customer service. NJDEP addressed the internal debate over the concept of customers with a decision to change the name of the focus area from customer focus to constituent focus for use in the department. The environment itself was identified by many as the major "customer." People who worked in the state parks looked at trees and animal as important constituents. As a regulatory agency, NJDEP took very seriously its responsibility to the environment, but that did not necessarily translate into a common understanding or agreement on the beneficiaries of its efforts. The prevailing response was, "We're regulatory; we don't have customers. The people with whom we interact may like us or not like us." The outcome was a shared understanding of the constituents and beneficiaries of NJDEP's services. In its Governor's Award application, NJDEP acknowledged that its constituent philosophy recognized not only citizens but also wildlife and ecosystems as beneficiaries of the department's work. It used unique measures to demonstrate results, such as voter support for environmental issues.[21] It also dealt with the questions on market performance by explaining that government agencies cannot expand their markets and that it was therefore not applicable.

- ■ Ascertain whether your leadership team is committed to making a difference. Much of the work that NJDEP was able to accomplish in its assessment processes was made possible because of the clear message that the effort had the support of management. As Tucci put it, people "heard enough times" that the head of the agency supported it. The importance of senior management support can be seen by comparing the support of the leadership of NJDEP at the beginning of this process and at the end. The initiative and support of Assistant Commissioner Tuminski and the support of Commissioner Shinn were what started the program and kept it going. The next set of leaders did not feel the same way about the Baldrige framework, and the program was not integrated enough to continue without support. Leaders need to both articulate their support and talk about the value of the process to the agency to create the staff buy-in necessary for the effort to succeed.

The most difficult lesson, which is related to but somewhat broader than leadership support, is the difficulty of maintaining existing systems in the face of government transitions. With a change in administration, the infrastructure of leadership support can fall away, and executive leadership support is critical. The transition from one administration to another almost always involves a review of programs and, often, results in a change of priorities. Tucci acknowledged that appointed agency leaders have a short window in which to accomplish their priorities, and, as a result, newly appointed leaders must often focus on short-term benefits.

The difficult question for those involved was why, when they had such a common focus, they could not sustain the process regardless of who was in leadership positions. If they had the chance to do it over again, what they would have done differently is to make sure that the assessment process was institutionalized and seen as part of how the agency does business. After winning the bronze-level Governor's Award, they did not apply again. Genovay feels that the organization should have continued to apply with a goal of obtaining gold-level recognition. Looking back, Tucci says the key in a change of administration is to clearly articulate the value of the process to the department.

Figure 7.3   The City of Coral Springs, Florida.

Local Government: Coral Springs, Florida 2007 Baldrige National Quality Award (nonprofit category)

Coral Springs, Florida, was incorporated as a city in 1963 and operates under a commission–manager form of government with five elected commissioners and an appointed city manager. It describes itself in its Baldrige application (Coral Springs, 2007) as a "city government with a corporate management model" and a "high performing municipal corporation."[22] There are currently over 132,000 residents, making it the 13th largest city in the state of Florida. The city's mission is to be the "Nation's premier community in which to live, work, and raise a family."[23] In terms of structure, there are seven operating departments, seven support departments, and four wholly owned subsidiaries (Coral Springs, 2007) (Figure 7.3).

Focusing on things "we know are important for our customers," Coral Springs has identified seven strategic priority areas[24]:

- Customer-involved government.
- Financial health and economic development.
- Excellence in education.
- Neighborhood and environmental vitality.
- Youth development and family values.
- Strength in diversity.
- Traffic, mobility, and connectivity.

Those involved with the Baldrige-winning processes of the City of Coral Springs will tell you that this was not a quick or an easy journey. According to Susan Grant, director of human resources, the city has been working on quality for 15 years so far. The route to becoming the first local-government winner of the Baldrige National Quality Award began in 1993 when the city manager decided to "change how they did things" and look for ways to improve government operations. The city began by examining a variety of different management models including such programs as management by objectives and quality circles and by studying Deming's work on quality. A management retreat was held to determine the best way to proceed, and the city decided on a total quality management approach.

The first effort under the TQM approach was a customer service upgrade designed to boost operations and service delivery by emphasizing an approach described by Grant as "customer-focused and quality-oriented." The program included the development and implementation of standards for customer service, along with customer surveys and customer service training. Other strategies included using advisory boards for input and mining customer complaints for information. The customer service initiative was a positive experience for employees and constituents. In a teleconference sponsored by the International City/County Management Association (ICMA), Deputy City Manager Ellen Liston described how important it is to gather information from customers rather than assuming that you know best what they need. She said that when you implement quality processes, you must consider, "What's in it for our customer? They don't get an award…. They get the results."[25]

In 1995, the city introduced a new business model that included strategic and business planning systems. Up to that point, Grant says, the city was "reacting." This new model reflected a change in approach that included a reliance on data in decision making. A strategic plan sets out the city's strategic priorities and a set of key intended outcomes. The plan is put into practice through a business plan, which addresses the initiatives to be taken and the allocation of resources.

Adopting a policy of continuing improvement meant the introduction of many initiatives designed to improve the city's effectiveness, not all of which were popular or successful. An early effort to introduce self-directed work teams did not work well and was quickly abandoned (Heflin, 2007a).

Members of city management first learned about the Baldrige Award and its Criteria for Performance Excellence through the State of Florida's Sterling Award, a state-wide award program that uses the Baldrige Criteria. According to Grant, they saw the Sterling Award as a structured, existing framework they could use to evaluate the work they had already undertaken. The city made its first application for the Sterling Award in 1995. It did not have staff specifically dedicated to quality; instead, it assembled a cross-functional writing team made up of staff members considered to be subject matter experts, who were assigned to the criteria category that matched their areas of expertise. As an example, the human resource director was responsible for working on the workforce category, and a representative of the city manager's office worked on the leadership category. A few staff members who were trained as Sterling or Baldrige examiners became part of the team. Together, members completed a self-assessment and put together a three-year action plan. Christine Heflin (2007a, 2007b, 2008) wrote that the first application did not describe processes and that, while some results were reported, there was not enough information about trends (Heflin, 2007a). In addition to having a limited number of results to report, Grant adds that team members had no comparative data. The Sterling Award program conducts site visits for everyone who applies and provided the city with a feedback report. Grant says the bottom line for that first year was that the city "received a zero in every results category" with no reported strengths.[26]

Despite this initial result, the city was committed to the process and continued to use the team to conduct organizational self-evaluations and function as an implementation team. The team was responsible for conducting the assessment, identifying the gaps, prioritizing them, and putting plans in place to close the gaps. Team members placed an emphasis on developing internal capacity for assessment, and one strategy they used was to increase their in-house knowledge and understanding of the criteria and requirements by having additional city employees trained as Sterling Award examiners. They used a train-the-trainer approach in which professional consultants trained an employee cadre of internal consultants. Some of the specific steps improvements made based on feedback reports were as follows:

- They increased the focus on management reporting rather than just collecting data.
- They created alignment throughout city government by linking individual performance objectives for employees to departmental- and city-level objectives and to the key intended outcomes.
- They instituted environmental scanning and the identification of strategic priorities using community visioning retreats.
- They instituted multiple means of communication with their constituents, both residents and business, including websites, an on-line "help desk," e-newsletters, and a magazine.

Coral Springs expects its entire workforce to treat quality the way it does business. Each employee receives training, including introduction to quality and empowerment. Grant describes the content of the training program as focusing first on cultural change before getting into quality processes and specific quality tools such as Pareto diagrams. Coral Springs also identified four core values and created a direct link between these values and the day-to-day business of the city:

- Customer focused.
- Empowered employees.
- Leadership.
- Continuous improvement.

The values form the basis for employee performance evaluations, as each employee is evaluated in each of these categories. The city also uses these values as the basis for excellence awards, which are presented in each of the four categories. The city collects constituent input through city-wide surveys and discussion forums and by taking services to places where people need them, like City Hall in the Mall (Figure 7.4). They conduct semiannual "Slice of the Springs" meetings where residents can meet the city employees, including police, fire, and code officials, who work in their geographic "slice" of Coral Springs.

Coral Springs applied for the Sterling Award again in 1996. Although it did not win, it used the feedback report to set goals for improvement in preparation for the next application. It applied a third time in 1997 and became the first government agency to win the Sterling Award. According to Grant, this award also made it the first state or local government to win a state-level award based on the Baldrige criteria. The city continued to conduct annual self-assessments each year and, in 2003, became the first two-time winner of the Sterling Award. But that was not its only achievement. The city applied for and won several national, regional, and local awards during this time period (Figure 7.4).

When the Baldrige organization announced a pilot program to include the nonprofit sector in the national Baldrige Award process in 2006, city management members saw this as the next level in their quality journey. Using the same team process, they prepared and submitted an application for the pilot. They were 1 of 10 government and nonprofit agencies that applied and 1 of only 2 selected to receive a site

Figure 7.4 The City of Coral Springs—City Hall in the Mall.

visit. The feedback report the city received after the site visit contained strengths and opportunities for improvement in each of the categories. Three areas in particular were identified for improvement: (1) a more systematic process for gathering information and making comparisons; (2) succession planning; and (3) knowledge sharing throughout the organization. Grant says that these outcomes "were consistent with what we expected," and they worked on these areas during the next year.[27]

Nonprofit organizations would officially be eligible for the upcoming year's Baldrige Award, and Coral Springs intended to apply. It believed it would need to significantly increase its score if it was to have a chance to actually win the Baldrige Award. With the support of top management, it set a target of a 100-point increase in its score (out of a possible total score of 1,000 points) and went to work on its 2007 application. Staff members who had trained as examiners served as "criteria police—reviewing the work to make sure every question and every part of every question was answered."[28]

Despite all the progress to date, this was a challenging event in part due to the financial climate. At the same time the city was preparing the application, a budget-cutting process was taking place. Concerned that the proposed cuts would impact public perception of its ability to provide service, it focused on providing as much information as possible to customers, legislators, and the public through a variety of media. Process leaders kept employees focused on the idea of the Baldrige Award as a goal that would bring them a level of national prestige. After submitting its application and going through a site visit, it was named the first local government recipients of the Baldrige Award. City leaders went to Washington, D.C., to accept the award and were invited to the White House. Grant says, however, that they are "prouder of the results that led to the award." The award was the "means to the end of getting better."[29]

Challenges

In addition to a difficult fiscal environment, Coral Springs dealt successfully with a number of challenges in implementing its assessment and improvement program:

- Responding to employee concerns. In the initial stages of implementing quality management, Liston says that employees often reacted to the idea by saying that they did not understand why an additional burden was being placed on them when they already had so much to do. The administration kept responding with a consistent message: It was not an additional work; rather, it is a way of doing business. She says that "employees hate the phrase 'do more with less.' It's that we rethink the way we do things, and work smarter, not harder."[30] Employees will believe this only when they see management walking the talk every day. They emphasize continual communication with employees, including payroll stuffers, e-mails, and quarterly communication meetings in which the city manager meets with every employee at every location.

The result is a very collaborative approach to continuous improvement. One of the most significant early initiatives was an organizational restructuring to flatten city government, which the city describes on its website by saying it "was stressful, but it worked." When quality processes were initially introduced, the city adopted a no-layoff policy to relieve employee concerns that they would lose their job because of the quality initiative. Liston says that being lean has the advantage of empowering employees, since they do not have enough employees to micromanage.

■ Identify appropriate sources for benchmarking. Coral Springs benchmarks city results against other local government agencies both in its geographical area and nationally. Finding comparisons was difficult during the early stages of implementing quality processes. Grant points out that measures such as police response time and crime rate have to be benchmarked within the public sector to have meaning. Coral Springs developed networks through the ICMA consortium that provide a common set of measures shared by a number of government agencies. It also credits the ICMA Center for Performance Measurement, saying that the use of its templates allows its outcomes to be compared with those of many other government organizations. The city also participates in a Florida benchmarking comparison group.

■ Concerns about the use of public information. Although Coral Springs has implemented a comprehensive program for collecting constituent information, it also notes the problem with conducting satisfaction surveys in the public sector. As Grant points out, "Everything is public record. It's risky if customers tell you they don't like x, y, or z" because "the information can be used against you."[31]

■ Containing the expenses associated with award processes. A consideration for government agencies is the cost of applying for a national-level award. The application fees can run several thousand dollars, on top of which there are fees for site visits. Grant described a situation she was aware of where a city that won a quality award became the subject of negative media attention because of the money spent on the application rather than the city receiving positive press for winning. Coral Springs was fortunate enough to have the local business community underwrite the cost of the site visit.

Lessons Learned

■ The only thing those involved with the process would do differently is to start measuring things earlier. They also learned that when it comes to measurement, one of the most critical lessons learned is that simpler is better. In the initial stages of quality improvement, the city went from not having any results to measuring too many things. Throughout its many awards and process improvements, it has refined and reduced the number of key measures to a vital few—

in other words, tracking fewer but higher quality measures. This information is made available in user-friendly information and budget documents.

■ Early on, says Grant, city management members believed "that we had to address everything by teams," which she terms a mistake.[32] Teams were initially appointed "all over the city" and told to work on problems. However, if the problem statements weren't well defined, the teams were not successful. Learning from this experience, members of management established a number of cross-functional process improvement teams for mission critical problems, including problem-solving teams and standing teams for specific programs and services, and made sure that they had the resources necessary. A total of 28 of these teams were used between 1994 and 2006 along with over 20 special department teams, and employees are actively encouraged to participate in such teams. Two of the cross-functional teams, the Emergency Management Services (EMS) "Time=Life" team, which assessed approaches to EMS delivery, and the traffic "CSI" (Citation System Improvement) team both competed in and won regional and state recognition. The EMS team also won fourth place in a national competition. The teams all use a six-step problem-solving model. All new employees are taught this model as part of their orientation.[33]

■ Those involved with the Coral Springs Sterling and Baldrige applications noted several issues that arise when government organizations use award criteria based on the language of business. According to Grant, one of the areas they found troublesome was language concerning supplier relationships and purchasing. Like many government organizations, they are required to conduct bidding as defined by statute and law, which generally means that they are required to take the low bid. Coral Springs has modified its purchasing regulations to include quality considerations in the award process but realizes that this language might still be problematic for many other government agencies that may not have gotten that far in changing their purchasing process. Another concept that differs in the private and public sectors is succession planning. Because the elected officials can appoint a city manager, it may not be possible to develop someone who can walk into that position.

■ The leadership of Coral Springs has been able to sustain the commitment to quality over 13 years, and Liston explains that it takes a lot of work. They have consistently done self-assessments every year. Throughout its quality journey, the city received the support and endorsement of its commissioners. This level of support is no doubt a result of the city's efforts to include the commissioners in the process. Since beginning the process, it has had a complete turnover in elected commissioners. Liston believes that the role of those involved in this process is to explain to the commission why this is so important to the city, and the large role that continuous improvement plays in the positive results the city has achieved. The communication between the city and the commissioners includes a new commissioner orientation and strategic planning workshops. City administrators provide key planning information to their commissioners in a workshop format. Rather than giving them a book of data, they sit down with them and discuss the information so that the commissioners can make what Liston called "informed critical decisions."[33]

■ The management of Coral Springs felt strongly that for the assessment and improvement processes to be successful, it could not be perceived as a single person's responsibility. By design, no one has the word *quality* in his or her job title. Instead, the core values and quality concepts are integrated into everything they do.

Summary

What conclusions can be drawn from the stories of these three organizations? Their experiences with assessment cover self-assessments as well as application to a number of different award programs at the organizational, state, and national level, but they have several elements in common. Examining these commonalities can provide guidance for public sector agencies undertaking an assessment process, regardless of the model used or whether that process is part of an award program or an internal self-evaluation process:

1. Take a systematic approach to assessment and improvement. All three agencies undertook assessments using a structured framework that identified the critical areas for evaluation and provided a process for collecting, analyzing, and acting on the information. After assessing the organization, each agency embarked on an effort to translate the knowledge gained into improvements. While results can be achieved from a single assessment, the road that each of these organizations followed prior to receiving an award generally took several years, during which the assessment and improvement cycle was repeated on an annual basis to build on the information received and the results achieved. Each year spent engaging in quality practices, assessment, and improvement increases staff knowledge about the process, about the level and type of information needed, and about how to use the information. The use of a structured process also facilitates comparisons from year to year and allows agencies to assess their progress over time.

2. Obtain feedback from external sources. All three agencies cited the external feedback that they received as a valuable source of information. Sources of feedback can include constituents, peer organizations, benchmarking consortia, and award programs. Coral Springs and ARDEC both incorporated information from their constituents as part of their assessment process, and all three engaged in some level of benchmarking. External feedback provided the agencies with a different perspective and a chance to see themselves as others—constituents, beneficiaries, and peers—see them. Feedback can be

more formal, such as the feedback received from the award programs in response to applications and following site visits, or as informal as asking people who know the organization whether the information developed in an assessment "rings true."

3. Engage employees in the assessment process. A key theme in all three cases is the need to engage as many employees as possible in the process. Each of the organizations established a core team that was responsible for collecting and analyzing the information needed to assess the organization. In some cases, it was a dedicated assignment for a period of time, but most often it was done in conjunction with team members' regular work assignments and responsibilities. Involvement extended beyond the core team, as other staff members functioned as writers, reviewers, site visit escorts, or sources of information. Communication became a primary method of engagement for those who were not specifically involved in the process. Keeping employees involved in what was being done through presentations, training, and e-mails and sharing the results with the entire organization were some of the strategies used.

4. Understand that this is an organizational commitment. Assessment and improvement were not limited to certain processes or areas. There was a deliberate effort in all three agencies to make sure that all parts of their organization were involved. Creating a culture of assessment and improvement can require a shift in the existing organizational culture, which can include recognizing that government agencies have identifiable beneficiaries and constituents, accepting the need to share information across organizational lines, and stepping out of a day-to-day focus to understand that improvement is possible and desirable. Success for these agencies came from incorporating assessment and improvement into all staff members' regular job processes by linking it to their jobs and making it part of their everyday work.

6. Recognize that this is a learning process. All of the organizations implemented some kind of training program for employees on quality practices and the assessment methodology. The skills required to assess an organization can be learned and improved on through subsequent assessments. They also supported staff members who wanted to go beyond a basic understanding of the processes by encouraging people to become trained as examiners and to bring the information back to improve the assessment effort.

7. Have the support of senior leaders. The initial question in undertaking an assessment is whether your leadership team is committed to making a difference. The level of that support can make a real difference. In some cases such as ARDEC, the impetus for assessment came from the organizational leader. Coral Springs involved not only city management but the city commissioners in understanding the importance and the benefits of assessment. NJDEP initially became involved in assessment due to the strong support of the agency's leaders, but their case also shows how the absence of such support can affect a program. When the leadership changed, the support for the program went

away; while those involved were able to sustain it for a time, it was eventually eliminated.

Notes

1. ARDEC, http://www.pica.army.mil/PicatinnyPublic/organizations/ardec/index.asp
2. Brad Sampson, ARDEC, e-mail correspondence with the author, 6/24/08.
3. Ibid, March 13, 2008.
4. Ibid.
5. ARDEC Baldrige application, p. 4.
6. E-mail correspondence from Brad Sampson, ARDEC, June 17, 2008.
7. Remarks of ARDEC director Joseph Lannon. Accessed September 7, 2008, from http://www.nist.gov/speeches/lannon_042308.html
8. Ibid.
9. Sampson interview, June 25, 2008.
10. Ibid.
11. 2000 Governor's Award Application—New Jersey Department of Environmental Protection (NJDEP) and NJSA 13:1D-1 et seq.
12. 2000 Governor's Award.
13. Joseph Genovay, NJDEP, interview, September 16, 2008.
14. Mark Tucci, NJDEP, interview, March 17, 2008.
15. 2000 Governor's Award.
16. Tucci interview.
17. Genovay interview.
18. 2000 Governor's Award.
19. Tucci interview.
20. Genovay interview.
21. 2000 Governor's Award.
22. City of Coral Springs Baldrige application.
23. City of Coral Springs, http://www.coralsprings.org/
24. Ibid.
25. Ellen Liston, ICMA teleconference with author, "Why the Baldrige Quality Model Works in Local Government." Liston discussed the processes and decisions that led to Coral Springs's successful application for the Baldrige Award, January 24, 2008.
26. Susan Grant, City of Coral Springs, interview, August 18, 2008.
27. Ibid.
28. Heflin (2008c, p. 3).
29. Grant interview.
30. ICMA teleconference.
31. Grant interview.
32. Ibid.
33. City of Coral Springs (see note 23).
34. ICMA teleconference.

Chapter 8

The Future of Assessment

What is the future of assessment in public sector organizations? How can the use of assessment processes best be promoted in government organizations, and how can assessment and improvement be made part of the culture of the organization? What can be done to increase awareness about the benefits of assessment?

Government, with its diverse responsibilities and far-reaching services, is a part of the day-to-day lives of all Americans. The work performed by those who make their careers in government agencies plays a critical role in determining the quality of life for those who live, work, or engage in some way with their communities. As a result, there are many compelling reasons why those who lead these agencies and those who work in public sector organizations must continue to improve their operations—not the least of which is that the challenges facing these organizations will continue to grow as the increasing demand for services struggles for balance against the available resources. Making the best possible use of those resources requires efficiency and effectiveness, and an appreciation for the need to examine not just outcomes but also organizations to see how they might be improved. Government has come a long way in addressing this need. Government agencies at the federal, state, and local level routinely engage in planning and budgeting processes that rely on outcome data and performance measures to gauge their success in providing services. Public sector organizations regularly engage in sophisticated project management processes. Many professional organizations support excellence in government service and provide the knowledge, and often the tools, needed to obtain this information and to encourage continuous improvement. However, the full potential of many such agencies is hampered by the lack of overall framework through which to evaluate efficiency, effectiveness, and the opportunities for improvement. Agencies need to establish a perspective that looks at the organization as a whole and examines how its various parts, programs, and priorities interact and then use that information to create a culture in which people routinely look to see how they might make their agency more capable of serving the needs of its constituents. While an assessment process must take into consideration the external environment in which an organization operates, it is primarily an inward-looking process. Assessment looks not only at outcomes but also at all the organizational components that contribute to the way those outcomes are obtained. Those who manage government agencies may have great intentions of increasing their effectiveness and efficiency, but assessment processes provide a structure that can focus those efforts and engage staff members in asking the questions that lead to positive organizational change.

The use of organizational assessment processes has proved to be a viable first step in any improvement effort, and over the years there has been a steady increase in efforts to introduce the use of these processes. The Baldrige National Quality Program was instrumental in introducing organizational assessment and proving its potential in the business world. That model was subsequently expanded through the development of state-level awards programs modeled after the Baldrige Award and supplemented by various programs to recognize excellence at the federal, state, and local levels. As tools for applying organizational assessment to government organizations have become available, their potential has increasingly been recognized. Structured organizational assessment processes provide a way for government organizations to examine and understand their current operations, to determine their strengths and opportunities for improvement, to prioritize their efforts, and to measure their level of progress toward improvement goals.

As Holzer and Callahan (1998) point out in their book *Government at Work*, professional public administrators are dedicated to provide increasingly effective and innovative services to ensure the best possible lives for their constituents. What must be done, then, to encourage and enable them to implement assessment processes that will support the continuous improvement of government's ability to achieve those goals? The future of assessment must include a focus on knowledge dissemination, improved tools and processes, and the development of linkages between assessment and resource allocation (Figure 8.1).

The Need to Identify and Disseminate Best Practices in Government Assessment

There are literally thousands of government organizations in the United States when the different levels and the different agencies at each level are taken into account, each of which has developed programs and processes for addressing the needs of its jurisdictions. There is currently no available inventory of programs that

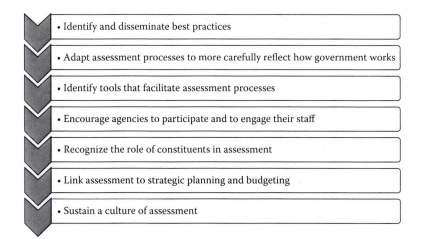

Figure 8.1 Building the future of public sector assessment practices.

would allows us to estimate how many of these organizations have implemented organizational assessment processes, but the number is surely increasing thanks to the many national, state, and local organizations that promote quality and assessment. There are, however, many more government agencies that have not engaged in structured assessments for any number of reasons, including a lack of familiarity with the process and its potential benefits or the time and resources required and the perceived effort needed.

This book has presented case studies and examples of just a few of the many government agencies that are using assessment processes successfully to improve their organizations and to enhance their ability to serve their constituents. Without a doubt, there are many more such stories out there. Their successes demonstrate that it is possible to incorporate assessment into government with positive and useful outcomes. Government agencies at all levels are stretched often to the limit of their ability to provide services. The example of these assessment leaders can be the key to convincing them that the investment of time and resources in assessment is worthwhile. Those who are already actively engaged in assessment can be considered, in the terminology of diffusion of innovation theory, the early adopters. Sharing their experiences can help create the necessary momentum in thought and action to increase the use of assessment processes by others. But what is the best way to do that? A number of questions require further thought and collaborative research.

The challenge in sharing best practices is to figure out how to make them readily available to both academic and practitioner audiences. Case studies and lists of best practices are available on websites associated with various programs, but these programs and resources may not be known to these various potential audiences. Information is presented in a passive way; that is, it is available to be found. How do we take passive resources and create active resources by bringing the information to practitioners and those who study public administration? How do we ensure that it is incorporated in public administration programs and classes to inspire the next generation of public servants? And, frankly, how do we translate the available academic research on assessment so that it can reach and benefit today's public administrators? Last, but not least, how do we present the information in a way that inspires public administrators to adopt a culture of assessment?

The Need for Continued Adaptation of Assessment Models

To make assessment processes attractive to and viable for federal, state, and local government organizations and other public agencies that could benefit from their use, they must be perceived as applicable. Each of the available models—whether it is the Baldrige Criteria, the Public Sector Assessment and Improvement Model, or any other assessment model—must adapt to the needs of government by specifically identifying and then incorporating the requirements, culture, and language of the public sector. Government administrators and employees must be able to "see themselves" in the questions and descriptions.

One of the reasons the Malcolm Baldrige National Quality Award has been so very effective throughout the United States in identifying the most successful organizations and promoting excellence across sectors is that it speaks so well to the critical performance factors associated with business, health care, and education. However, there is a need for models and materials with increased customization to address the needs of specific types of organizations within sectors. The success of Baldrige-based efforts such as *Excellence in Higher Education* (Ruben, 2007a), which addresses a very specific section (colleges and universities) of the broader education sector, shows that this can have a very positive impact.

Jeff Weinrach of Quality New Mexico points out that the current Baldrige criteria for business and non-profit organizations do not fully integrate the language of government and nonprofits into the questions themselves. Instead, they often present them in italics in the accompanying explanatory notes. He believes, as do many others, that future adaptation of the Baldrige Criteria to produce a version for government and nonprofit organizations is likely, in the same way that the education and health-care versions developed. In the meantime, he says, the role of organizations like his is to talk to government agencies about how to interpret the language to make it usable (Weinrach, 2008).

In the same way that government employees wince when they are told to be more like business, they know that their critical performance factors differ in many ways from those of the business sector. Realistically, the availability of models that focus on the priorities of government and that use identifiable examples that resonate with staff at all levels will go a long way. By making organizational assessment programs more applicable to the public sector, it increases the likelihood that they will be used.

Identifying Tools That Facilitate Assessment Processes

Unlike businesses, whose improved performance might generate increased financial or human resources that can be reinvested in quality improvement efforts, the time and resources available to conduct assessment processes in government organizations can often be limited. Undertaking an assessment process, even with a model or set of criteria to guide the process, can be somewhat intimidating for organizations. While the models explain what questions to ask, agencies must still figure out how to answer them. Therefore, expanding the use of assessment processes in government may rely on the ability of public administrators to find ways to make the process as user-friendly as possible.

One way to accomplish this can be through the development of assessment tools that support the process, educate employees, and assist in completing the information-collection and data-analysis stages. Some tools are already available; one example is a "wheel" model used by the State of Utah (adapted from a model by Mary Campbell), which can be used to help define performance measures for every organizational activity or process by identifying, for each of five groups of stakeholders (beneficiaries, recipients, funders/authorizers, managers/enablers, and producers/partners), who they are, what they want to know, and the metric that will be used to produce that information. Another example is Quality New Mexico's workbook of foundational questions that can be used to help prepare an organizational profile.

Going forward, what others tools can be developed to assist agencies with the assessment process? We have scratched only the surface of the available technology, including online conferencing, collaborative documents, and programs for analyzing information.

Finding New Ways to Encourage Governments to Participate and to Engage Their Staff

Assessment processes are most effective when they include, at a minimum, broad cross-sections of organizations. That can present a challenge to both large and small agencies that must sustain a full range of activities while engaging in an assessment process. Public administrators not only need to understand the value of assessment itself but also must be made aware that the quality of an assessment is enhanced when staff members representing the many different demographics of the organization are able to participate. How can we convince organizational leaders that assessment will not be an added burden on an already burdened staff? This is a two-part question that involves first making assessment an accepted and valued organizational activity that factors into resource allocation on a par with budgeting and strategic planning. Second, participation in an assessment must be a valued activity regarded not as an extracurricular activity but as a key part of a staff member's responsibilities.

The challenges of participation also include finding better ways to assist government organizations. Quality New Mexico's Weinrach suggests that part of the future of assessment, especially for states such as his where the size of the state provides logistical challenges in working with rural communities to improve their processes, is the use of technology such as distance learning, the Internet, and other related technology to enable the participation of more communities and more people.

Increased Recognition of the Role of Constituents in Assessment

Many proponents of assessment also advocate the inclusion of constituents in the assessment process. The level of constituent involvement in developing programs and processes for government varies, but in many cases the role accorded to them is growing. An argument can be made that a true assessment cannot take place without some understanding of the satisfaction levels of constituents. There are many well-understood and accepted reasons for incorporating constituent data, but allowing constituents to actually participate in the process is more controversial. In terms of assessment, constituents must always be a primary focus—if not in terms of participation, then in terms of the mission and the effectiveness of agency operations. Government performs its services for the benefits of constituents; therefore, the most critical assessments will reflect whether the outcomes achieved accomplish this goal.

Linking Assessment Processes to Strategic Planning and Budgeting

Assessment and improvement are both important processes but are most effective when they are linked. While assessment creates the awareness of what can be done, awareness itself does not move the organization forward. An assessment process that identifies opportunities for improvement is one thing, but if few or none of those recommendations are enacted, it will be that much more difficult for leaders and employees to justify participation in the future, to say nothing of the frustration that results. It must be accompanied by the development and implementation of improvement plans. Implementation of improvements requires that they be consistent with the mission and vision of the organization, and factored into the other goals and objectives the organization has set.

Often resources must be assigned. Efforts to link the outcomes of assessment processes to strategic planning and future budgets have not always been successful, but establishing links between those processes may be the key to institutionalizing assessment efforts. The State of Utah has made great strides in linking performance measures to agency budget requests and the allocation of resources. It has also created a focus on identifying enterprise-wide initiatives and providing funding to functions and programs that are linked to these initiatives.

Finding Ways to Sustain a Culture of Assessment That Do Not Rely on a Single Champion

Having a highly placed and visible champion in the organization can be extremely helpful to those implementing an assessment process. It provides a signal to those who hold the necessary resources (time, information, and people) that this effort is in the best interests of the agency. However, one of the challenges for assessment is finding ways to prevent programs from being linked to a particular person or political appointee and therefore subject to abandonment if that person leaves or the administration changes. Mark Tucci of the New Jersey Department of Environmental Protection suggests that one strategy to do this is to communicate the benefits achieved through existing assessment programs to new administrators. Sustaining organizational assessment programs depends on the ability to prevent the disruption of these processes due to political changes. Those who would promote assessment in government need to be able to convey a sense of its importance to the internal operation and effectiveness of the organization and to get both internal and external constituents to recognize that improvement is not political.

Conclusion

Using structured organizational assessment processes offers public sector organizations an opportunity to examine and improve their operations and to create a workplace culture and climate that facilitates excellence. It challenges leaders and employees at all levels to focus on the mission and goals of the agency and to identify ways of working together—as an organization rather than as individual processes and programs—to provide the best possible services to constituents. Assessment can be a powerful tool for articulating the strengths of the programs and services government provides and for conveying that information to its constituents as well as for identifying and creating a case for current and future needs.

Introducing and sustaining assessment as part of an organization's culture can provide the critical feedback that not only enables higher levels of performance but that also engages the workforce in a way that uses their knowledge and abilities in accomplishing the mission. The responsibility of agency leaders is to introduce, support, and sustain assessment. At its most fundamental, assessment is not just a process. It is a way of thinking about what services are provided, how they are being provided, and how the people who provide them are being supported and enabled to perform the critical functions of government.

Appendix A: The Public Sector Assessment and Improvement Model

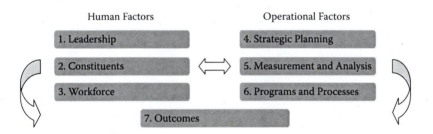

Human Factors

1. Leadership
2. Constituents
3. Workforce

Operational Factors

4. Strategic Planning
5. Measurement and Analysis
6. Programs and Processes

7. Outcomes

Organizational Profile

Organizational Purpose

1. What is the mission of the organization? What is the enabling legislation that establishes the organization and its purposes? What changes have been made to that legislation to expand or change those original purposes and responsibilities?
2. What jurisdiction does this organization represent? What are the demographic features of the jurisdiction?

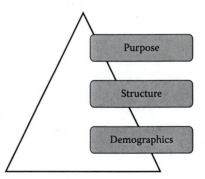

Structure

1. How is the agency organized? Describe the structure including the levels of the organization, its divisions or subunits, and its links to other agencies such as commissions or boards that may fall under its jurisdiction.
2. What is the management structure?
3. Are there other levels of government to which this organization reports? What are they, and what are the primary points of contact? What degree of autonomy exists between these levels of government?
4. Where is the organization located, including its primary location or head-quarters and other major facilities including regional locations and points of service?

Demographics

1. How many employees are in this organization? How has this number changed over time?
2. What are the major job categories and the number of people currently assigned to each?
3. Who are the labor representatives?

Human Factors

Category 1: Leadership

Leadership Structure and Practices

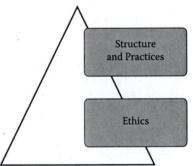

- What is the leadership structure? Who is included when we talk about leaders?
- What actions do leaders take to communicate and build a commitment to the mission across the organization?
- What steps do leaders take to define their priorities and make sure they are clear and understood across the organization?
- How do leaders review and monitor performance and progress on plans and goals?
- How do leaders promote a focus on the needs of beneficiaries and constituents: the people for whom you provide services?
- How do senior leaders build public and legislative support for the organization's priorities and plans? How successful are those efforts?
- In what ways are leaders visible to and accessible to employees?
- What steps do leaders take to advocate for the agency and its needs?

- How do leaders at all levels of the organization share their expertise and experience with the organization?

Ethical Leadership

- What do leaders do to emphasize the importance of integrity and ethical behavior across the agency?
- What actions do leaders take to demonstrate their personal integrity and to promote ethical behavior? How do they model ethical behavior?
- What are the areas of potential ethical concern for the organization (e.g., conflicts of interest, bidding processes, nepotism, inappropriate influence)? What mechanisms are in place to address each of these areas?
- What impact do the agency's operations have on the community in which it is located? What impact do they have on the environment? How are these addressed in a proactive manner?
- What are the legal and regulatory requirements that pertain to the organization's operations, and how are these requirements and associated standards met? How is this information made known throughout the organization?

Category 2: Constituents

Identifying Constituents

- What major constituent groups benefit from the work of the organization?
- What are the primary programs and services provided to each group?
- What other constituents groups have an interest in the services provided, even if they are not direct beneficiaries?
- How are these groups changing? What constituent groups have been added or are anticipated to change in the next two years?

Assessing Constituent Needs, Expectations, and Satisfaction

- What information is collected on a regular basis about the needs and priorities of each of these groups? How is it collected, and how often is it collected?
- How is this information used to anticipate future needs?
- How do you determine current satisfaction levels of individuals, groups, and organizations with the services provided?
- What are the most critical needs and expectations of each constituent group?

- What changes are anticipated in the critical needs and expectations of these groups over the next one to five years?
- How, and to what degree, does the organization seek diversity in the participation of constituents—that is, drawing participation from many groups that may have different viewpoints rather than from only those that share the same policy perspective?

Building Constituent Relationships

- What actions are taken to include constituent needs, expectations, perspectives, and satisfaction levels in project planning?
- How do you incorporate this information in performance measures and standards, such as standards regarding waiting times, telephone call-back response time, and responding to letters of complaint or in terms of expectations for service?
- How is information about programs and services in general and about specific projects made available to constituents (e.g., public forums, newsletters, websites)?
- What staff groups have regular and significant contact with members of constituent groups? How does this contact take place, and how is the quality of the interaction monitored?
- What steps are taken to ensure that people have access to programs or services at times and places that are convenient and appropriate to their needs?
- What methods are used to identify and assist people who need special assistance or accommodations to enable them to use the agency's services?
- What processes are in place for people to provide feedback about programs and services?

Category 3: Workforce Focus

Workforce Planning

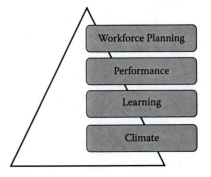

- What process is used to identify current and future workforce needs? How frequently are anticipated workforce needs reviewed?
- What are the critical jobs in your organization without which the work of the organization could not be done?
- What functions if any are currently outsourced?
- What are the core competencies and skills for each major employee group or job category? What steps are taken to anticipate new skills that will be needed in the future?

- How are current skill sets and competencies assessed?
- What processes are in place to ensure that new employees are recruited in a manner that recognizes and supports diversity?
- What formal processes are in place to address succession planning and retention of organizational knowledge?
- Are career development processes, including career counseling and mentoring, in place? How accessible are these processes to the workforce as a whole?
- How are collaborative work practices including cross-training, cross-organizational teams, and task forces used to increase employee knowledge and abilities?
- How is demographic information tracked and used in workforce planning?

Performance Assessment and Recognition

- What systems are in place to review performance review and to provide feedback? How do these systems encourage outstanding performance?
- Do performance review systems encourage excellence in both individual performance and team performance and collaboration?
- How is individual and team excellence recognized and reinforced?

Learning and Professional Development

- How are new knowledge, skills, and capabilities needed by staff identified?
- What methods (e.g., classroom, online, webcasts, subject matter experts, on-the-job training, contracted training, tuition reimbursement) are used to make training and professional development available and accessible to employees?
- What standards or goals exist for ensuring the amount of training made available to all employees?
- How are professional development programs evaluated?
- What are the major subject areas or categories of training and professional development available to staff?

Workplace Climate

- What processes are in place to assess and improve workplace health, safety, and ergonomics?
- What procedures are in place to ensure a secure workplace where employees will be free from harm?
- How does the agency ensure that the workplace is free from discrimination and harassment?
- How does the agency ensure that the workplace is prepared for emergencies, natural, health, or environmental disasters, and security emergencies? What plans exist, and how are they communicated to staff and reinforced?

- What is the relationship between organizational leaders and employee representatives, such as unions or associations? How are communications between the organization and these groups maintained?
- What methods (e.g., surveys, interviews, exit interviews or measures of staff retention, absenteeism, productivity) are used to assess the workplace climate and staff satisfaction levels? How and how often is this satisfaction and climate information gathered?

Operational Factors

Category 4: Strategic Planning

Strategic Plan Development

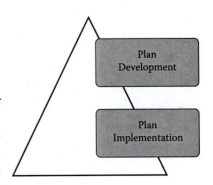

- Is there a formal, adopted statement of the organization's mission and vision?
- To what extent is the mission defined by law or regulation? What are the applicable laws and regulations, and how is this information made known to employees?
- Has the organization identified its core values and communicated them to employees?
- How does the organization translate the mission and vision into plans and goals?
- Is there a formal, documented strategic planning process? If so, what are the major steps in the process? Does it take place on a regularly scheduled basis?
- Does the planning process include an analysis of the current environment (strengths, weaknesses, opportunities, and threats) as well as information from any previous organizational assessments, self-studies, and internal or external audits or reviews?
- How are staff members involved in the planning process? How is staff input and feedback encouraged and incorporated in the planning process?
- How are goals, strategies, and action plans determined for all levels of the organization?
- How does the planning process incorporate information about the following:
    - Trends in the jurisdiction (e.g., the city, district, county, or state)?
    - Funding issues and resources (both current and anticipated)?
    - Legislative environment and pending or proposed legislation?
    - Organizational capabilities?
    - Information on needs and expectations of constituents?
    - Human, fiscal, and other resources needed to accomplish the mission?
- How does the planning process align human and fiscal resources with identified goals?

- How are goals, strategies, and action steps established?
- What actions are taken to ensure that plans throughout the organization are aligned with the larger organizational goals and plans?

Implementing the Strategic Plan

- What steps are taken to communicate the plan to all employees and to build commitment for the plan throughout the organization?
- What steps are taken to ensure that people have a clear understanding of the goals, strategies, and actions to be taken?
- How is the plan implemented? Who is responsible for its implementation?
- How is progress toward goals, objectives, strategies, and actions monitored?
- What processes are in place to adapt the plan for changes in available fiscal and human resources, organizational capabilities, and unanticipated obstacles, challenges, and opportunities?
- What performance measures or key performance indicators are used to measure progress toward goals, strategies, and action plans?
- What steps are taken to ensure that organizational decision making at all levels is guided by the strategic plan?

Category 5: Measurement and Analysis

Information

- What information is collected about major work programs and processes?
- How is information collected and disseminated so it is available for use?
- What information is required by regulatory or other external agencies?
- Are information systems user-friendly?
- What actions are taken to ensure the integrity, reliability, accuracy, timeliness, and security of data and information?
- What safeguards are in place to protect data security and employee/constituent privacy considerations?

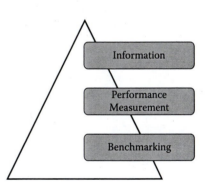

Performance Measurement

- What performance measures are used to determine the organization's performance against the mission, plans, and goals?
- How are performance measures or indicators developed?
- How are performance indicators reported throughout your organization?

■ How does the agency review performance measures to make sure that they reflect current priorities?

Benchmarking

■ How does the agency use data and information to compare current outcomes and measures with the outcomes from previous years?
■ How does the agency compare its information with that of other organizations to evaluate outcomes and achievements? What organizations are currently used for benchmarking, and why were they selected? Do the organizations chosen reflect government agencies at the same or other levels of government or those in other sectors?

Category 6: Programs and Processes

Core Programs, Services, and Processes

■ What are the organization's core programs and services?
■ What are the major processes associated with each core program or service?
■ What constituent groups are served by each program or service?
■ How are new programs or services developed?
■ What steps are taken to ensure that core processes are appropriately standardized, documented, and monitored?
■ How do you ensure that new and existing processes make the best use of available technology?
■ What performance measures or indicators are used to assess the effectiveness and efficiency of core processes?
■ How often are core processes reviewed and (if needed) redesigned?

Administrative Support Processes

■ What are the organization's most important administrative support processes?
■ What steps are taken to ensure that administrative support processes are appropriately standardized, documented, and monitored?
■ How do you ensure that new and existing administrative support processes make the best use of available technology?

- What performance measures or indicators are used to assess the effectiveness and efficiency of administrative support processes?
- How often are support processes reviewed and (if needed) redesigned?

Category 7: Results

Performance Measures and Results

For each of the other six categories:

- What are the results associated with each measure of organizational performance?
- How do these outcomes compare to information from the previous years?
- How do these outcomes compare with established targets or goals?

Appendix B: The Public Sector Assessment and Improvement Model—Short Form

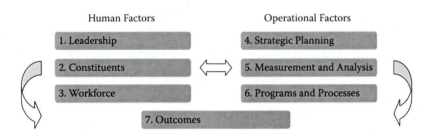

Human Factors

Operational Factors

1. Leadership

2. Constituents

3. Workforce

4. Strategic Planning

5. Measurement and Analysis

6. Programs and Processes

7. Outcomes

Based on the same Public Sector Assessment and Improvement Model (PSAI), the short form provides a way for agencies to:

- Use a pilot project to build support for a full assessment.
- Conduct a preliminary assessment to determine organizational readiness.
- Undertake a quick assessment to determine priority areas on which to focus a full assessment.

This abbreviated version of the PSAI model is in questionnaire format. It consists of statements about values, information, or behaviors that would, generally speaking, predict positive outcomes in a full assessment. Participants are asked to estimate whether each statement:

- Is a valid description of the organization being assessed.
- Is a valid description of many parts of the organization.

- Is a valid description some parts of the organization.
- Is not a valid description of the organization.

Human Factors

Leadership

	Valid across the Organization	Valid for Many Parts	Valid for Some Parts	Not a Valid Description
Leaders are visible to and accessible to members of the organization.				
Leaders have made their priorities clear throughout the organization.				
Leaders exhibit a focus on beneficiaries and constituents.				
Leaders have a commitment to ethical behavior.				

Constituents

	Valid across the Organization	Valid for Many Parts	Valid for Some Parts	Not a Valid Description
The major constituent groups can be readily identified.				
Information about the most critical needs and expectations of constituents is collected and shared.				
Constituent information is incorporated in planning efforts.				

	Valid across the Organization	Valid for Many Parts	Valid for Some Parts	Not a Valid Description
Constituent satisfaction with services is assessed on a regular basis.				
Performance measures include expectations for constituent service.				
Attention is paid to whether constituents have access to services.				

Workforce

	Valid across the Organization	Valid for Many Parts	Valid for Some Parts	Not a Valid Description
A process exists to identify current and future workforce needs.				
Core competencies have been identified for all employee groups or job titles.				
Recruitment processes support diversity.				
Excellence in individual and team performance is supported and recognized.				
Professional development opportunities are available to all employee groups.				
Workplace safety and security are assessed on a regular basis.				
Practices are in place to ensure the workplace is free from discrimination.				

Strategic Planning

	Valid across the Organization	Valid for Many Parts	Valid for Some Parts	Not a Valid Description
The organization has a formal mission statement, which is available to leaders, staff members, and constituents.				
The vision that leaders have for the organization has been shared with and is known to the staff.				
The organization's core values have been defined and communicated to staff.				
There is a formal, documented strategic planning process.				
Staff input and feedback are included in the planning process.				
The planning process aligns human and fiscal resources with identified goals.				
The strategic plan is communicated throughout the organization.				

Measurement and Analysis

	Valid across the Organization	Valid for Many Parts	Valid for Some Parts	Not a Valid Description
Information about major work programs and processes is collected and disseminated for use.				

	Valid across the Organization	*Valid for Many Parts*	*Valid for Some Parts*	*Not a Valid Description*
Safeguards are in place to protect data security and employee/constituent privacy.				
Performance measures are used to determine progress against the mission, plans, and goals.				
Data and information are used to compare current outcomes with the outcomes from previous years.				
Information is compared (benchmarked) with that of other organizations.				

Programs and Processes

	Valid across the Organization	*Valid for Many Parts*	*Valid for Some Parts*	*Not a Valid Description*
The major processes associated with core programs and services are documented and reviewed on a regular basis.				
Performance measures are used to assess the effectiveness and efficiency of core processes.				
Processes and programs made the best possible use of available technology.				

Outcomes

For each of the PSAI categories, how do the available performance outcomes compare with the information for the previous year?

	Much More Positive	Somewhat Positive	Same/ Level	Somewhat Negative	Much More Negative
Leadership					
Constituents					
Workforce					
Strategic planning					
Measurement and analysis					
Programs and processes					

Appendix C: Exercises

The following exercises can be used to develop a sense of the decisions to be made and options that exist in planning and implementing an assessment process.

Chapter 1: Organizational Assessment and the Public Sector

1-1. You are the director of Child Services in a large human services agency, and you believe that an assessment process would be helpful in improving the way that the agency as a whole operates. You raise the issue with the newly appointed head of the agency. He doesn't reject the idea, but it clearly isn't high on his list of priorities. You feel strongly that it would help your area, in particular, as well as the rest of the agency. What actions could you take?

Chapter 2: Assessment as a Communication Process

2-1. The leaders of your agency have decided to implement an organizational assessment, and you are directed to prepare a communication plan that details how information about the proposed assessment will be made available to employees. What types of communication will you use, and to whom will they be directed? Draft an announcement from your agency head explaining what will happen and why.

2-2. You are the team leader for an assessment process. Consider and explain the steps you would take to identify the best internal and external information sources.

Chapter 3: Applying Assessment Practices in the Public Sector

3-1. You have been assigned to develop information about performance measures available in the public sector. Think about three government agencies at different levels in the same field: the U.S. Department of Education, a state Department of Education, and a local school board. What performance measures would be most important to each? Would they have any performance measures in common?

Chapter 4: The Public Sector Assessment and Improvement Model

4-1. Using the Public Sector Assessment and Improvement Model, write a proposal for applying it to your organization, including anticipated resources, time frames, and methodology.

Chapter 5: Implementing a Self-Assessment Program

5-1. You are charged with implementing an assessment process in a transportation agency that includes many different occupational groups. You wish to include four primary groups in the assessment process: engineers, community relations specialists, human resource specialists, and highway maintenance staff. How would you structure the process in a way that recognizes the constituents of each group, differing priorities, and different levels of availability? What factors must be taken into consideration?

5-2. One type of information that exists in an agency is the stories that are shared between employees and help shape the culture and identity of the agency. What are some of the stories told in and about your organization of which you are personally aware? What are some of the stories told in your area to "set the stage" for newcomers to the organization?

Chapter 6: Assessment, Improvement, and the Process of Organizational Change

6-1. You have completed an organizational assessment process and identified and prioritized the opportunities for improvement. As part of the process of implementing those opportunities, you need to address potential resistance to change. What are the significant groups within your agency that have the ability to support or impede this change effort, and how can they be made part of the process?

Chapter 7: Case Studies and Best Practices

7-1. You are about to face a change of administration and want to take steps to ensure that your current program of annual organizational self-assessments continues. Consider the experiences of the New Jersey Department of Environmental Protection and the City of Coral Springs. What factors contributed to the ability or inability to sustain a program of assessment and improvement? What actions do you think are critical to efforts to institutionalize such a program so that it can withstand changes of administration?

Appendix D: Tools for Organizational Change Efforts

Assessing Organizational Identity

A strategy that can be used in preparing to implement organizational change is to get a sense of what employees believe is the organization's identity. One method for gathering this information is through an employee survey (see the exercise titled "Assessing Organizational Identity"). Asking four brief open-ended questions will provide information that can spark discussion and ultimately lead to greater understanding. While the questions are fairly straightforward, many organizations are surprised at the diversity of answers generated, even within very small work units.

The first question asks participants what they believe are the three most important functions of the agency. The purpose of this question is to determine whether there is a shared sense of the core mission and the relative criticality of the operations. As an example, the list of the most important functions from an assessment of a physical plant/facilities division included the following:

- Maintain/repair physical plant.
- Provide support services: printing and office supplies.
- Future planning for facilities.
- Energy management.

These answers seem fairly straightforward. The question is how many of those taking the survey responded to this question by identifying core maintenance and support functions and how many selected the more future-oriented functions such as energy management or planning. The answer might indicate whether the division sees itself as a response and repair operation or as a facilities planning and management unit. In this case, energy management was not identified as a core part of the organization's mission, although the director of the division believed it was the most important priority. Similarly, an administrative division may want to see whether its employees see their core mission as enforcing rules or providing services to employees. A call center manager might want to know whether employees view their job as "answering phones" as opposed to "solving employees' problems."

Survey: Assessing Organizational Identity

What do you believe are the three most important functions of your agency?

1.

2.

3.

On what three factors do you believe the effectiveness of your agency should be judged?

1.

2.

3.

What are the three greatest strengths of your agency?

1.

2.

3.

What are the three most important opportunities for improvement?

1.

2.

3.

Table A4.1 Participant-Identified Measures for Judging Effectiveness

Effectiveness Measure	Before Assessment	After Assessment
Customer satisfaction	17%	22%
Effective & efficient utilization of resources	13%	13%
Compliance with laws and regulations	7%	4%
Timeliness of services performed (meeting deadlines)	13%	4%
Quality of work completed/product/service	17%	13%
Morale of staff	3%	0%
Are future needs planned for	3%	9%
Results/deliverables/outcomes	3%	13%

When the responses are compiled, they can be analyzed to determine how convergent (similar) or divergent (different) the responses are. There will generally be some differences, especially those related to job location and job category. Generally speaking, employees should have a common idea of the most important overall mission and functions. However, if the range of answers shows some marked differences, there may not be a shared sense of organizational identity across the workforce.

The second question, which asks how the effectiveness of the organization should be judged, can provide a sense of the criteria that employees believe is being used by constituents to assess the performance of the organization. This can also be an indicator of what employees believe are the core functions, based on what they believe people outside the organization see as priorities. This example (Table A4.1) shows some changes in how the participants in an organizational assessment identified the factors for judging the effectiveness of their agency before participating in the assessment process and after participating. The difference in perception reflects discussions that took place during the course of the organizational assessment. The increased focus on results, deliverables, and outcomes can be a result of the emphasis on these three concepts during the assessment process. Interestingly, there was a decrease in the number of people who identified timeliness as a measure of effectiveness. During the assessment, the participants decided that timeliness, while normally a measure of customer satisfaction, was directly linked to the level of resources the division had to accomplish their work. Rather than focus on providing timely but potentially inadequate service, the participants decided that quality of service and overall customer satisfaction would be better measures.

The last two questions in this survey, about the strengths and opportunities for improvement, provide another way to look at whether employees are in agreement about the way they interpret the operation of the agency.

Assessing Organizational Identification

Please answer the items in this question as they apply to [name of organization]:

For each of the following items, indicate how strongly you agree:

1 = Strongly agree
2 = Agree somewhat
3 = Neutral
4 = Disagree somewhat
5 = Strongly disagree

a. When someone criticizes [name of organization], it feels like a personal insult.
b. I am very interested in what others think about [name of organization].
c. When I talk about [name of organization], I usually say "we" rather than "they."
d. The [name of organization]'s successes are my successes.
e. When someone praises [name of organization], it feels like a personal compliment.
f. If a story in the media criticized [name of organization], I would feel embarrassed.

A composite score can be developed from the responses to the individual questions. The more strongly a person agrees with these questions, the stronger his or her level of organizational identification; the lower the score, the higher the level of identification (adapted from a scale developed by Mael and Ashforth 1992).

Glossary

Appreciative inquiry: A method of evaluation and assessment that, rather than looking at poor performance, focuses attention on times and events when the organization has performed well and examines what made those successes possible.

Assessment: A systematic process for examining an organization to create a shared understanding of the current state of the elements that are critical to the successful achievement of its purposes.

Baldrige National Quality Award ("Baldrige"): A widely recognized program, operated by the National Institute of Standards and Technology of the U.S. Department of Commerce, which is designed to recognize excellence in organizations by assessing their performance in seven categories that represent critical organizational functions. See also Malcolm Baldrige National Quality Award.

Benchmarking: The process of comparing one organization, or the functions, processes, and results of that organization, with another; commonly used to identify, study, and emulate best practices or to compare an organization with its peers or the leading agencies in its field.

Beneficiaries: The people and organizations who benefit from the impact of the work of government, either as direct users of government services or through the general benefit to society of government's actions.

Consensus: A process through which individual participants reach an agreement that can be supported by all parties involved.

Constituents: The people and organizations that have an interest in the operation of government.

Continuous improvement: A way of conducting operations so that processes are continually reviewed for opportunities to improve the functioning of the organization.

Core process: A series of systematic steps that carry out the activities of a core program.

Core program: A program that carries out the mission of the organization.

Criteria for Performance Excellence: A set of questions in seven major categories used in the Baldrige National Quality Program to collect the information needed for an organizational assessment process.

Communication: The exchange of information to create shared meaning.

Dashboard: A visual display of performance measures that allows the user to quickly determine the current state of a selected set of critical indicators.

Deployment: The process through which a particular practice is adopted throughout an organization; it may also refer to the extent to which a practice is deployed.

Diffusion of innovation: The process through which information about new ideas is communication, adopted, and accepted by the members of a group.

Excellence in Higher Education: A program for organizational assessment in colleges and universities, which is an adaptation of the Baldrige National Quality Program, to include the culture and language of higher education.

Facilitator: A person who supports the assessment process by providing direction to groups as they engage in assessment activities.

Government Performance and Results Act (GPRA): A federal government program enacted to improve the performance of federal agencies.

Improvement plan: A plan of action created as an outcome of an assessment process, which identifies the highest priority opportunities for improvement and assigns specific responsibilities, time frames, and action steps for to enact the proposed improvements.

Improvement priorities: Opportunities for improvement resulting from an assessment that have been selected as the highest priorities for implementation.

Incremental change: A change process in which adjustments are made to existing processes and in which the intended outcome is visible to the members of the organization.

Interpersonal communication: The process and methods through which individuals communicate with each other individually or in groups.

Leaders (or leadership): The person or persons who are identified as leaders for purposes of assessing the performance of organizational leadership.

Malcolm Baldrige National Quality Award: An award presented annually to recognize excellence in business, nonprofit, health-care, and education organizations. See also Baldrige National Quality Program.

Mission: The defining purpose for which an organization exists.

Mission statement: A statement of purpose that is generally written and disseminated to employees and constituents.

Negotiation: The process through which two or more parties discuss their differences to reach common agreement on an issue.

Operationalize: A way of presenting a concept or idea so that it can be understood and measured.

Opportunities for improvement: Organizational structures, processes, practices, or procedures that have been identified in an assessment process as having the potential to benefit from change and improvement.

Organizational assessment: A systematic process for examining an organization to create a shared understanding of the current state of the factors that are critical to the successful achievement of its purposes.

Organizational change: The process through which an organization moves from its current state to a different and more desirable state.

Organizational climate: The current state of the organization as perceived by its employees, encompassing morale, perceived treatment, and interpersonal relationships.

Organizational culture: The shared values, beliefs, and norms held by an organization.

Organizational communication: The process through which members of the organization share information to create meaning.

Organizational development: A process that uses behavioral science to create organizational and personal learning and to build a case for change in organizations.

Organizational identity: What the members of the organization believe to be the definition of its purposes and central characteristics.

Organizational identification: The way an individual views his or her connection to the organization.

Outcome measures: A set of metrics that describe the outcomes achieved by the organization.

Participant: An individual who takes part in or plays an active role in an organizational assessment process.

Performance Assessment Rating Tool (PART): A federal government program for evaluating agency performance and goal achievement.

Performance measurement: A systematic process for identifying key performance indicators and measuring the relative progress over a period of time.

Performance measures: The key performance indicators selected to represent progress toward organizational goals and objectives.

Process: A series of steps through which an organization carries out a specific program or action.

Process improvement: A quality methodology in which processes are systematically examined to determine opportunities for improvement.

Program: A set of operations used to enact a set of goals and objectives.

Quality: A state in which the operations, processes, and programs of an organization are enacted in a way that produces the optimum levels of achievement.

Quality Circles: A program popular in the 1980s that empowered teams of employees to identify problems, to analyze the related processes, and to recommend (and in some cases to implement) ways to improve them.

Quality improvement: A philosophy in which organizations and their programs and processes are reviewed, analyzed, and revised to improve the outcomes.

Robust: A description used to indicate that a program or process is particularly strong, successful, or thoroughly deployed throughout an organization.

Self-Assessment: An assessment process that uses the members of an organization as the participants and source of information as opposed to an external assessors, such as a consultant or auditor.

Strategic planning: A systematic process through which the members and leaders of an organization determine the goals, objectives, strategies, and action plans necessary to move the organization to its desired level of performance.

Strengths: Programs, processes, or behaviors that are performed well.

Support process: A series of steps that enacts a support program.

Support program: A program that provides support services, such as human resources, accounting, facilities management, or information technology, in support of the core programs of the organization.

SWOT Analysis: An assessment tool in which the participants compile lists of the strengths, weaknesses, opportunities, and threats that they see in the organization

Systems approach or systems theory: Recognizing that organizations are made up of various interlocking systems and examining the way that they function together.

Total quality management (TQM): A way of conducting and managing operations that emphasizes the review and improvement of performance and processes so that the best possible quality can be obtained.

Transformational change: An organizational change process in which major changes are instituted that are discontinuous with current operations.

Values: Personal and organizational characteristics that are expected of the members of an organization; characteristics, attitudes, and approaches that the members of the organization have the right to expect from each other in the performance of their jobs.

Vision: A statement of what the organization sees as its ultimate goal or performance.

Assessment Resources: Websites

Alliance for Performance Excellence: http://www.baldrigepe.org/alliance/
American Society for Public Administration: http://www.aspanet.org
Association of Government Accountants: http://www.aga.org
Baldrige National Quality Program: http://www.quality.nist.gov

Center for Performance Measurement, International City/County Management Association (ICMA): http://www.icma.org

Center for Organizational Development and Leadership, Rutgers University: http://www.odl.rutgers.edu

City of Coral Springs, Florida (Baldrige page): http://www.coralsprings.org/baldrige/index.cfm

ExpectMore.gov: http://www.whitehouse.gov/omb/expectmore/about.html

Florida Sterling Award: http://www.floridasterling.com

Governing Magazine: http://www.governing.com

Government Innovators Network, Harvard University: http://www.innovations.harvard.edu/

International City/County Management Association: http://www.icma.org

National Academy of Public Administration: http://www.napawash.org/pc_government_performance/about.html

National Center for Public Productivity: http://www.ncpp.us

National Governors Association Center for Best Practices: http://www.nga.org

Quality New Mexico: http://www.qualitynewmexico.org

Results.gov: http://www.whitehouse.gov/results/

United States Army Armament Research, Development and Engineering Center: http://www.pica.army.mil/PicatinnyPublic/organizations/ardec/index.asp

Washington State Quality Award: http://www.wsqa.net

Bibliography

Albert, S. and Whetten, D. (1985). Organizational Identity. *Research in Organizational Behavior,* Vol. 7, 263–297.

Altheide, D. and Johnson, J. (1980). *Bureaucratic Propaganda.* Boston: Allyn and Bacon.

Ammons, D. (1999). A Proper Mentality for Benchmarking. *Public Administration Review,* Vol. 59, No. 2, 105–123.

Anderson, D. and Anderson, L. (2001). *Beyond Change Management.* San Francisco: Jossey-Bass.

Arcaro, J. (1998). *The President's Quality Award Program Self Assessment Process for Federal, State, and Local Government.* Boca Raton, FL: CRC Press.

Argyris, C. (1982). *Reasoning, Learning, and Action.* San Francisco: Jossey-Bass.

Argyris, C. (1992). *On Organizational Learning.* Cambridge, MA: Blackwell Publishers.

Austin, J., Klimoski, R., and Hunt, S. (1996). Dilemmatics in Public Sector Assessment: A Framework for Developing and Evaluating Selection Systems. *Human Performance,* Vol. 9, No. 3, 177–198.

Aydin, E. and Rice, R.E. (1992). Bringing Social Worlds Together: Computers as Catalysts for New Interactions in Health Care Organizations. *Journal of Health and Social Behavior,* Vol. 33, No. 2, 168–185.

Babicz, G. (2002). Assessing the Baldrige Award. *Quality,* Vol. 41, No. 11, 36.

Baldrige National Quality Program (2003a). *Getting Started.* National Institute of Standards and Technology, Department of Commerce, Gaithersburg, MD.

Baldrige National Quality Program (2003b). *Why Apply?* National Institute of Standards and Technology, Department of Commerce, Gaithersburg, MD.

Baldrige National Quality Program (2007a). *Criteria for Performance Excellence 2007.* National Institute of Standards and Technology, Department of Commerce, Gaithersburg, MD.

Baldrige National Quality Program (2007b). *Criteria for Performance Excellence in Education 2007.* National Institute of Standards and Technology, Department of Commerce, Gaithersburg, MD.

Baldrige National Quality Program (2007c). *Criteria for Performance Excellence in Health Care 2007.* National Institute of Standards and Technology, Department of Commerce, Gaithersburg, MD.

Baldrige National Quality Program (2008). *Commerce Secretary Gutierrez Joins President Bush in Announcing 2008 Baldrige National Quality Awards.* http://www.nist.gov/public_affairs/releases/2008baldrigerecipients.htm. National Institute of Standards and Technology, Department of Commerce, Gaithersburg, MD.

Beckhard, R. (1969). *Organizational Development: Strategies and Models*. Reading, MA: Addison-Wesley.

Behn, R. (2003). Why Measure Performance? Different Purposes Require Different Measures. *Public Administration Review*, Vol. 63, No. 5, 586–606.

Behn, R. (2008). On Why, to Improve Performance, Management Is Rarely Enough. *Bob Behn's Public Management Report*, Vol. 5, No. 9. http://www.hks.harvard.edu/thebehnreport/ May2008.pdf

Berman, E. (1998). *Productivity in Public and Non-Profit Organizations: Strategies and Techniques*. Thousand Oaks, CA: Sage Publications.

Berman, E. (2002). How Useful Is Performance Measurement? *Public Performance & Management Review*, Vol. 25, No. 4, 348–351.

Berman, E. and Wang, X. (2000, September–October). Performance Measurement in US Counties: Capacity for Reform. *Public Administration Review*, Vol. 60, No. 5, 409–434.

Berman, E. and West, J. (1995a). Municipal Commitment to Total Quality Management: A Survey of Recent Progress. *Public Administration Review*, Vol. 55, No. 1, 57–66.

Berman, E. and West, J. (1995b). TQM in American Cities: Hypotheses Regarding Commitment and Impact. *Journal of Public Administration Research & Theory*, Vol. 5, No. 2, 213–231.

Blackburn, R. and Rosen, B. (1993). Total Quality and Human Resource Management: Lessons Learned from Baldrige Award-Winning Companies. *Academy of Management Executive*, Vol. 7, No. 3, 49–67.

Boyne, G. (2006). Strategies for Public Service Turnaround. *Administration and Society*, Vol. 38, No. 3, 365–388.

Boyne, G. and Chen, A. (2007). Performance Targets and Public Service Improvement. *Journal of Public Administration Research and Theory*, Vol. 17, No. 3, 455–477.

Boyne, G., Gould-Williams, J., Law, J., and Walker, R. (2004). Toward the Self-Evaluating Organization? An Empirical Test of the Wildavsky Model. *Public Administration Review*, Vol. 64, No. 4, 463–473.

Boyne, G., Meier, K., O'Toole Jr., L., and Walker, R. (Eds.). (2006). *Public Service Performance: Perspectives on Measurement and Management*. New York: Cambridge University Press.

Bozeman, B. and Kingsly, G. (1998). Risk Culture in Public and Private Organizations. *Public Administration Review*, Vol. 58, No. 2, 109–118.

Calhoun, J.M. (2002). Using the Baldrige Criteria to Manage and Assess the Performance of Your Organization. *Journal for Quality & Participation*, Vol. 25, No. 2, 45–53.

Carr, D. and Littman, I. (1990). *Excellence in Government: Total Quality Management in the 1990s*. Arlington, VA: Coopers and Lybrand.

Cheney, G. (1983). On the Various and Changing Meanings of Organizational Membership: A Field Study of Organizational Identification. *Communication Monographs*, Vol. 50, 342–362.

Cheney, G. and Tompkins, P.R. (1987). Coming to Terms with Organizational Identification and Commitment. *Central States Speech Journal*, Vol. 38, No. 1, 1–15.

Chuan, T.K. and Soon, L.C. (2000). A Detailed Trends Analysis of National Quality Awards World-Wide. *Total Quality Management*, Vol. 11, No. 8, 1065–1080.

City of Coral Springs, Florida. (2008). A to Z Guide to City and Community Services. www.coralsprings.org/publications/AtoZguide.pdf

Coe, C. (2003). A Report Card on Report Cards. *Public Performance Management Review*, Vol. 27, No. 2, 53–76.

Coggburn, J. and Schneider, S. (2003). The Quality of Management and Government Performance: An Empirical Analysis of the American State. *Public Administration Review*, Vol. 63, No. 2, 206–213.

Coggburn, J. and Schneider, S. (2003). The Relationship between State Government Performance and State Quality of Life. *International Journal of Public Administration*, Vol. 26, No. 12, 1337–1354.

Collins, J. and Porras, J. (1994). *Built to Last*. New York: Harper Collins.

Committee on Governmental Affairs, United States Senate. (1993). Report on the Government Performance and Results Act of 1993. http://www.whitehouse.gov/omb/mgmt-gpra/gprptm.html

Conference Board. (1993). *Sustaining Total Quality*. New York: Conference Board.

Conference Board. (1995). *In Pursuit of Quality: Views from the Leading Edge*. New York: Conference Board.

Connor, P. (1997, November–December). Total Quality Management: A Selective Commentary on Its Human Dimensions. *Public Administration Review*, Vol. 57, No. 6, 501–509.

Cornin, M. (2004). Continuous Improvement in a New York State School District. Unpublished dissertation. Rutgers, The State University of New Jersey, New Brunswick, NJ.

Coplin, W. and Dwyer, C. (2000). *Does Your Government Measure Up?* Syracuse, NY: Community Benchmarks Program, Maxwell School of Citizenship and Public Affairs, Syracuse University.

Curkovic, S., Menyk, S., Calantone, R., and Handfield, R. (2000). Validating the Malcolm Baldrige National Quality Award Framework through Structural Equation Modeling. *International Journal of Production Research*, Vol. 38, No. 4, 765–791.

DeCarlo, N. and Sterett, W.K. (1995). History of the Malcolm Baldrige National Quality Award. In Brent D. Ruben (Ed.), *Quality in Higher Education* (pp. 79–96). New Brunswick, NJ: Transaction Publishers.

Deetz, S. (1995). *Transforming Communication Transforming Business*. Cresskill, NJ: Hampton Press.

Dilulio, J., Garvey, G., and Kettl, D. (1993). *Improving Government Performance: An Owner's Manual*. Washington, DC: Brookings Institution Press.

Douglas, T. and Fredenhall, L. (2004). Evaluating the Deming Management Model of Total Quality in Services. *Decision Sciences*, Vol. 35, No. 3, 393–422.

Dubnick, M. (2005). Accountability and the Promise of Performance. *Public Performance Management Review*, Vol. 28, No. 3, 376–417.

Dutton, J. and Dukerich, J. (1991). Keeping an Eye on the Mirror: Image and Identity in Organizational Adaptation. *Academy of Management Journal*, Vol. 34, No. 3, 517–554.

Eagle, K. (2004, October). The Origins and Evolution of Charlotte's Corporate Scorecard. *Government Finance Review*, Vol. 20, No. 5, 16–22.

Etzione, A. (1964). *Modern Organizations*. Englewood Cliffs, NJ: Prentice Hall.

Fernandez, S. and Rainey, H. (2006, March–April). Managing Successful Organizational Change in the Public Sector. *Public Administration Review*, Vol. 66, No. 2, 168–176.

Folz, D. (2004, March). Service Quality and Benchmarking the Performance of Municipal Services. *Public Administration Review*, Vol. 64, No. 2, 209–220.

Fredrickson, D. and Fredrickson, H. (2006). *Measuring the Performance of the Hollow State*. Washington, DC: Georgetown University Press.

Frohman, A. (1997, Winter). Igniting Organizational Change from Below: The Power of Personal Initiative. *Organizational Dynamics*, Vol. 25, No. 3, 39–52.

Gabriel, Y. (2000). *Storytelling in Organizations*. New York: Oxford University Press.

Gilliland, M. (2004). Leading a Public University: Lessons Learned in Choosing the Possibility of Quantum Results rather than Incremental Improvement. *Public Administration Review*, Vol. 64, No. 3, 372–377.

Gore, A. (1995). *Common Sense Government*. New York: Random House.

Government Accounting Office. (1991). *Management Practice: U.S. Companies Improve Performance through Quality Efforts* (NSAID-91-190). Washington, DC: Government Accounting Office.

Government Accounting Office. (2004). *Performance Budgeting: OMB's Program Assessment Rating Tool Presents Operational Challenges for Budget and Performance Integration— Statement of Paul S. Posner*. Washington, DC: Government Accounting Office.

Government Accounting Office. (2008). *Lessons Learned for the Next Administration on Using Performance Information to Improve Results: Statement of Bernice Steinhardt, Director Strategic Issues* (GAO-08-1026T). Washington, DC: Government Accounting Office.

George, S. and Weimerskirch, A. (1994). *Total Quality Management*. New York: John Wiley & Sons Inc.

Haass, R. (1994). *The Power to Persuade*. Boston: Houghton Mifflin Company.

Haavind, R. (1992). *The Road to the Baldrige Award: Quest for Total Quality*. Stoneham, MA: Butterworth-Heinemann.

Harsell, D. (2003). The Government Performance and Results Act: Assessing Its Effects on Careerist and Political Appointee Relations. Paper prepared for the 2003 meeting of the American Political Science Assoc.

Hart, C.L. and Bogan, C.E. (1992). *The Baldrige*. New York: McGraw-Hill Inc.

Heaphy, M.S. and Gruska, G.F. (1995). *The Malcolm Baldrige National Quality Award: A Yardstick for Quality Growth*. Reading, MA: Addison-Wesley Publishing Company.

Heflin, C. (2007a). Has Coral Springs Found the Holy Grail?—From Sterling to Baldrige. *Public Sector Digest*. August.

Heflin, C. (2007b). Has Coral Springs Found the Holy Grail?—From Sterling to Baldrige. *Public Sector Digest*. October.

Heflin, C. (2008). Has Coral Springs Found the Holy Grail?—From Sterling to Baldrige. *Public Sector Digest*. February.

Heinrich, C. (2004). Performance Management as Administrative Reform: Is It Improving Government Performance? *Public Finance and Management*, Vol. 4, No. 3, 240–246.

Herzik, E. (1988). Government Productivity, Effectiveness, and Public Policy. *Policy Studies Review*, Vol. 7, No. 3, 684–691.

Higgs, M. and Rowland, D. (2005). All Changes Great and Small: Exploring Approaches to Change and Its Leadership. *Journal of Change Management*, Vol. 5, No. 2, 121–151.

Himm, A. (1993). *Does Quality Work? A Review of Relevant Studies*. New York: Conference Board.

Hogan, T.J. The Applicability of the Malcolm Baldrige National Quality Award Criteria to the Evaluation of Quality in Collegiate Administrative Services. Unpublished dissertation. Ohio University, Athens, OH.

Holzer, M. and Callahan, K. (1998). *Government at Work*. Thousand Oaks, CA: Sage Publications.

Hsieh, A., Chou, C., and Chen, C. (2002). Job Standardization and Service Quality: A Closer Look at the Application of Total Quality Management to the Public Sector. *Total Quality Management,* Vol. 13, No. 7, 899–912.

Hunt, V. (1993). *Quality Management for Government.* Milwaukee: ASQC Quality Press.

Hutton, D.W. (2000). *From Baldrige to the Bottom Line.* Milwaukee: ASQ Quality Press.

Immordino, K. (2006). The Impact of Structured Organizational Self-Assessment Processes on Issue Identification and Prioritization. Unpublished dissertation.

Ingraham, P. (Ed.). (2007). *In Pursuit of Performance: Management Systems in State and Local Government.* Baltimore: Johns Hopkins University Press.

Irr, F., Kalnbach, C., and Smith, M. (2003, Summer). The Real Story behind the Commandant's Performance Challenge. *Journal for Quality & Participation,* Vol. 26, No. 2, 41–45.

Irvin, J. and Stansbury, J. (2004). Citizen Participation in Decision Making: Is It Worth the Effort? *Public Administration Review,* Vol. 64, No. 1, 55–65.

Jick, T. (1995). Accelerating Change for Competitive Advantage. *Organizational Dynamics,* Vol. 14, No. 1, 77–82.

Kanter, R.M. (1991a). Change: Where to Begin. *Harvard Business Review,* Vol. 69, No. 4, 8–9.

Kanter, R.M. (1991b, May–June). Transcending Business Boundaries: 12,000 World Managers View Change. *Harvard Business Review,* Vol. 69, 151–164.

Kaplan, R. (2001). Strategic Performance Measurement and Management in Nonprofit Organizations. *Nonprofit Management and Leadership,* Vol. 11, No. 3, 353–370.

Kaplan, R. and Norton, D. (1992). The Balanced Scorecard—Measures that Drive Performance. *Harvard Business Review,* Vol. 70, No. 1, 71–79.

Kaplan R. and Norton, D. (1996). *Balanced Scorecard: Translating Strategy into Action.* Boston: Harvard Business School Press.

Katz, D., Gutek, B., Kahn, R., and Barton, E. (1975). *Bureaucratic Encounters: A Pilot Study in the Evaluation of Government Services.* Ann Arbor: University of Michigan.

Kearney, R. and Berman, E. (Eds.). (1999). *Public Sector Performance: Management, Motivation and Measurement.* Boulder, CO: Westview Press.

Keehly, P., Medlin, S., MacBride, S., and Longmire, L. (1997). *Benchmarking for Best Practices in the Public Sector.* San Francisco: Jossey-Bass.

Kemelgor, B., Johnson, S., and Srinivasan, S. (2000, January–February). Forces Driving Organizational Change: A Business School Perspective. *Journal of Education for Business,* Vol. 75, No. 3, 133–137.

Kravchuk, R. and Schack, R. (1996). Designing Effective Performance Measurement Systems under the Government Performance and Results Act. *Public Administration Review,* Vol. 56, No. 4, 348–359.

Krzykowski, B. (2008). Far-Sighted: Long Range Focus Allows City Government to Celebrate Baldrige Recognition. http://www.asq.org/quality-progress/2008/06/baldrige-national-quality-program/far-sighted.html

Kulik, T. (1998). *The Continuing Search for Performance Excellence.* New York: Conference Board.

Leith, J. (1997). *Implementing Performance Measurement in Government.* Washington, DC: Government Finance Officers Association.

Lewin, K. (1951). *Field Theory in Social Science.* Westport, CT: Greenwood Press.

Long, E. and Franklin, A.L. (2004). The Paradox of Implementing the Government Performance and Results Act: Top-Down Direction for Bottom-Up Implementation. *Public Administration Review,* Vol. 64, No. 3, 309–319.

Mael, F. and Ashforth, B. (1992). Alumni and their alma mater: A partial test of the reformulated model of organizational identification. *Journal of Organizational Behavior.* 13, 103–123.

Mahoney, F.X. and Thor, C.G. (1994). *The TQM Trilogy.* New York: American Management Association.

Mehta, P. (2000). President's Quality Program Honors Government Organizations. *Quality Progress*, Vol. 33, No. 8, 57–62.

Michelson, E. (2006). Approaches to Research and Development Performance Assessment in the United States: An Evaluation of Recent Trends. *Science and Public Policy*, Vol. 33, No. 8, 546–560.

Neves, J. and Nakhai, B. (1993). The Baldrige Award Framework for Teaching Total Quality Management. *Journal of Education for Business,* Vol. 69, No. 2, 121–125.

Niven, P. (2005). *Balanced Scorecard Diagnostics: Maintaining Maximum Performance.* Hoboken, NJ: John Wiley and Sons.

Niven, P. (2008). *Balanced Scorecard: Step by Step for Government and Non-Profit Agencies.* Hoboken, NJ: John Wiley and Sons.

Nystrom, P. and Starbuck, W. (Eds.). (1981). *Handbook of Organizational Design* (vol. 2). New York: Oxford University Press.

Oman, R., Damours, S., Smith, T., and Uscher, A. (1992). *Management Analysis in Public Organizations.* New York: Quorum Books.

Orr, M. and West, D. (2007). Citizen Evaluations of Local Police: Personal Experience or Symbolic Attitudes? *Administration and Society,* Vol. 38, No. 6, 649–668.

Osbourne, D. and Gaebler, T. (1992). *Reinventing Government.* Reading, MA: Addison-Wesley Publishing.

Pace, R. and Faules, D. (1993). *Organizational Communication.* Allyn & Bacon.

Pannirselvam, G. and Ferguson, L. (2001). A Study of the Relationships between the Baldrige Categories. *International Journal of Quality & Reliability,* Vol. 18, No. 1, 14–34.

Pannirselvam, G., Siferd, S., and Ruch, W. (1998, October). Validation of the Arizona Governor's Quality Award Criteria: A Test of the Baldrige Criteria. *Journal of Operations Management*, Vol. 16, No. 5, 529–550.

Pascale, R., Millemann, M., and Gioja, L. (1997, November–December). Changing the Way We Change. *Harvard Business Review*, 127–139.

Pederson, L. (2002). *Performance-Oriented Management: A Practical Guide for Government Agencies.* Vienna, VA: Management Concepts, Inc.

Phillips, J. (2004). An Application of the Balanced Scorecard to Public Transit System Performance Assessment. *Transportation Journal*, Vol. 43, No. 1, 26–55.

Popovich, M. (Ed.). (1998). *Creating High Performance Government Organizations.* San Francisco: Jossey-Bass.

Powell, C. and Persico, J. (1996). *My American Journey.* New York: Ballantine Books.

Przasnyski, Z. and Tai, L.S. (2002). Stock Performance of Malcolm Baldrige National Quality Award Winning Companies. *Total Quality Management,* Vol. 13, No. 4, 475–488.

Purser, R. and Petranker, J. (2005). Unfreezing the Future: Exploring the Dynamic of Time in Organizational Change. *Journal of Applied Behavioral Science*, Vol. 41, No. 2, 182–203.

Quality Digest. (1996). Army Research Center Targets Quality. http://www.qualitydigest.com/aug/army.html

Radin, B. (1998). The Government Performance and Results Act (GPRA): Hydra-Headed Monster or Flexible Management Tool? *Public Administration Review*, Vol. 58, No. 4, 307–316.

Raven, B. (1995). The Bases of Power: Origins and Recent Developments. In S. Corman, S. Banks, C. Bantz, and M. Mayer (Eds.), *Foundations of Organizational Communication.* White Plains, NY: Longman Publishers. p. 271–288.

Redburn, F., Shea, R., and Buss, T. (Eds.). (2008). *Performance Management and Budgeting: How Governments Can Learn from Experience.* Armonk, NY: M.E. Sharpe.

Robert Wood Johnson University Hospital at Hamilton. (2004). Application Summary for the Baldrige National Quality Award. www.rwjhamilton.org/baldrige1/appsummary. pdf

Rogers, E. (1995). *Diffusion of Innovations.* New York: Free Press.

Rosenberg, A. (2007). *Army Facility Wins National Quality Award.* www.govexec.com/story-page.cfm?articleid=387458dcn=e_ndw.

Ruben, B. (1995). *Quality in Higher Education.* New Brunswick, NJ: Transaction Publishers.

Ruben, B. (2002). Integrating Organizational Assessment, Planning, and Improvement: Making organizational Self-Study and Change Everyday Activities. Unpublished manuscript. New Brunswick, NJ.

Ruben, B. (2004). *Pursuing Excellence in Higher Education.* San Francisco: Jossey-Bass.

Ruben, B. (2005). The Center for Organizational Development at Rutgers University: A Case Study. *Advances in Developing Human Resources,* Vol. 7, No. 3, 368–395.

Ruben, B. (2007a). *Excellence in Higher Education: A Baldrige-Based Guide to Organizational Assessment, Improvement and Leadership.* Washington, DC: National Association of College and University Business Officers.

Ruben, B. (2007b). *Excellence in Higher Education: A Baldrige-Based Guide to Organizational Assessment, Improvement and Leadership. Workbook and Scoring Guide.* Washington, DC: National Association of College and University Business Officers.

Ruben, B., Connaughton, S., Immordino, K., and Lopez, J. (2004, July). Paper presented at the annual meeting of the National Consortium for Continuous Improvement in Higher Education, Milwaukee, WI.

Ruben, B. and Immordino, K. (2006a). *Excellence in the Public Sector: A Baldrige-Based Guide to Organizational Assessment, Improvement and Leadership.* New Brunswick, NJ: Rutgers University.

Ruben, B. and Immordino, K. (2006b). *Excellence in the Public Sector: A Baldrige-Based Guide to Organizational Assessment, Improvement and Leadership. Workbook and Scoring Guide.* New Brunswick, NJ: Rutgers University.

Rusaw, A. (1998). *Transforming the Character of Public Organizations: Techniques for Change Agents.* Westport, CT: Quorum Books.

Schachter, H. (2007, September–October). Does Frederick Taylor's Ghost Still Haunt the Halls of Government? A Look at the Concept of Governmental Efficiency in Our Time. *Public Administration Review,* Vol. 67, No. 5, 800–810.

Schein, E. (1980). *Organizational Psychology.* Englewood Cliffs, NJ: Prentice-Hall.

Schein, E. (1992). *Organizational Culture and Leadership.* San Francisco: Jossey-Bass.

Scott, C. (1997). Identification with Multiple Targets in a Geographically Dispersed Organization. *Management Communication Quarterly,* Vol. 10, No. 4, 491–522.

Scott, C., Connaughton, S., Diaz-Saenz, H., Maguire, K., Ramirez, R., Richardson, B., et al. (1999). The Impacts of Communication and Multiple Identifications on Intent to Leave. *Management Communication Quarterly,* Vol. 12, No. 3, 400–435.

Scott, S. and Lane, V. (2000). A Stakeholder Approach to Organizational Identity. *Academy of Management Review,* Vol. 25, No. 1, 43–62.

Senge, P. (1990). *The Fifth Discipline: The Art and Practice of the Learning Organization.* New York: Doubleday.

Shirks, A., Weeks, W.B., and Stein, A. (2002). Baldrige Based Quality Awards: Veterans Health Administration's 3-Year Experience. *Quality Management in Health Care,* Vol. 10, No. 3, 47–54.

Spechler, J.W. (1993). *Managing Quality in America's Most Admired Companies.* San Francisco: Berrett-Koehler Publishers.

Sweeney, S. and Charlesworth, J. (Eds.). (1963). Achieving Excellence in the Public Service. Philadelphia: American Academy of Political and Social Service.

Syfert, P., Elliott, N., and Schumacher, L. (1998). Charlotte Adopts the Balanced Scorecard. *American City and County,* Vol. 113, No. 11, 32.

The Most Amazing Innovations of 2004 (2004, November 29). *Time Magazine.*

Van de Ven, A. and Poole, M. (1995). Explaining Development and Change in Organizations. *Academy of Management Review,* Vol. 20, No. 3, 510–540.

Van de Ven, A. and Poole, M. (2005). Alternative Approaches for Studying Organizational Change. *Organizational Studies,* Vol. 26, No. 9, 1377–1404.

Van Wart, M. and Dicke, L. (Eds.). (2008). *Administrative Leadership in the Public Sector.* Armonk, NY: M.E. Sharpe.

Vokurka, R.J. (2001). The Baldrige at 14. *Journal for Quality and Participation*, Vol. 24, No. 2, 13–19.

Wallace, M., Fertig, M., and Schneller, E. (Eds.). (2007). *Managing Change in the Public Services.* Malden, MA: Blackwell Publishing.

Walters, J. (2006). Rivals with a Cause. http://www.Governing.com/manage/pm/perf0606.htm (accessed March 15, 2008).

Walters, L., Aydelotte, J., and Miller, J. (2000). Putting More Public in Policy Analysis. *Public Administration Review,* Vol. 60, No. 4, 349.

Weisbord, M. (1987). *Productive Workplaces.* San Francisco: Jossey Bass.

Willem, A. and Buelens, M. (2007). Knowledge Sharing in Public Sector Organizations. *Journal of Public Administration Research and Theory,* Vol. 17, No. 4, 581–606.

Wisniewski, M. and Donnelly, M. (1996). Measuring Service Quality in the Public Sector: The Potential for SERVQUAL. *Total Quality Management,* Vol. 7, No. 4, 357–365.

Witherspoon, P. (1997). *Communicating Leadership.* Boston: Allyn and Bacon.

Yang, K. and Callahan, K. (2007, March–April). Citizen Involvement Efforts and Bureaucratic Responsiveness: Participatory Values, Stakeholder Pressures, and Administrative Practicality. *Public Administration Review*, Vol. 67, No. 2, 249–264.

Younis, T. (1997). Customers' Expectations of Public Sector Services: Does Quality Have Its Limits? *Total Quality Management,* Vol. 8, No. 4, 115–129.

Interviews

Jeffrey Weinrach, Director, Quality New Mexico (August 6, 2008) telephone interview

Mark Tucci, Director, Human Resources, New Jersey Department of Environmental Protection (March 17, 2008) Trenton, NJ

Alfred Brenner, Director of the Division of Support Services, New Jersey Department of Transportation (June 20, 2008) Ewing, NJ

Brad Sampson, Army Armament Research Development and Engineering Center (June 25, 2008) telephone interview

Susan Grant, Director of Human Resources, City of Coral Springs, Florida (August 18, 2008) telephone interview

Joseph Genovay, Manager, New Jersey Department of Environmental Protection (September 16, 2008) Trenton, NJ

Michael Hanson, Office of the Governor, State of Utah (June 23, 2008) telephone interview

Gary Allen, Virginia DOT (February 13, 2000) telephone interview

Email Correspondence

Susan Fourney, Managing Editor, *Governing Magazine* (March 12, 2007)

Brad Sampson, Army Armament Research Development and Engineering Center (March 13; June 17, 24, October 23, 2008)

Michael Hanson, Office of the Governor, State of Utah (July 11; August 11, 2008)

Maria Fuentes-Archilla, Public Information Officer, City of Coral Springs, Florida (May 2, 2008)

Jeffrey Weinrach, Director, Quality New Mexico (February 19, 2009; July 18, 2008)

Natalie Lemke, American Society for Quality (June 27, 2008)

Webcast

International City and County Management Association (2008, January 24). Why the Baldrige Quality Model Works in Local Government.

Index